MORALITY IN AMERICAN POLITICS

MORALITY

IN

AMERICAN POLITICS

BY GEORGE A. GRAHAM

RANDOM HOUSE   NEW YORK

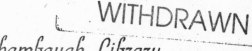

First Printing
Copyright, 1952, by George A. Graham
All rights reserved under International and
Pan-American Copyright Conventions.
Published in New York by Random House, Inc.,
and simultaneously in Toronto, Canada, by
Random House of Canada, Limited.
Library of Congress Catalog Card Number: 52-7142
Manufactured in the United States of America
by H. Wolff, New York
Designed by Jerome Kuhl

To the women
in my life:
Mother,
Mary,
Rosanna,
Lora,
little Mary,
and their friends

PREFACE

No justification is needed for a book on morals and politics. The two subjects are by nature linked, and both are fundamental in modern civilization. Americans are embarrassed in 1952 by evidence of official misconduct revealed in legislative investigations, disciplinary action by administrators, the prosecution of public officials, and the full publicity given to these events in an election year. Yet the consensus of thoughtful observers who have a long perspective is that ethical standards in government are higher than they used to be and that the vast majority of public officials are honest and faithful. Many also believe that ethical standards in government are higher than in the business world and other walks of life. Even if these conclusions be accepted without qualification, they give no grounds for complacence; for the need for high standards has grown faster than the standards, and the degree of compliance with approved standards is far from satisfactory.

Confronted with a situation of this sort, men react in different ways. Many look for a scapegoat and a panacea. Some helpful soul always wisely observes that we need better men in office; and the pessimistic say that nothing can be done. This book is an attempt to point up some of the more basic aspects of the morals problem; and the reader will note the author's view that although the problem has far-reaching ramifications, much can be done and many people can help.

The book is in part a by-product from an uncompleted study of "America's Capacity to Govern," which has been aided materially by a grant from the Rockefeller Foundation. My interest in the problem was sharpened by serving in 1951 as a consultant to the distinguished "ethics subcommittee" of the Senate Committee on Labor and Public Welfare (Douglas, chairman, Aiken, Humphrey, Morse, Neely), and I have made extensive use of the committee's published hearings and reports. Princeton University authorities, with characteristic encouragement and generosity, made it possible for me to go ahead with the writing during the winter of 1951-52. I am greatly indebted to my colleagues in the Department of Politics for assistance: Harold Sprout, Hubert Wilson, Edgar Lane, and especially to Marver Bernstein, who for five months took over some of my more onerous academic duties and so made the book possible.

The Princeton University Library has provided ideal facilities and working space; and Miss Helen Fairbanks, special librarian in charge of the Public Administration Collection, has given invaluable bibliographical assistance. For patiently deciphering my longhand and typing the manuscript, I am indebted to Mrs. Elizabeth P. Sangston, Miss Marianne J. Ehrenborg, and Miss Nan Benamon. I am grateful to the editor, Saxe Commins, for his understanding and vigor as well as for the skillful use of his big red pencil. Despite the challenge of the subject, I would not have attempted to set down my views for publication except for the urging of my colleague, Whitney J. Oates, who argues persuasively, *de gustibus disputandum*.

GEORGE A. GRAHAM

Princeton, New Jersey
May 15, 1952

CONTENTS

MORALITY IN AMERICAN POLITICS

I

AMERICAN POLITICS—THE CHARACTERS AND THEIR ROLES

A thoughtful American who attempts to analyze his own attitudes usually finds that he views American politics with mixed and somewhat inconsistent feelings.

Proud as he is of the democratic institutions of self-government conceived and established by the great men of American politics, he does not actually enjoy self-government. Frequently he neglects even the minimal chores of registering to vote and casting his ballot. On the basis of statistics alone, it is un-American to register and vote regularly in all primaries and elections.[1]

Representative government is a wonderful thing but representatives, and others who give their time to public affairs, are to him "politicians," who as a class constitute one of the lowest orders of American society. Probing his mind further, the thoughtful American finds that he venerates Adams, Washington, Jefferson, Hamilton, Madison, Jackson, Lincoln and other political heroes of the past, but he habitually heaps abuse

3

on the political leaders of his own day—just as his fathers did before him. The great Americans are honored because of their contributions to American government, but to him government itself is inherently an evil thing.

Although government in general is considered bad, and this has always been the popular view, specific functions have been added one after the other to the responsibilities of government, and each specific function seems very good to a lot of people. Similarly the individual representatives, public officials, or civil servants whom one knows personally seem to be pretty fine folks. No one is down on the public-school teachers, the public-health nurses, the county agents, the letter carriers, or even the cop on the corner, particularly if he knows them. It is just the group of employees and officials as a whole and in the abstract that is scorned.

Perhaps what Americans yearn for is complete mechanization of politics. Not a dictator but a political automat is the subconscious ideal, a well-engineered electronic device, a composite voting-vending-calculating-servicing machine to satisfy the needs of the worthy citizen on schedule, operated solely from nickels in the slot, and entirely free of emotional involvement. Although Americans have been content at times to turn over city or county affairs to local "machines" they have always found those machines disappointingly personal and human, hence frail and unsatisfactory. Hope dies hard, and new varieties of political apparatus have been welcomed—the direct primary, the initiative and referendum, and proportional representation, for example. None of these contributions measures up to the modern standards of being fully automatic and completely impersonal, but this defect is sometimes forgotten.

Realism compels the thoughtful American to accept the fact that he will have to be content with "manual" operation of the machinery of government, at least for some time, but the yearning for the impersonal and automatic survives in the "ambiguous they" of current political discussion. "They ought to pass a law." "They ought to do something about it." "They ought not to allow that." These are phrases which the average person hears and uses almost daily, and he sometimes acts on the assumption that government is a mechanical device which requires no more attention from him than the radio, the oil burner, or the refrigerator.

Do the inconsistent political attitudes of American life grow out of the direct personal experiences of living Americans? Or are they conventional word pictures that are in the air and which a man only half accepts, employing them like hand-me-down sayings to express his feelings of the moment? Or does the confusion arise from the co-existence of half-accepted traditional attitudes and half-interpreted direct experience?

Whatever the source, the paradox of America's traditionally mingled pride and shame in its politics, and its almost indiscriminate honoring of the long dead and its dishonoring of the living in the field of public affairs has some significance. At the very least the paradox indicates that Americans of this generation have not thought through their political situation and their political problems. Perhaps through neglect they have forgotten the fundamental facts of the nature of representative government in a democratic society.

The Cast of Characters: The Big Three

In attempting to reach conclusions regarding morality in American politics a useful first step is to note the principal elements in the political system, which is a mixture of both old and new features. The old elements are the legislative, executive and judicial "branches of government," the "big three" of tradition, which once dominated the game almost completely. The galaxy of stars who drafted the Constitution of the United States gave more attention to legislative power, to creating the Congress and to defining its authority than to any other subject. Their decisions are embodied in Article 1, which although not quite 200 printed lines in length,[2] more than twice as long as any other article. The legislative assembly has always been the heart of representative government, and the framers of the Constitution, rich in political experience and aware of the lessons of political history, especially their own, started with legislative power and the legislative body in creating a new government.

The executive came next in literary order and also in importance; and when the decision was made to set up a strong and unified executive in the President of the United States, his powers, duties and method of selection could be defined in Article 2, which is approximately eighty lines of print, less than half as long as the legislative article. Article 3 on the judicial power is a matter of only about thirty lines, packed with meaning for the future, as were all parts of the Constitution, famous for its lucid brevity.

Certain characteristics of the three branches of government should be noted. They were deliberately created by the constitutional convention which Jefferson, who was not a member, being absent as a diplomat in France, called an "assembly of demigods." The three branches are equal in having constitutional status. That is, each is a creature of the Constitution, with certain powers secured to it by the Constitution. But they are otherwise quite different and unequal in their constitutional character, for only Congress is created in completeness by the Constitution, and only Congress has generic powers. No one has added to or subtracted from the powers of Congress, except by reinterpreting or amending the Constitution itself, and the composition of Congress has changed only through amendment (No. 17 providing for direct election of Senators), through the admission of new states to the Union and through Acts of Congress itself in reapportioning the membership of the House of Representatives after each decennial census, as required by the Constitution. Although the 82nd Congress, weighted down with 160 years of precedents, conventions, and (some hamstringing) traditions, is a quite different body from the first Congress, the first was a complete, if not mature, political organism.

The executive, in contrast, was quite incomplete. The entire executive branch, except the chief executive (and the Vice President), has been created since by Acts of Congress or under the authority of such Acts and could be abolished by the Congress.

If the executive was incomplete, the judiciary was more so. The Constitution provided that there should be one supreme court but left its composition and the composition of all other federal courts to the Congress. These also could be altered or abolished (except possibly the Supreme Court) by Acts of Congress. Article 3 is concerned chiefly with the tenure of federal judges and the jurisdiction of federal courts.

The constitutional separateness and the degree of independence which each of the three branches has in the exercise of its functions is famous as the threefold "separation of powers." It was a new departure in modern times, and a deliberate creation of men who were both experienced and learned, but it was not original. The idea goes back to the Grecian Pentateuch of all Western politics, where a three-way separation of powers is suggested in Aristotle's *Politics* (Book IV, Ch. 14.). It was elaborated and advocated as a safeguard to freedom by Locke and Montesquieu with whose ideas Madison and his colleagues in the constitutional convention were quite familiar. The contribution of the framers of the Constitution to the art of politics, in this connection, was their refinement and skillful application of the doctrine of separation of powers and their combining it with "checks and balances." The separation was in essence a primary division of labor and as such was in accord with experience, but it was not *isolation* of powers. In fact, each branch of government was deliberately made dependent upon one or both of the others.

Examples of this principle of "checks and balances" are numerous: Congress legislates, but the executive and the courts carry laws into effect; Acts of Congress are also subject to the President's veto, which may be overridden by a two-thirds vote in both houses; the President is chief executive, but Congress authorizes programs, determines the organic structure, prescribes procedure, and appropriates funds—frequently in great detail; the Senate shares in the executive's functions in giving its advice and consent to the making of treaties and to most of the important executive appointments and the appointment of judges; Congress may also remove both executive officials and judges through the impeachment process; the courts are independent in trying cases brought before them, including questions of the constitutionality of Acts of Congress and of state legislatures, but theirs is a passive role; someone else initiates all actions; the executive prosecutes, and the President makes appointments to the bench and also has the power of pardon.

A few state governments had experimented with the separation-of-powers idea during the years of the Confederation before the Constitution of the United States was drafted, and Madison and his colleagues of the constitutional convention were familiar with their experience; but the division of labor was not so clear and legislative hegemony was much stronger in the state governments. Most of the early state governments were completely dominated by the legislature; the executive and the courts were weak and under legislative control. The states, in time, learning from experience and influenced by the federal Constitution, came to follow the threefold separation-of-powers plan. But although some state constitutions set forth the separation-of-powers doctrine in extreme form, most of them fell short of the federal example in developing their governmental institutions. In the states today, the legislative domination still tends to be greater than in the federal government, despite the dramatic development of the office of governor. The state executive tends to lack the strength of the federal executive; and the state judiciary, in comparison with the federal courts, is relatively weak and less independent.

The separation-of-powers principle in American politics is famous, but not well understood. Points too often overlooked are the primacy of the legislative body in the trilogy, and the distinctly inferior role of the courts in the day-to-day business of government. Although each member is essential, the "big three" have not been and cannot be equal partners. An even more important point is the rationale for separating the legislative, executive, and judicial processes. The historic objective was a very practical one—to avoid the unfair discrimination which almost always arises when a government takes action on particular matters without a pre-established principle or policy to guide it. By first determining the policy on the basis of general considerations, a government makes more probable the consistent treatment of individual cases, which is an essential ingredient of justice. It helps to have the rules understood before a game starts.

A second practical objective was to get the benefit of specialization inherent in a rational division of labor. Historically legislative assemblies have been unexcelled in establishing broad policies generally satisfactory to the public, but have never been found suited to the daily conduct of public affairs, an executive function, or to the trial of numerous specific legal controversies, the historic mission of courts. These rather obvious points should be noted for the reason that if legislative, executive and judicial institutions develop in such a way that this division of labor is not preserved, the entire separation-of-powers scheme loses its meaning.

The Cast of Characters: New Members

The men of the constitutional convention did a remarkably complete job. The government they designed began to operate quickly and was successful in governing the country from the beginning. To the 1789 cast of characters, however, three new and important members have been added which have radically changed the drama of American politics. The advent of one of these was feared, a second would have been regarded with horror if it had been foreseen, and the third was expected but not understood.

The feared member was the party system. Since democratic suffrage had yet to be established, the political leaders of the American colonies naturally thought of parties in terms of the aristocratic factions which schemed, maneuvered, or warred for power among the monarchies of Europe, or in terms of the contemporary behavior of contending groups in the first state governments. So dissatisfied were the framers of the Constitution with the political parties of their experience that they hoped to avoid entirely or greatly minimize party politics in the new government, and urged adoption of the new Constitution on the ground that it would tend "to break and control the violence of faction." [3] Although party lines began to form before the constitutional convention was well under way, Washington, after two terms as President of the new government, still held to the eighteenth-century antipathy for parties and in his farewell address warned his countrymen deliberately and at length "in the most solemn manner against the baneful effects of the Spirit of Party, generally." [4] He argued powerfully that in a country equipped with democratic institutions of representative government political parties are thoroughly subversive. His warnings were ineffective. During the nineteenth century political parties became an integral part of the political system, making fundamental changes in the constitution without altering a line of the constitutional document, playing a dominant part in government, and going through substantial organic changes of their own.

The sincere and bitter denunciations of parties by Washington and Madison actually apply more accurately, in fact with amazing precision, to the economic pressure groups which have come to play so important a part in American politics of the twentieth century. Madison was concerned about "the violence of factions," and saw that "the most common and durable source of factions has been the various and unequal distribution of property." . . . "A landed interest, a manufacturing interest, a mercantile interest, a moneyed interest, with many lesser interests, grow up of necessity in civilized nations. . . . The regulation of these various and interfering interests forms the principal task of modern legislation, and involves the spirit of party and faction in the necessary and ordinary operations of the government." [5] This sounds quite modern to twentieth-century citizens; but what Madison could not foresee was the aggressive and skillful way in which these regulated interests themselves set about to regulate the state itself in all of its activities, legislative, executive, and judicial. They have come to be organized bodies entirely independent of the traditional political parties. "The activities of pressure groups were once thought to be merely a segment of American politics. It would be more accurate, today, to say that the political parties themselves have become a segment of a much vaster system of pressure politics, a year-round business with an infinite variety of forms and almost unlimited funds." [6] What Madison and Washington feared has happened, not so much in the political parties of the nineteenth century, as in the pressure groups of the twentieth. The warnings of these wise and practical men make solemn reading today because after 150 years they are so timely.

The third new member of the governing cast is the vast administrative structure and administrative staff of government—a coral growth, of small pieces added one at a time, constantly beaten upon by waves of criticism, but slowly built up to meet the demands of a people who have been consistently anti-government in attitude. It is a tough structure, not easily torn down. Its vitality is firmly based on the character of the tasks that it performs, most of which seem to be essential to modern life. Services are expanded and curtailed from time to time, but they are seldom stopped entirely. Battleships were put in moth balls after World War II, but the Navy was not discontinued. Daily mail deliveries can be reduced, but it is hard to drop even a single category of postal services. Congress may cut the budget, and the staff, of the Federal Communications Commission, but it does not stop regulating the air waves. The functions of state and local governments are even more inelastic; the municipalities in particular are in effect consumers' co-operatives providing essential services of all sorts—public schools, police protection, fire protection, street systems, rapid-transit facilities, parks and beaches, health protection, water supply, sometimes other public-utility services, sanitation, etc.

The administrative structure today is vast as well as relatively stable. The largest executive departments of the federal government are bigger enterprises by far than the largest business concerns, and more complex in their range of ethical, technical and managerial problems. Any one of the three largest executive departments of the federal government (Army, Post Office, Navy) has a larger working force than the Ford Motor Company, the Bethlehem Steel Corporation, Swift and Co., and the Aluminum Company of America, all combined.[7] One of the smaller departments such as Interior, eighth or ninth in size among federal agencies, with 55,-000 to 65,000 employees,[8] is larger in number of employees than all except a handful of manufacturing corporations. The number of civilian employees in the federal government has increased from a little more than 200,000 in 1900 to a little more than 600,000 in 1930, to 1,000,000 in 1940, and to 2,100,000 in 1950.[9] Between 1940 and 1950 the number of federal civilian employees swelled to more than 3,000,000 during World War II, and then dropped below 2,000,000 (and was continuing to drop) before the Korean conflict began. Rearmament and partial mobilization increased the number of federal workers again to more than 2,500,000 men and women in 1951.

Federal employment tends to fluctuate in accordance with

the scale of the government's defense program. Employment in state and local governments is more stable, and is greater in total than federal employment except during the peak of total war, *e.g.*, 1945. State and local governments had a working force of 3,400,000 in 1940 compared with the federal government's 1,000,000 and in 1950 the state and local force of 4,200,000 was just twice that of Uncle Sam's.[10]

Governmental expenditures also reflect the role of public administration in the governmental process. Comparing the years 1929 and 1949, the expenditures of all governments in the United States totaled just $10.22 billions in 1929 and were 9.8 per cent of the gross national product.[11] In 1949 the expenditures of all governments totaled $59.7 billions, and were 23.3 per cent of the gross national product of the country. The change in percentage has come chiefly in the federal government. State and local expenditures were almost the same percentage of gross national product in 1949 (7.2 per cent) as in 1929 (7.3 per cent). Now that the national problems of economic stability and international security have been accepted as functions of the national government, its financial burdens and administrative problems will continue to be large.

Size alone is not the most significant factor in making administration a new force in American politics. More important are the positive character of the governmental functions, the wide variety of specific programs which require an active working force, and the substantial discretion which administrators have in carrying on their work. Public administration not only has an impact on the prosperity and welfare of the nation; it is an integral part of the economy, and most changes in government policy grow out of what the government is already doing. The administrative experience of government is perhaps its prime source of ideas for modifying or improving legislation, and the discretionary power delegated to administrators in many fields gives them a critical role in shaping public policy.

Public administration is obviously an important new member of the cast in the present drama of politics, but opinions differ as to the nature of the role. Hero or villain? A leading part or just a mass of "extras" filling up the scenery? Again the contrast between general and specific views is evident. There has scarcely been a year in the last half-century when someone has not written a book or a series of articles on the perils of bureaucracy; and the frequent cry of wolf! wolf! does not mean that there is no danger. But when specific administrative organizations are considered there are always numerous and convincing character references. The most expensive function of government, national defense, which also tends to be most bureaucratic, is an obvious example. Although the defense departments are costly, full of bureaucratic zeal, convicted of error, authoritarian, and at times scornful of the civilian, they still have high standing and a touch of glamour. With lesser agencies the situation is much the same. Nothing is less popular than regulation, but when anyone suggests tinkering with the Interstate Commerce Commission the railroads rally immediately to its defense; they want it left just as it is! The National Labor Relations Board was subject to severe criticism for a decade before the storm broke, leaving in its wake not destruction but reincarnation and an assured future. The state public-utility commissions, once simultaneously cheered and booed by different parts of the public, are now venerable characters with plenty of friends in the industry. Public administration is neither hero nor villain, but the play cannot go on without it.

The Public—Phantom or Reality?

The enigma in American politics is the public itself. Confidence in the public's powers and virtues has waxed and waned almost as often as the moon. Revolutionary enthusiasm for the common man's capacities to govern had somewhat moderated when the Constitution was written, but extra-legal changes quickly transformed the President from a remote figure to be chosen indirectly by a select group, into a great popular leader elected, although not nominated, by the people. Every loss of faith in the public has been followed eventually by a renewed drive for more democratic politics. Universal suffrage, direct primaries, popular election of the Senate, and the initiative, referendum, and recall are landmarks of this swinging pendulum. For the past thirty years, however, there has been persistent pessimism about the public's capacity to act as a rational force.

Any system of representative government is based upon ultimate public decision in political matters, and when the system of representative government is democratic the public must be large, as it is in the United States. The system cannot possibly work if the public does not do its part. Lincoln's phrase "of the people, by the people, and for the people" is as true as it is dramatic. Government cannot be for the people unless it is of them and by them, and the ultimate test of government's being of and by the people is its being in fact for them.

But what is the public's role? How much is it reasonable to expect? And who are the public? The answer to these questions is not clear in the minds of Americans today. At one extreme is the historic conception of the rational citizen, a dignified eighteenth-century figure in knee breeches and powdered wig, who gave most of his time to affairs of state in a highly intelligent way. At the other extreme is the neurotic public implied by many present-day appeals of both politicians and commercial advertisers, who seem to say that man is moved so largely by his fears, passions, and prejudices that his reason is of little consequence. If these extreme views are unrealistic, and if the public is in fact moved by both reason and emotion, the question becomes one of proportion and degree. How many members of the public are accustomed to think rationally about political matters? How many deliberately make it a practice to try to get the evidence and to view it dispassionately? If there is even a small number of men and women of this stamp, scattered widely throughout American society, perhaps the public's political competence is not in danger. If the number is substantial, democratic confidence in the public is fully justified; for all students of mankind, the cynics as well as the optimists, recognize that men follow leaders in their opinions as well as their actions, and that a few active thinkers influence many who are more passive.

The public's capacity for intelligent decision is not something unchangeable, nor is it solely a function of the voter. Political practices and methods which encourage or discourage dispassionate analysis have a bearing, and so does the clarity with which issues are presented and political responsibilities are fixed. If all political leaders make an emotional appeal to fear and prejudice, the public has little chance to be discriminating in its judgment. It needs to have the facts presented and discussed objectively by at least a few persons who seek its attention in order to have a choice. Similarly, if the machinery of government becomes so complex in its design or in its operation that the public cannot tell who is responsible for legislative and executive decisions, the public's capacity to govern is reduced, through no fault of its own. If "people have an obligation not to be 'suckers'," [12] as the Ethics Subcommittee of the Senate has suggested, the citizen also has a right to a reasonably clear system of executive responsibility in administering public affairs, and to an understandable legislative process. This point is emphasized by what is one of the oldest maxims of representative government—authority and responsibility must be clearly fixed if the system is to work. To subvert this principle by a committee system, rules of legislative procedure, or purely traditional arrangements is just as serious in the Congress as to deny the public the forms of representation.

The public also has a right to expect adherence to at least the common standards of professional ethics among its political representatives as a class. This is no more than decent respect for the principles of division of labor and specialization underlying modern life. Existing specialization is tolerable only because a man can have at least moderate confidence in the honesty, reliability, and good faith of the advice he receives from his doctor, dentist, lawyer, architect, teacher, or other professional person. He has a certain amount of skepticism; he likes to hear the reasons, and sometimes the patient decides not to take the medicine and to get another doctor; but the layman does not have to verify everything that his numerous professional advisers tell him. Most of the time he can rely upon the judgment and integrity of the professional man.

Although the profession of politics has important differences from the other professions, it must inevitably be subject to at least equivalent standards of integrity and competence. Otherwise his political duties would take the citizen's full time. Delegation to the Representative in Congress or the physician at the medical center makes sense only when normally he can be relied upon.

The phantom public is less of a phantom than the cynics would have us believe, but there is evidence that the public is not entirely happy with its present lot or fully effective in its present role. Enigma that it is among the principal characters in American politics, the public is still the strong member of the cast although it is the least articulate one.

The problem of morality in politics involves them all—legislature, the executive, the courts, public administration, parties, pressure groups, and the public. Moral problems, moral standards, moral failures and moral achievements are involved in the structure of political institutions, and they are so treated in the chapters which follow. The moral problems of any man, in government or out, can be appreciated only when one understands the conditions under which the man lives.

II

MORALS AND POLITICS

Views as to the moral nature of politics differ widely. Some men believe politics to be inherently amoral. They argue that states cannot be and are not bound by the moral code that governs individual men. Others think politics essentially immoral, for they note the tendency of men in politics (as in other phases of life) to fall short of approved moral standards, and they overlook the fact that moral failures in politics receive more attention than do moral failures in any other field, except perhaps religion. Influence peddling, for example, makes the front page when it involves government, while in purely inter-business transactions it is seldom given a line on the financial page. However, men in politics can count on being reminded of the truth of Lord Acton's famous phrase "all power corrupts, and absolute power corrupts absolutely."

The varied points of view from which the subject can be approached make for some confusion, but the morality of politics as a social process, the morality of the American system, and morality of men in politics, although different matters, are related. Moral standards for states, statesmen, and the system in which they operate are all derived from a common source, the cultural and religious heritage of the country. Although states are obviously not individuals, and their ethical problems differ, what is wrong for an individual, in dealing with his fellow men, obviously does not become right simply because he does it through an organized group—pressure group, party, state, or nation.

A significant phase of the moral problem, also, is the interaction of the political system and the ethical standards of politicians upon each other. The logical starting point in trying to get questions of political morality straight, however, is the moral nature of authority in the American political system of representative government. Fortunately, this is relatively clear.

The Moral Basis of Politics

Representative government in the United States has English roots, but they are in English local self-government, and in the municipal corporations and chartered companies of merchant adventurers, such as the Virginia Company, rather than in the English Parliament, which was a rival as well as an example. In fact, self-government in America owes more to the necessities of the situation in the early colonies than to legal precedent. It was not possible to administer the new colonies from England. To deal with their problems and to overcome difficulties that faced them, the participation of colonists themselves was rather quickly recognized to be essential. The needed realism and motivation could not be secured otherwise. To a very considerable extent the vitality of the institution of self-government stems from the conditions of American life. In both law and fact the responsibility for survival was on the shoulders of the colonists, and over the course of 169 years they came in fact and habit to exercise the powers of self-government.

When during the eighteenth century the government in England attempted to impose unacceptable policies on the Englishmen in America, it was too late; they had actually become Americans, and revolution followed, perhaps unavoidably. Revolution did not come immediately, however, and questions of the nature of political authority and of political institutions were thoroughly analyzed and discussed. When the Declaration of Independence was finally written and signed, it reflected not merely the views of the chief draftsman, Thomas Jefferson, or of the drafting committee of five, or of the fifty-six signers; it was an expression of consensus.[1] It stated the ideas and the arguments upon which the revolutionists agreed. It summarized the convictions of men who were willing to fight for self-government and who did so. The Declaration of Independence is therefore a most significant part of the American Constitution.

In it are implicit three great principles, corroborated and developed by later events of war and peace, which are basic in the American political system. They are fundamental constitutional principles more elemental and more deeply founded even than the great constitutional document drafted eleven years later, at the Philadelphia convention.

The first great principle is the generic principle that political authority has only a moral basis, rationally determined. Governments derive no authority merely from the fact that they exist. The revolutionary statesmen recognized the power of tradition and inertia. "Prudence, indeed, will dictate," they said, "that Governments long established should not be changed for light and transient causes; and accordingly all experience has shown, that mankind are more disposed to suffer, while evils are sufferable, than to right themselves by abolishing the forms to which they are accustomed." But they denied that tradition or physical force gives validity to government, and argued that when causes are more than "light and transient," and when the failures of government to fulfill its proper ends are serious and continued, there is a right *and a duty* of revolution.[2]

A second great fundamental is the critical principle that the public interest is the criterion by which political actions must be judged—not an individual interest, not a group interest, not even the interest of a majority group. This is implicit in the ideas that "All men are created equal" and that it is the function of governments to secure to them all their God-given and "unalienable rights" ("among these are life, liberty, and the pursuit of happiness"). The fact that the public interest includes the interest of all, not merely the interest of a majority, was recognized more fully in the decisions of the constitutional convention, which attempted to provide for effective majority rule but with limited powers, and with clear protection for minority rights. In setting up the federal government the Fathers of the Republic attempted to act on the fundamental principle that if the interests of no group are pushed too far, the interests of all are reconcilable. This criterion of the public interest is basic in both the Declaration and the Constitution. The comprehensiveness of this standard makes it both more ambitious and more subtle than "the greatest good of the greatest number," and it is feasible only if there is in government both vigor and restraint. The tacit qualification (of human slavery) upon this universal concept may be said to have been expunged and expiated in the bloody Civil War for which Lincoln's Gettysburg address is perhaps the appropriate commemorative constitutional document.

Fully as significant as the moving passages of the opening paragraphs of the Declaration of Independence are the twenty-seven paragraphs which follow, each one detailing a specific failure of the British government to respect the public interest in its dealings with the colonies. The rational and pragmatic test was applied. The British government lacked authority in America because it had seriously neglected and abused the welfare of Americans; they thought it was not in fact governing for the American public interest. "Let facts be submitted to a candid world."

A third great precept is the organic principle of representation—of governments "deriving their just powers from the consent of the governed." Its negation gave moral fervor to the Revolution, and its positive application permeated the Constitution which begins "We the people of the United States . . . do ordain and establish this Constitution for the United States of America." The tenth amendment, the last item in the "bill of rights," adopted in 1791, makes explicit the popular sovereignty which is implicit in the body of the Constitution. "The powers not delegated to the United States by the Constitution, nor prohibited by it to the States, are reserved to the States respectively, or to the people." Article 1 gives to Congress "all legislative powers herein granted" and enumerates them, and it also specifies in detail a series of limitations both substantive and procedural. State constitutions have followed the same basic plan. There is no hereditary political power in the United States. There is no inherent political power. There is no prerogative. Public officials derive both their power and their office from the public, and it has been a consistent endeavor of constitution-makers to insure that officials will act for and in the interest of the public. It is not possible to make this certain by constitutional machinery alone, but in America it is not left to any transcendental process. The consistent tendency has been to favor objective institutional arrangements that will increase the probability that officials will act in the public interest.

The power of these ideas comes not chiefly from their having been stated or followed in the great political documents, some of which have legal status, but from their fundamental validity. After more than a century and a half of uniquely American political experience (as long as the period since the Revolution) the statesmen of the Revolutionary period had insight into the nature of politics that went deep. Heavy responsibility and extensive practice in self-government matured them, and economic pressure hardened them. Judged by the standards of today, however, the amazing thing about the politicians of the eighteenth century is the high level of their analysis of the problems of politics. They felt the need to justify their course; they chose to justify their decisions on moral grounds; and they appealed to reason, arguing the facts, not without emotion, but with an honest attempt to be clear, and on grounds that could be generalized. They treated their specific problems in a way that had general validity. The result was a consensus and moral force which made possible, first revolution, and, second, the still more difficult achievement of continental unity in a new nation of commonwealths in which the centrifugal forces of localism and particularism were already very strong. In combining the rational and the moral, the early leaders of the Republic were drawing upon the same basic forces that have been so largely responsible for the progress and the strength of Western culture in modern times.

The American political system, to be understood, must be seen in its setting as the westernmost development of Western culture. Deep religious conviction had been as important as economic pressure in settling the colonies, and the intellectual leaders of the new nation recognized the authority of Hebrew-Greek-Christian thought as to man, his nature, his obligations, and his role in life. These men had moral courage, moral conviction, and moral force. They knew where they stood and for what they stood. In the hierarchy of laws—federal constitution, federal statutes, state constitutions, and state statutes—which has become so characteristic of American politics, there is a still higher law: "The Laws of Nature and of Nature's God," which is the first premise of the Declaration of Independence.

From its first moment of independence the nation has avowed the highest moral standards known to man. Its political system and its political decisions must be justified rationally by these standards. This is the first and oldest constitutional principle of American politics. Such a standard has given trouble and it is bound to do so again, but it also gives direction to American politics.

Moral principles are fundamental in the American political system. When issues arise which are recognized as moral issues, they take precedence. But why is it that so few problems of day-to-day politics are recognized as raising any ethical questions in themselves, or that ethical questions are treated as subordinate, secondary, or inconsequential? The explanation lies in the context of American life, and in the attitudes and habits which have grown out of American experience during the past century. The tendency to overlook or minimize basic ethical issues in public affairs is influenced by many factors, among them a belief in the automatic qualities of the economic system and in the inherent mechanical stability of the system of representative government, great emphasis upon constitutionalism and legalism, and very substantial achievement in safeguarding the welfare, status, and freedom of the individual man and woman in American life.

Early Success and Moral Apathy

The last factor comes first in chronological order. The emphasis given to the equality and the rights of man by political leaders of the Revolutionary period was carried into the Constitution of the United States and into subsequent public policy. Property and tax-paying qualifications for voting were removed in one state after another, and were not established in the new Western states. The battle to establish universal suffrage for men (except slaves) was largely won by the time of Jackson's election in 1828. The rich resources of the Western territories and Western states, combined with the policy of selling land to the public in small tracts at low prices and the later homestead policy kept the door of opportunity open and made it possible for the average man to win comparative economic security through his own hard work. The progressive industrialization of the country during the past century with its high productivity, high wages, and mass production of goods for an assured continental market greatly enhanced the welfare and the physical security of the individual in America. More recently the New Deal social-security program further protected individuals against adverse consequences of the industrial system. The policy of free general public education, furthermore, has brought individual cultural development within the reach of the vast majority of each generation —the poor as well as the rich. So great a majority of Americans, therefore, today enjoy personal freedom, reasonable economic security and a social status unrestricted by a rigid class system that they are inclined to take for granted the basic human rights which were uppermost in the minds of many leading Americans 175 years earlier.

The very considerable success in achieving the early goals which were closely related to the God-given and unalienable rights of man has tended to take them out of political discussion. It is hard for the majority to realize emotionally that there are still minorities which are not so well off, even though they know it intellectually. For example, it is hard to arouse much public concern about defending civil liberties, for so few men have suffered loss of their civil liberties. The third degree is tolerated because a limited group in society bears the brunt of it; the rest have no direct experience with illegal force. The post-Civil War discriminatory restrictions on voting and the intimidation to prevent Negro citizens from voting in some areas of the South are grave problems that cannot be quieted until they are solved, for the evidence that they exist is persuasive. But here also most people do not see the attack on civil liberties in operation. The affected minority experience it; the majority know of it only by hearsay. The present policy of passing upon the loyalty of federal employees by methods which do not come up to the standards of American justice-according-to-law have not concerned the general public very greatly. Federal employees are only a portion of the total body of public servants, and only a tiny portion of them has been adversely affected by the so-called loyalty program. (It is no comfort to remember that disregard of the majority for discrimination against select minorities was characteristic of Nazi Germany.) The general public tends not to be aroused to political action about strictly moral issues until they become acute or general, which is infrequent.

Amoral Economics

In modern politics the issues which attract the most attention and which are the center of the greatest pressures by organized groups come under the general label of "economic" questions. This category almost by definition seems to preclude any intrinsic ethical issues. The assumption appears to be that an economic problem has no moral aspects. If this assumption is accepted, moral issues arise in connection with economic problems only in the political methods and processes by which they are handled. That is, for example, a price-control law involves no intrinsic moral issues; they arise only if there is bribery, venality, or other improper action in the passage of the law or in its enforcement.

This primary role of economic questions in public affairs and the secondary character of moral issues is reflected in the report of the Douglas Committee of the Senate on Ethical Standards in Government.[3] "The forces that would drive public servants from the straight and narrow path of virtue center chiefly upon a limited area, the area in which Government is heavily 'action-laden.' This is the area in which there are big economic stakes, where the decisions of legislators and administrators directly affect the business, or the property, or the income of particular groups or individuals. The abuses of discretion or the exploitation of power are most serious chiefly where the Government is dispensing valuable rights and privileges, constructing extensive public works, spending vast sums for military supplies and equipment, making loans, granting direct or indirect subsidies, levying taxes, and regulating the activities of privileged monopolies or economic practices in which there is a public interest."

Senator Humphrey, in the hearings of the Committee on Ethical Standards, discussed the question,[4] "Where does corruption come in?" and noted that it was the result of pressure for important economic concessions upon "political appointees" at the high policy level. The revelations of corruption which gave rise to the committee's inquiry, he said:

> . . . dealt with a particular area of the Government. . . . We are not referring to the Old-Age Pension or Unemployment Compensation. There has been no scandal around that. What does this involve? It involves an activity of the Government that can do a particular economic favor or act in behalf of people in business or in behalf of people in some form of enterprise. In other words, Teapot Dome dealt with oil, and it took an oil company to make a Secretary of the Interior a crook. RFC dealt with loans and it took somebody that wanted to get a loan to buy somebody a mink coat. What I am trying to get at is that the broad areas of the Government, the great area of our Government that performs the little day-by-day services like the person who polices around the Washington Monument—I do not believe there is any corruption there. I have not heard any exposed— or the guard at Lincoln Memorial or the Food and Drug Administration, or the Children's Bureau, or the Smithsonian Institution, or the Library of Congress, or the rank-and-file agencies like the extension agencies around the country; nobody has pointed out much corruption on them. Where does the corruption come in? Does it not come from where you have two things—a substantial economic reward, not a two-bit one, or a favor to a very limited group, which reward or favor is administered by a political appointee—I repeat, by a political appointee. I have noticed that you find very few instances in all the history of our Government in terms of investigations, and there have been investigations going on since 1798, where an established civil service, particularly since the days of the civil-service law back in the late 1880's, that the civil servant as such has been involved in the corruption. It has been on the two bases. First of all, we had the corruption in giving of land, by whom?—political appointees. Next we had the corruption in reference to the big Teapot Dome on oil; by whom?—political appointees. In the Veterans Administration; by whom?—political appointees. Then we are supposed to have had some alleged corruption in recent days; by whom?—people confirmed by the Congress, honorable men, supposedly, from private life. But the favor was granted to whom? To a particular economic group.

So I think we have a limited area here in the Government in a sense that when we get right down to it, the problem of ethics that we are coming up to comes up from certain revelations. What revelations? Shipbuilding, for example; the Maritime Commission. Surplus ships to whom? To somebody who wants to make a fast dollar, not to grandma or old-age pensions. Somebody who wants a loan. To build what? To build a hotel, a race track, or something else. Government has entered upon a new field of activity where its benefits or gifts or its emoluments go to a limited group.

The tendency to relegate moral considerations to the procedures by which the substance of policies is determined purely on "economic" or "political" merits was noted by the Committee on Ethical Standards. The extemporaneous remarks of Senator Humphrey in the Committee hearings highlight this paradox.[5]

Senator Douglas, and myself, in the 81st Congress, went into the tax law of this country. We had a great time. We did not make too much progress, but we had a very interesting experience and I personally found it very educational. We had twelve so-called tax loopholes that we discussed as amendments to the tax bill. The Congress of the United States had legislated special privileges and no one even thought it improper. All of these exemptions in the excess-profits tax, all the exemptions that Senator Douglas tried to plug in the Renegotiation Act—I think it is the world's worst act—lead to the possibility of the most vile form of corruption. It will take men of the greatest moral integrity to administer this act without fear of suspicion. We have the law of depletion and allowance. I think that is improper. But who am I? Nobody gets as steamed up as they do about the mink coat. I think it is improper to have some of the exemptions in the excess-profits tax. I think it was improper that the insurance companies did not pay any Federal income taxes for two years. That only amounted to $147,000,000, and here is a $9,000 mink coat that gets the headlines.

I am not condoning the mink coat. I think that is inexcusable, and has brought to our attention a very sad moral condition. But what this Senator is trying to drive at is that you have a problem in this country that if you can get the law fixed, that is, those who want special privilege make the special privilege legal by getting the law. Therefore it does not become illegal any more, and after long use it is not improper. You know you can get used to jumping on one leg.

So sooner or later that which was termed "illegal" becomes proper.

Where do you draw the line? My code of ethics is this, that while it is terrible and it ought to be prosecuted, and I had a little record in doing so as a municipal official, slot machine, one-armed bandits, that is corruption, but it is not any more illegal than stealing the iron ore out of Northern Minnesota and not paying a fair share of the tax on it. But they made that legal by getting the tax fixed. They just say it is politics. Not to me. It is part of my region. I do not think people have the right to exploit the resources of this country. Is it proper to go out and exploit the forests? Here is the Forestry Service. I have not found anybody being accused of being a crook in that Service.

I do not know if I can tie this up, except there seems to be two patterns. On the one hand you have government involved in the economic activity. The men would not be corrupt in the Government if they were not corrupted from the outside. I think we need better men . . . You cannot possibly find a man who is going to withstand all the pressure if the community on the outside is filled with economic vultures. They are going to find somebody who is going to break down sooner or later. So as the preceding witness said, this goes deeper than the Bureau of the Budget, and the executive agencies, and frankly a lot of it goes right down to Congress, where we make the basic law of the land. When we can withdraw the act of 1872 on this whole matter of officials of Government going back to private industry, and representing their industries before the ones they were acquainted with; when we can have the kind of contract settlement that we have; when the Congress of the United States passes a war-assets program that permits the disposal of Government property without due consideration of value. This comes right back here. You know all you have to do is legislate a pattern. Pass a law there shall be no more sin. No one apparently legally commits any sin. It depends on what your moral standards are. We have two things here. Illegality and a proper evaluation of what is adequate morality, and morality is intangible. It is hard to place your fingers on what is moral and immoral.

The report of the Committee on Ethical Standards also called attention to this anomaly.[6] "We should also realize that morality is violated not merely by politicians and by the weak, but also frequently by the strong and powerful, who sometimes are able to have their antisocial acts approved by legislation or court action. The medieval English quatrain about the way in which the common lands were enclosed and taken over by the nobility of England has also real meaning for our times:

> The law locks up both man and woman
> Who steals the goose from off the common,
> But lets the greater felon loose
> Who steals the common from the goose."

The Automatic Economic System

The tendency to play down or entirely ignore the ethical questions imbedded in the substance of economic issues can be explained partly in terms of certain notions which many Americans have about the automatic qualities of the economy; the idea of the economic order which has dominated American thinking for many years is that it is a machine largely automatic in quality. It seems to require only occasional oiling or adjusting to keep it running. Anything more than this is called "interference." We have clung desperately to the idea that competition of investors, businessmen, employees, and farmers so integrates the efforts of all that no matter what each does or tries to do for his own benefit, the effect is to benefit all. That is, we have assumed an economic system in which both prosperity and justice are inherent; moral issues are resolved automatically by the "system."

There are a number of reasons why the idea of an automatic economic "system" has a hold on Americans. One is the familiar habit of wishful thinking. It would be nice to have such a system. It is only a short step from that to thinking that we do have it.

A second is the inevitable lag in adjusting ideas to changed situations; the period of adjustment may be unusually long among a people not much given to theorizing, and events have moved swiftly. In 1952 it is easy to forget that agriculture dominated the American economy during most of the nine-teenth century, and that it was highly competitive agriculture.[7] The trust movement did not make itself felt until the 1880's and the anti-trust legislation of 1890 and 1914 seemed at the time to be a direct reply, even though the effectiveness of these measures was difficult to assess.[8] The Federal Reserve legislation of 1913 looked like a similar reply to the threat of centralized financial domination symbolized by "Wall Street." [9] Its effects were also difficult to measure. Doubts about the inherent perfection of the economic system were muffled by the boom of the 1920's, and the first real challenge to the concept of automatism was the shock of the severe and pro-longed depression which ended that decade. Perhaps prosperity and progress were not inherent functions of the American econ-omy after all.

The illusion was fractured but not shattered. Wartime pros-perity and the post-war boom have glued up the cracks. The depression has become a sort of dark chapter in our past, best not to be talked about. One could almost believe that there was no depression, and that the New Deal was a dream (good or bad depending upon your point of view). We see only "prosperity" ahead and we have not yet discovered the full significance of inflation. The idea of a mechanical econ-omy dies hard.

The high degree of specialization and intense personal con-centration which have characterized American business also influenced American belief in an automatic economic order. In the eighties and nineties men began to feel the pressure of business demands; the older men began to drop out of active politics and the younger men felt that they could not afford to enter it. (They also began to withdraw from social, cultural, recreational, and religious affairs.) Concentration became the rule, and it was thought to be a necessity. The Mark Hannas and Tom Johnsons who made the contrary choice and gave up business for politics were freaks who came to be regarded as sinister or dangerous. When the leading men in the rising industry of their day were concentrating on a single industry, a single company, or a single product—steel, oil, soap, tobacco, air brakes, or an automobile, it was not difficult to assume that the economy was self-regulating even though each businessman sought to utilize political as well as economic forces for the furtherance of his business. This assumption was reinforced by the fact that businessmen sought to utilize those forces only for the benefit of their businesses. That was "tending to business," and if everybody was doing so the business system must be automatic.

A factor confirming this impression was doubtless the steady increase in wealth.[10] If the rule is to tend strictly to the business of getting ahead, and if individual fortunes and the national wealth grow apace, it is easy to think that the increase in wealth is a function of the system rather than of the situation, and that the system is mechanically stable.

Probably as influential as anything in determining American attitudes is the fact that personal competition has always been keen and still is in American business. Businessmen work hard and rivalry is strong. Individual enterprise is a reality even though Adam Smith would hardly admit that our form of business organization is one of private enterprise. Business seeks talent and the door of opportunity is open. Nepotism and favoritism are not so strong as in foreign countries, and able young men do not have to have family influence to get a start. It is easy to identify the strong personal competition of American business with a fully competitive economy, although the two are quite different things from the customer's point of view.

Despite the strength of our desire to forget the shock of the depression to the American idea of a mechanical economy, there is no doubt of the reality of the shock. Under no other circumstances could the Temporary National Economic Commission have been created to survey the wreckage of 1929. Among other things, the TNEC served to document the fact that "big business" did exist. It also recognized that to competition and monopoly, as we had previously understood them, American business had added something new, a third area of quasi-monopoly or limited competition. We were in the midst of painfully pondering this situation when the Wagner Act, like a magic wand, created "big labor" where before there had been a largely unorganized labor force.[11] Then only a little more slowly "big agriculture" [12] came on the scene conceived by the New Deal and nourished by World War II.

To one trying to look at the scene objectively it would seem that the American economy has almost completely changed in character in the past fifty to seventy-five years,[13] but that nevertheless our conventional ideas about it, our subconscious assumptions, or our wishful views, have not changed very much. We have renamed the picture rather ingeniously. We don't call it "individualism," "rugged" or otherwise; that would be a little strong. We don't even say very much about "private property." "Free enterprise" is the new term that carries with it the old connotation of automatism and does so without explicitly challenging the obvious facts of life.

It is a good term. There is much freedom and a lot of enterprise in American economic life, and these are qualities which deserve recognition. It is a good economy to which the term refers, even though it is very obviously a "political economy."

We seem to be reconciled to that also. The American economy of free enterprise is the best in the world. Most of us believe this even without being told it by the advertisements in the periodicals of wide circulation, by the enclosures in pay envelopes, by the reprints clipped to dividend checks, and by the more ostentatiously patriotic radio commentators. We have reason to believe it. But we are beginning to doubt that the *system* is fully automatic in its capacity to produce "prosperity." Skepticism might be carried one step further, that is, to ask for evidence that justice and equity are inherent in the play (which is sometimes highly political) of "economic forces." Labeling a question "economic" does not *ipso facto* exclude all moral considerations.

The Automatic System of Representative Government

A factor which has encouraged the tendency to minimize ethical considerations is a similar rather widespread belief in the inherent stability of the American system of representative government. We see in our political system with its historic emphasis on constitutionalism, federalism, delegated powers, limitations on power, division of powers, checks and balances, and extensive elections a mechanism which produces both stability and progress—automatically. It is a marvelous contrivance which manufactures responsible government from the total political activity of somewhat irresponsible people. Our political system makes officials responsible while freeing everyone else from the burden of responsibility. This is a comforting mental picture of the American system of government.

Of all modern conveniences which American ingenuity has devised, this governmental mechanism is by far the greatest.

Relying on the unerring wisdom of the machine, each of us is at liberty to concentrate his efforts so as to get as much for himself as he can from the state, by whatever means are not effectively prohibited, and the result will be order, progress, and prosperity for all. The pulling and hauling of individuals and groups for advantage leads inevitably to equilibrium. The electronic wisdom and the gyroscopic stability of the American system of representative government are so great that it can integrate the unrestrained efforts of all irresponsible individuals, and from this complex of forces create responsible government. This is the perfect philosophy to accompany pressure politics.

Americans, to be sure, are realists. We know that no system is perfect and say so repeatedly. The weak spot in our system, almost all agree, is to be found in the "politicians," who sometimes are sadly lacking in wisdom, courage, or integrity. Although this weakness in the "human element" is a matter of universal regret, we are confident that our system of government is so rugged that it can absorb a lot of mismanagement without serious consequences. We have the situation so well diagnosed that if anything goes wrong, that is, if we don't like the situation in which we find ourselves, we know immediately that the trouble lies with "the politicians in Washington." On this point at least Americans are a united people.

The progressive collapse of democratic representative government in Europe was disturbing, but could be explained on various grounds which distinguished Europe from America. In Italy representative government was new and not well established. Germany never had been really democratic, and the authoritarian tradition was strong. Spain was a bitter episode for all Americans—a state consumed by violence in which "good" and "evil" forces (according to our differing perspectives) were strangely mixed; but of course representative procedures were even newer in Spain. The collapse of representative government in France was more disturbing. We suspected there were other explanations than being overrun by a ruthless foe; but it was difficult to distinguish cause and effect. Furthermore, none of these countries had the American system. All were copying the British parliamentary model, and that is clearly something different from our own. Even here encouragement could be derived from the stability of representative government in Britain itself and in Norway, Sweden, Denmark, Holland, and Belgium. Perhaps the net effect of the European reverses was further to convince us of the virtues and the inherent stability of the American system.

Legalism

Closely related to the concept of an automatic political order is the legalism which is so well established in American life. Although the manner in which the Constitution of the United States was drafted and adopted and the document itself make it clear that it is the instrument by which authority is delegated from the people to public officials to be used in the public interest, and that it is not an independent source of authority, there is a tendency to attribute to the Constitution an almost divine personality, and to venerate it as a source of authority in itself. Similarly there is a tendency to assume that what is legal, touching public affairs, is also right. A well-known example is the field of tax law. The generally accepted standard that it is right to avoid paying taxes by all legal means was both emphasized and challenged in the hearings of the Senate Committee on Ethical Standards. Senator Aiken brought up the subject [14] by referring to an article

. . . on the financial pages of the New York *Times* this morning which states that the Textron Corp. has sold a mill to Vanderbilt University, the mill being in Charlotte, N. C. . . . Vanderbilt University has leased the mill back to the Textron Corp. There is to be no change whatsoever in the operation of the mill. The article stated that by this transaction, State and Federal taxes would not have to be paid on the property. In other words, the University and Textron Corp. share the tax-evasion profits. That is what it amounts to.

Senator Fulbright. That is right.

Senator Aiken. That is just as dishonest as if it were prohibited by law, and that is something that probably law could cure.

Senator Fulbright. That is right.

Senator Aiken. Why do we not have courage enough to cure it?

Senator Fulbright. To me that is a clever tax-avoidance scheme, and it can be reached by law, and it ought to be reached. That is nothing new. That has been going on in an ever-increasing way the last ten or fifteen years since taxes became so heavy.

Senator Aiken. Why does not Congress have courage to stop that?

Senator Fulbright. I am not on the committee, and I have not studied it particularly, but there is this thing that makes it difficult, perhaps. We do have a great sympathy for the plight of the private institutions. They are in a very difficult situation due to inflation on the one hand and low interest rates on the other, both of which come out of governmental policy.

Senator Aiken. The Textron Corp. is not in hard straits according to their recent financial report.

Senator Fulbright. That is true, but I mean the private institutions. I mean the participation of the private institutions is the element which, I imagine, has caused some reluctance to move into the field. They do not know how to save the private institutions, especially the small ones. I personally think it is a terrible thing to the private institutions to be driven out. I am not saying that is an excuse for not doing something because I imagine Textron is getting a windfall which they have no business getting. I do not approve of that system. We ought to find some more legitimate way to help the small institution. This kind of tax avoidance is not a proper thing at all, it seems to me. It has been done on a very large scale.

Senator Aiken. I suppose in this case Vanderbilt University, which probably needs money, will get part of it.

Senator Fulbright. This is right. That is the whole objective. Maybe they split it 50-50.

Senator Aiken. And the University for a consideration is letting itself be used for purposes of tax avoidance by the Textron Corp.

Senator Fulbright. I think that is true. I think the record ought to be clear that this is not new with Vanderbilt. New York University and one after the other of the big institutions have done that. Also, the University of Pennsylvania. They buy the huge buildings, Lit Brothers in Philadelphia, and Gimbel's that pay enormous real-estate taxes. They buy them and lease them back to the company. There are hundreds of thousands, if not millions of taxes saved.

Instead of the taxes going to the Government, it inures to the benefit of the two parties. That is an old device of at least eight or ten years.

Senator Aiken. It would be much better for the Government to collect taxes on the property and allocate a part of it for the cause of higher education.

A witness before the committee, an expert in tax law and tax administration, and a distinguished former public official, brought the ethics of tax evasion back into the discussion a little later:[15]

Mr. O'Connell [addressing Senator Aiken] . . . I do not believe that many people share the view that you expressed: That, in the absence of a change in the law, people would generally think that that type of arrangement was immoral. I do not think that is a theory accepted by people. I think generally the people think that the tax laws are perfectly technical, and it is fair game to take advantage of a loophole.

Senator Aiken. It is an indirect method of government supporting the institutions of higher learning. I think it is probably an expensive method in the long run.

Mr. O'Connell. I think it is true. What it amounts to is that the value of the tax-exempt privilege of the institution is divided up between the commercial enterprise, the tax-exempt institution, and usually the financial institution which supplies the money to the charitable institution to acquire the property. How the division is made, I have not figured out. Maybe they divide it equally, as Senator Fulbright says.

Senator Douglas. Do you think public opinion approves that?

Mr. O'Connell. I think generally you will find very little disapproval among people who deal with tax laws.

Senator Douglas. Perhaps not those who deal with tax laws, because they are professionals who are organized to find loopholes, but I think the general public disapproves of it.

Mr. O'Connell. I think it is not defensible as a general public matter, but I think the only way to handle it is by law.

Legalism is a constant in American politics.

Public Morals and the Problem of Corruption

To a considerable extent the responsibility for regulating the nation's economy has passed from the state capitals to Washington, and has lifted from the states a good bit of the economic pressure for special favors. The pressure of the eighteen eighties and eighteen nineties for generous corporation charters, the later demands for favorable public-utility franchises, and the campaigns to moderate the aggressive tendencies of the new (1911) state public-utility commissions will probably not be repeated. The issues of competition versus monopoly, of unemployment, of inflation, and of economic policy generally are now beyond the states.

State politics is no longer the center of interest for the leading industries of the country. State administrative activities, however, have increased in size and scope as the service functions of the states have grown (with federal aid) in such matters as highway systems, public-assistance programs, unemployment compensation, and expansion of state hospitals and public-health programs. These activities all carry with them certain pressures, but except where construction of public works, highways, bridges, and buildings is involved, they do not come from highly organized interests nor involve the same danger of corruption as formerly when valuable or exclusive economic privileges were at issue. In a sense Esau has sold his birthright and cannot do it again.

The state and local governments, however, still are almost completely responsible for the regulation of public morals. Crime is defined chiefly by state law and the law is chiefly enforced by local officials. Consequently state and local officials have to contend with one of the oldest and most virulent sources of corruption—commercialized vice and crime. This hazard affects them chiefly rather than the federal government, and partially explains their generally lower rating on the scale of ethical standards. This moral hazard is rooted in the double standard of public morality which requires that gambling and other forms of vice be prohibited or at least strictly regulated and which also provides numerous customers who furnish the ample funds to buy protection. When there is so rich a "racket," it is hard to evade its corrupting influence.

In times past reformers in politics occasionally came to the conclusion that the underworld was less dangerous to the public than predatory business interests. Benjamin Cohen, a witness before the Senate Subcommittee on Ethical Standards, recalled [16] "a story which may be apocryphal that used to be told in the old days, and they may not be so far remote, when it was thought that some of the public-utility companies had been active in raising campaign funds. . . . A gubernatorial candidate had to decide whether he would let the utilities or the gamblers finance his campaign, and he took the gamblers' money because he thought fewer strings were attached to their money." Senator Douglas reminded the committee that the famous reform mayors of Cleveland and Toledo,[17] "Tom Johnson and Golden Rule Jones, who were supposed to be very fine men, generally used the underworld as political allies against the private utility companies of the upper world with whom they were struggling."

The possibility of a tolerable choice between predatory interests in the upper- and underworld, as the witness and the committee noted, has been blasted. Senator Aiken warned the Committee on Ethical Standards,[18] citing his Vermont colleague, "I think if Senator Tobey were here he might have some comment to the effect that you do not always have gamblers on one side and utility people on the other . . . sometimes they join forces."

The revelations of the Kefauver Committee (Senate Special Committee to Investigate Organized Crime in Interstate Commerce) that crime is a highly organized big business, which penetrates both legitimate forms of business and politics, completely riddle the notion that there is any way of compromising with it, or that it can have a benign function.[19]

> Organized criminal gangs operating in interstate commerce are firmly entrenched in our large cities in the operation of many different gambling enterprises such as bookmaking, policy, slot machines, as well as in other rackets such as the sale and distribution of narcotics and commercialized prostitution. They are the survivors of the murderous underworld wars of the prohibition era. After the repeal of the prohibition laws, these groups and syndicates shifted their major criminal activities to gambling. However, many of the crime syndicates continued to take an interest in other rackets such as narcotics, prostitution, labor, and business racketeering, black marketing, etc.
>
> Criminal syndicates in this country make tremendous profits and are due primarily to the ability of such gangs and syndicates to secure monopolies in the illegal operations in which they are engaged. These monopolies are secured by persuasion, intimidation, violence, and murder. The committee found in some cities that law-enforcement officials aided and protected gangsters and racketeers to maintain their monopolistic position in particular rackets. Mobsters who attempted to compete with these entrenched criminal groups found that they and their followers were being subjected to arrest and prosecution while protected gang operations were left untouched. . . .
>
> Despite known arrest records and well-documented criminal reputations, the leading hoodlums in the country remain, for the most part, immune from prosecution and punishment, although underlings

of their gangs may, on occasion, be prosecuted and punished. This quasi-immunity of top-level mobsters can be ascribed to what is popularly known as the "fix." The fix is not always the direct payment of money to law-enforcement officials, although the committee has run across considerable evidence of such bribery. The fix may also come about through the acquisition of political power by contributions to political organizations or otherwise, by creating economic ties with apparently respectable and reputable businessmen and lawyers, and by buying public good will through charitable contributions and press relations.

Gambling profits are the principal support of big-time racketeering and gangsterism. These profits provide the financial resources whereby ordinary criminals are converted into big-time racketeers, political bosses, pseudo-businessmen, and alleged philanthropists. Thus, the two-dollar horse bettor and the five-cent numbers player are not only suckers because they are gambling against hopeless odds, but they also provide the moneys which enable underworld characters to undermine our institutions.

The legalization of gambling would not terminate the widespread predatory activities of criminal gangs and syndicates. The history of legalized gambling in Nevada and in other parts of the country gives no assurance that mobsters and racketeers can be converted into responsible businessmen through the simple process of obtaining State and local licenses for their gambling enterprises. Gambling, moreover, historically has been associated with cheating and corruption.

The committee has not seen any workable proposal for controlled gambling which would eliminate the gangsters or the corruption.

Rapid transmission of racing information and gambling information about other sporting events is indispensable to big-time bookmaking operations. This information is presently being provided by a monopoly operated by the Continental Press Service. The Continental Press Service, at critical times and in crucial places where monopoly of bookmaking is at stake, yields to the domination and control of the Accardo-Guzik-Fischetti crime syndicate, to which it is beholden for its own monopoly in the wire-service field. The wire service is so vital to large bookmakers that they are compelled to pay what the traffic will bear to the Continental Press Service. This makes it possible for the Accardo-Guzik-Fischetti crime syndicate to participate in the profits of bookmaking operations throughout the country. . . .

Crime is largely a local problem. It must be attacked primarily at the local level, with supplementary aid, where appropriate, from State and Federal authorities. The conduct of various forms of gambling enterprises, houses of prostitution, the distribution of narcotics, the use of intimidation, violence, and murder to achieve gang objectives are all violations of State laws. The public must insist upon local and State law-enforcement agencies meeting this challenge, and must not be deceived by the aura of romanticism and respectability, deliberately cultivated by the communities' top mobsters.

The Federal Government has the basic responsibility of helping the States and local governments in eliminating the interstate activities and interstate aspects of organized crime, and in facilitating exchange of information with appropriate safeguards between the Federal Government and local and State law-enforcement agencies as well as between law-enforcement agencies in the various States.

The task of dealing with organized crime is so great that the public must insist upon the fullest measure of co-operation between law-enforcement agencies at all levels of Government without buck-passing. The committee feels that it has fully demonstrated the need for such co-operation. The time for action has arrived.

Wide-open gambling operations and racketeering conditions are supported by out-and-out corruption in many places. The wide-open conditions which were found in these localities can easily be cleaned up by vigorous law enforcement. This has been demonstrated in the past in many different communities and has received added demonstration during the life of our committee. The outstanding example is Saratoga, N. Y., which ran wide open through the racing season of 1949 but was closed down tight in 1950.

Venal public officials have had the effrontery to testify before the committee that they were elected on "liberal" platforms calling for wide-open towns. The committee believes that these officials were put in office by gamblers and with gamblers' money, and that in the few cases where the public was convinced that gambling is good for business, this myth was deliberately propagated by the paid publicists of the gambling interests. In many wide-open communities, so-called political leaders and law-enforcement officials have sabotaged efforts of civic-minded citizens to combat such wide-open conditions and the crime and corruption that they entailed.

The Treasury of the United States has been defrauded of huge sums of money in tax revenues by racketeers and gangsters engaged in organized criminal activities. Huge sums in cash handled by racketeers and gangsters are not reflected in their income-tax returns. Income-tax returns filed with the Federal Government have been inadequate since, as a rule, they contained no listing of the sources of income nor any itemization of the expenses. Gangsters and racketeers, moreover, do not keep books and records from which it might be possible to check tax returns.

Mobsters and racketeers have been assisted by some tax accountants and tax lawyers in defrauding the Government. These accountants and lawyers have prepared and defended income-tax returns which they knew to be inadequate. At the very least, those who are guilty of such practices could be convicted of a misdemeanor and sent to jail for a year for every year in which they have failed to comply with the law.

The Bureau of Internal Revenue states that it has, to the best of its ability, considering its limited manpower, been investigating these returns. It states further that when it pursues the case of one of these individuals, it prefers to set up against him a case of criminal tax evasion which is a felony, rather than the lesser offense of failing to keep proper books and records, which is a misdemeanor.

Despite this, the [Kefauver] committee believes that the Bureau of Internal Revenue could, and should, make more frequent use of the sanctions provided for failure to keep proper books and records than it has heretofore. In any event, the Bureau of Internal Revenue should insist on adequate returns and proper books.

While the great majority of agents of the Bureau of Internal Revenue are honest and efficient, there have been relatively few instances in different parts of the country of lack of vigorous and effective action to collect income taxes from gangsters and racketeers.

A major question of legal ethics has arisen in that there are a number of lawyers in different parts of the country whose relations to organized criminal gangs and individual mobsters pass the line of reasonable representation. Such lawyers become true "mouthpieces" for the mob. In individual cases, they have become integral parts of the criminal conspiracy of their clients.

Evidence of the infiltration by organized criminals into legitimate business has been found, particularly in connection with the sale and distribution of liquor, real-estate operations, night clubs, hotels, automobile agencies, restaurants, taverns, cigarette-vending companies, juke-box concerns, laundries, the manufacture of clothing, and the transmission of racing and sport news. In some areas of legitimate activity, the committee has found evidence of the use by gangsters of the same methods of intimidation and violence as are used to secure monopolies in criminal enterprise. Gangster infiltration into business also aggravates the possibility of black markets during a period of national emergency such as we are now experiencing. Racketeers also have used labor unions as fronts to enable them to exploit legitimate businessmen.

In some instances legitimate businessmen have aided the interests of the underworld by awarding lucrative contracts to gangsters and mobsters in return for help in handling employees, defeating attempts at organization, and in breaking strikes. And the committee has had testimony showing that unions are used in the aid of racketeers and gangsters, particularly on the New York water front.

These well-considered and conservative conclusions of the Kefauver Committee supported by abundant evidence (a small sample was quite impressive to television viewers) give renewed emphasis to the fact that the essence of immorality in public affairs is ruthlessness, and that such ruthlessness is fundamentally hostile to democratic representative government and to civilization itself. The danger of ruthlessness is more obvious in the underworld, but it is not less real in other walks of life.

The Context of American Life

To lay the foundation for understanding morality in American politics it is not enough to review the basic constitutional principles underlying the political system, to get acquainted with the cast of characters in politics, and to note such varied moral problems as arise in economic policy, and administration of criminal justice. It is necessary also to consider certain features of American life more generally, for they shape and condition the goals, methods, and ethical standards of men in politics. "The morals of official conduct may be distinguished, but certainly not separated, from public morals generally. The moral standards of the country, indeed, provide the ethical environment which in turn conditions the standards of behavior of public officials. Low standards in the conduct of public affairs are a symptom of low standards in the country generally. High standards in the country are reflected in high standards in government." [20]

The late Harold Ickes, former Secretary of the Interior, put one aspect of this relationship bluntly[21]—"Within my knowledge, no public officer has ever bribed himself," and he also emphasized the fact that official morality is more than a political problem.[22] "By all means let us consider how to assist in the establishment of higher moral standards in the official conduct of the Government, but at the same time let us realize that we cannot hope to assist the Government in this regard unless we are willing to assist ourselves and each other in the establishment of higher moral standards as between man and man in private life." Politics is an important part, an integral part, but only a part of the total pattern of life.

Significant influences have been noted already: a trend toward moral apathy growing out of early success in protecting human rights and in promoting individual welfare; the tendency to assume that there is an automatic and inherently moral economy; reliance upon the system of representative government as if it were an automatic vending machine, supplying services on the stimulus of a coin in the slot; and the substitution of legalism for a moral code as a standard of conduct. Certain other features of American life should be pointed out also, not dogmatically, as in identifying old landmarks, but rather as one who searches the sky at night to discover the constellations amidst the confusing multitude of heavenly bodies. Perhaps this can be done best by asking questions.

Impersonality and Bigness

Does the impersonality of American life, as compared with mid-nineteenth-century conditions, tend to obscure moral issues and make men less sensitive to the interests and welfare of others? The growth in size of business organizations has made all men very small frogs in very large puddles. The transition from personal to corporate ownership of industry, with increasing reliance on professional management, and with ownership divided among a complex group of bondholders, preferred stockholders, and perhaps several varieties of common stockholders, has tended to impersonalize the economic life of the country. The trend also is to reduce all economic relationships to a contractual agreement which strictly limits the obligations of all parties. A great many of these contractual obligations, furthermore, can be repudiated, if they become inconvenient, and the damages adjusted with a money payment. In this impersonal way of doing business the personal commitment of the individual man to the enterprise of which he is a part is minimized, and obligation to other groups is avoided entirely.

Recognition of man as an individual and his recognition of others who are part of the same organization have become difficult; and persons outside his organization may be disregarded completely. The habit of mind is to narrow one's responsibilities, not to broaden them, and the natural emphasis of each person is upon his rights, not his duties. In fact, in this way of living there is little occasion to think through one's relations to the groups—economic, social, religious, political—of which he is a member; and there is even less inclination to think of the relations of one's own groups to other groups. If for some reason a man attempts to think through his relations to his fellows, the task seems hopelessly confusing. The scale, complexity, and impersonality of life appear to be too great to be fathomed.

The general tendency at this stage of confusion is to conclude that ethics have been lost from the vast world of economics and politics. Amorality is inherent in size. If one accepts this conclusion he inevitably resigns his own personality at the same time. If men are only cogs in machines, and merely units in statistical series, no one escapes. We all have numbers, not names, whether we wear them or not. Even the more luminous figures in the mass of humanity must realize that their light is dim when seen from a distance. If this view should be generally accepted, individualism as well as morals would fade and with them would go American life as we know it.

The Brandeisian view goes one step further—bigness is inherently bad. Although this view is obviously an attempt to find a simple explanation of a complex situation, a number of thoughtful people consciously accept it, and a much larger number do so unconsciously. Justice Brandeis, of course, was not the first to question the virtue of bigness. Adam Smith, writing in the eighteenth century, proved with rather conclusive evidence that a joint stock company could not succeed, except in a few fields (banking, insurance, and public utilities), in competition with individual ownerships and co-partnerships. He was, however, more concerned with the impersonality of the corporation than its size. Morris Ernst, an apostle of Brandeis, appearing before the Douglas Committee on Ethical Standards, argued the inherent susceptibility of big business and big government to unethical practices:[23]

> I am quite convinced as to the morals of business as to which I have quite professional familiarity, they are getting increasingly lower as the companies get bigger. . . . As I see it, when a company gets very

big, and I think it is true of the Government, there is less capacity to supervise. There is less intimacy in relationship. I analyzed . . . the Savings Banks of New York State, as a result of being a member of the Banking Commission for a decade, and proved without a doubt the greater laxity as the banks got bigger.

There is also a minimum point as well as optimum point of morale and efficiency. Below a certain point you have the sweatshop, the little guy, but after a savings bank in New York got over a half a billion dollars of people's nickels and dimes, it was incapable of that personal intimate relationship and supervision required to create decent adequate standards.

If clients of mine want a loan from the big insurance companies and lending institutions, it is my duty as their lawyer to say you have to go to the broker who knows the vice president in charge. That is fairly analogous to the kind of thing we are talking about in government. Nobody gets loans from the big companies or does business with the big companies, if he is sane, unless he finds a guy who knows the wife of the president or the vice president. That is part of America.

The only point I am making is that as the Government gets bigger, you are going to have an increased difficulty.

This is an extreme position. Few men today are persuaded that bigness is inherently and inevitably either inefficient or immoral, but it is clear that size and impersonality complicate the problems of both management and morals. Moral issues as well as questions of efficiency must be recognized and faced directly.

A corollary of large-scale organization that makes for impersonality is the extreme division of labor and specialization which characterize employment today, in the professions and agriculture as well as in commerce and industry. When one's economic contribution is to make only the part of a part of a total product which is used to manufacture other products that are eventually consumed by men who are never seen, it is difficult to escape the feeling of being a cog in an impersonal machine. The farm of 1952 is highly specialized in comparison with the farm of 1852, where varieties of food, clothing, and tools were manufactured. Medicine, the law, and academic life are also specialized to an extent not formerly known, contributing to the impression of impersonality in modern life. Moral obligations are more indirect than in the days of lesser specialization and more intimate producer-consumer relationships.

Impersonality and Urban Living

Urban living is also thought to contribute to impersonality, although this may be in part the illusion of country-bred sociologists. Comparison of the rural or village setting with the metropolis, however, does suggest that although the city man may have even more friends than his rural brother, they are so small a proportion of the people he meets that his general attitude is necessarily more impersonal. Whether the city's size actually contributes to immorality is another question which is not resolved. Nevertheless, the belief in superior rural virtue persists—in rural sections (which use it to defend their over-representation in state legislative bodies!).

An exchange between members of the Committee on Ethical Standards presents some of the different opinions on the problem:[24]

> *Senator Aiken.* . . . I believe it was Jefferson who predicted that when the United States became urbanized, it would become as corrupt as the nations of Europe were in that day. Have you any comment on that, whether the increasing control of government by the cities, very large cities, has had any effect on the morals of government?
>
> *Senator Fulbright.* Since you have asked me—it would not be very becoming for me, coming from one of the more rural areas, to make such invidious comparisons—but if you force me to answer you, I agree with Jefferson's view. I think the great influence of the largest metropolitan cities has not been beneficial to our democratic system.
>
> *Senator Douglas.* I must enter a demurrer at this point.
>
> *Senator Fulbright.* I thought the Senator would.

Senator Douglas. I do it not merely because I come from a large city, but I think also there is a great fallacy and an assumed superior virtue of rural life. What you have in the cities is the fact that there is a greater absolute magnitude of crime and corruption merely because the cities are larger. Therefore, there are more individual instances that occur, and the city newspapers are on the alert to point these out. I question whether relatively there is more vice, crime, and corruption in a city than in country districts, and I have lived in both. There is this further fact in the country districts: The newspapers on the whole suppress this, because they do not want to reflect on the neighbors. If I may put it this way, if you have a garbage dump for a community of 1,000 people on the outskirts of the city it is not very odoriferous. But the garbage dumped for a city of one million people, 1,000 times that, by sheer size, is repellent. Yet there may be no more garbage per capita in the larger community than in the small.

. . . When you magnify anything, it is more disturbing. I think you will find in the rural areas just as many murders per 1,000 population, just as many embezzlements, just as much unchastity, and I must protest against this smug and alleged superiority of rural districts which is used to perpetuate one of the greatest injustices of our political system, namely, the under-representation of cities.

Senator Fulbright. I do not agree there is a difference just in the size. I think there is a difference in kind between the two. I think in the bringing together of so many people as in the case of New York, that there is an irresponsibility that goes with that size. They are not subject to criticism of their neighbors, because they do not know them. They are always wandering around in this mass of people. In little towns the real discipline comes not from the law so much, but the fact that everybody knows what everybody is doing. That may be irritating to individuals, but actually I think it is the basis of discipline, either in small towns or rural areas. . . . Let me pursue it a little further. When you go to cities like New York, I am confident that Congressmen from those cities do not have and cannot have the same sense of responsibility as in areas where they are personally known to the people. I think the record will show it in such things as independence, voting records, and the part they play in the Congress itself. They are part of a machine. All they have to do is get along with whoever is running the machine, and that is based upon an entirely different consideration than in the case of the Congressman from some area in Vermont, or I would say in my own State. I do not think we have any inherent moral superiority, if that is what the Senator means.

I am not trying to leave that impression. I think the actual organization of society as it is in New York does something to this whole democratic process. It makes it different. Maybe it is as good, but it is different, and not in accord with the idea that Jefferson had, as to how a democratic system should be set up.

Senator Aiken. I think governments are definitely closer to people in rural communities. They watch the expenditure of their local funds closer. They know personally the candidates for office which the city voter does not know at all.

Senator Fulbright. That is the all-important thing.

Senator Aiken. Furthermore, your rural constituency deals directly with its elected officials and not through some office operated by what is commonly called ward heelers, or perhaps district managers sounds better.

Senator Douglas. Assembly district leaders, in New York; ward committeemen in Chicago.

Senator Aiken. The rural constituency deals directly with its elected official. It is quicker to discern his faults and knows better what to do about it. The voter in the city feels helpless to do anything about it. I say that the Senator from Illinois is a notable exception. The people felt they knew him. Whether they knew him personally or not, they felt they did, and they felt he represented their type of thinking, that he was honest and the kind of man they wanted in the Senate.

Senator Fulbright. He certainly was not the product of the machine. He is not trying to convince us that he came in here as the product of the Kelly-Nash machine, which is the typical situation in these big cities. It is in that sense we mean that he is an accident.

Senator Aiken. The exception proves the rule.

Senator Douglas. It puts me in a bad situation.

Senator Fulbright. You are outnumbered two to one; that is the only difficulty.

Senator Douglas. I think city life and city politics are unfairly disparaged.

Ruthlessness

A second question regarding the context of American life is perhaps related to the features which have been mentioned: Is there a growing tendency toward ruthlessness? Has restraint been thrown off, by economic interests in particular, with the feeling that it is necessary to be hardboiled and disregardful of the rights and interests of others in order to "get results"? The "ruthless competition" of the late nineteenth century which was concurrent with the trend toward monopoly and with early stages of the growth of big business now seems to have its counterpart also in big labor and big agriculture. Was the idealism of the Knights of Labor discredited by that organization's decline? Is the idealism of the Granger movement gone forever from farmer organizations? Have power and success misled strongly organized economic groups into thinking that there is no need for restraint in the complex and delicately adjusted society of today?

Almost no important social reforms are achieved without a fight at some stage. This fact gives politics its vitality. But when the underdog gets on top, what then? Political power in a self-governing society has to carry with it responsibility. Failure to learn this lesson could be disastrous.

Naïveté

A third question concerns the mental habits and attitudes of the American people. Are Americans of this generation philosophically naïve? Is there such an aversion for thinking about duties and obligations, about man's nature, about the relations of man to man, and about values, that Americans are unfitted for political decisions and for self-government? The evidence is not conclusive, but much of it suggests that compared with their forebears, and considering the great increase of knowledge and its availability, Americans of today are somewhat unsophisticated on fundamental questions of meaning and value.

Despite the wealth of ability in successive generations of Americans, the country has not produced philosophers, theologians, or even economic theorists in proportion to its size, vitality, or general intellectual capacity. Among the philosophers who has there been since Jefferson of comparable stature? Indigenous American religious leaders are known for their emphasis on specialized aspects of religious truth, or as organizers, rather than as comprehensive contributors to theology. Basic American economic theory is still largely imported. Attention and energy during the past century have been turned to immediate, tangible, and graphic objectives, rather than to philosophical problems. Perhaps this tendency has characterized American intellectual life as well as industry, commerce, and agriculture. In engineering and science, American achievements in solving difficult specific problems are well known. In the social sciences and humanities, has there not been the same tendency to concentrate on problems and projects? Valuable clinical observation, statistical analyses, and studies of trends have been done. The study of public opinion has been carried farther than anywhere else in the world, with the polling industry as a by-product. No other nation has approached American scholars in producing an organized body of knowledge about public administration, about international relations, and about governmental institutions. But the emphasis has been upon analysis, not synthesis. Political theory is in the grip of the historically minded. In an effort to be scientific, social scientists have concentrated on data and avoided reflection. Scholars as well as men of affairs have been too busy to think.

The testimony of a number of witnesses before the Douglas Committee on Ethical Standards called attention to characteristics of American life that can be considered part of this tendency to avoid or pass over fundamental questions of nature, meaning, and value. The Committee, being deliberately tentative, summarized this testimony in a series of questions: [25]

1. Is there a secular trend in America which creates a new moral problem? Have the churches declined as a training ground for moral conduct? If such a trend exists and should continue, what will be the consequences?

2. Do people have an overweening desire for wide social approval which makes them less independent in their judgments, less loyal to ancient values, and more inclined to go along with the sentiment or the practice of the moment?

3. Are Americans as citizens and voters prone to be undiscriminating in their thinking? Do they lack the skepticism to reserve judgment until evidence is presented? Do they tend to lump together whole categories of people or situations without discriminating as to significant differences? If these traits of a politically immature people should be found to exist, would they indicate some degree of gullibility as to reckless charges, smear tactics, and emotionalism generally? Would they not raise some question as to the American capacity to deal realistically with complex issues and to avoid beguiling panaceas or wishful thinking?

4. Is there a dominantly emotional outlook on public affairs and politics that leads to inconsistent attitudes and violent changes in opinion? . . . Moods of optimism and pessimism come in rapid succession. Fears of scarcity are not quieted before fears of surplus appear. A sanguine mood in regard to international affairs gives way quickly to the fear of total war. Fluctuations in popular feeling seem to be much greater than can be explained by changes in the facts.

5. Is there a general ignorance of the basic ethical and political ideas upon which American institutions were founded? Are Americans unaware of the ideas and principles which really control them today? If such ignorance exists, how does it affect capacity to deal with present-day problems of public affairs?

Double Standards

A fourth question regarding the American context has to do with double standards. The Committee on Ethical Standards noted "the simultaneous existence of conflicting codes of conduct"—double standards of morality.[26]

"Double standards are more prevalent than most men realize and are, perhaps, at the root of the problem of ethics in government. The free American society with its system of democratic and representative government is based upon some of the highest ideals of Jewish-Christian-Greek thought, and it could not have developed as it has without those basic ideals as a moving force in the life of successive generations. The man who sweareth to his own hurt and changeth not is essential in both the business and political worlds. In maintaining the effectiveness of an organization, the character of men in key positions is recognized to be as important as their intelligence. Americans venerate Washington for his integrity, and Lincoln for his unswerving dedication to the Union. These judgments reflect the enduring values of basic American ideals.

"The accepted ideals are challenged daily, however, by contrary values. The clever man who makes a 'fast buck' gets a certain amount of acclaim, provided he makes enough of them. The political trickster frequently can claim his rewards—if he wins. There is a tolerance in American life for unscrupulous methods which bring immediate rewards, even though those methods, if they should become universal, would destroy the very society in which they are tolerated.

"Veneration for the principle of government according to law has its inverse side—an erroneous assumption that what is lawful is right. Although this is an untruth which authoritarian governments of all varieties have demonstrated vividly and recently, representative governments also must be on guard lest they make the same mistake. Where discretion exists in making law, the law itself is not a sufficient guide. Legality is not enough.

"Examples of double standards can be found in all walks of life today. The credit system of the country is based upon faithfulness in meeting obligations, and banks are long-established fiduciary institutions, yet some bankers have felt no compunctions about using RFC refinancing to rid themselves of bad risks. The businessman's code is to be independent and stand on his own feet, but some organized industries, as well as other economic groups [this presumably includes organized agriculture and organized labor], do not hesitate to use all possible political force to secure highly favorable decisions from legislators and administrators at the public expense. A fair system of representation is a sacred element in the American political system, yet some politicians light-heartedly steal representation from the citizens of their own States by creating grossly disproportionate congressional districts, and from rival parties by gerrymandering boundaries. The same situation is often found in State legislative districts. The claim of Congress to moral authority is based upon its representative character, yet have not the two Houses sometimes challenged the representative principle in their internal distribution of offices? . . .

"There is in American life a double standard, one highly responsible in its warm feeling for the welfare of our fellows, and the other coldly irresponsible in its single-minded devotion to direct personal advantage. The ruthless standard is epitomized by the traditional comment that 'business is business' or 'politics is politics.' When the two realms of economics and politics are combined, however, there is a clear danger to society from aggressive and self-centered policies. If economic capacity and political power are combined and used indiscriminately for the personal gain of individuals, groups and classes, is there any assurance that America as we know it can survive?"

In this quick listing of some of the features in the context of American life which have an important bearing on the problem of morality in politics, the categories are not intended to be rigidly mutually exclusive. They are obviously interrelated and some are probably aspects of broader and more obscure characteristics. They suffice to make the point, however, that one must constantly refer to the context in thinking about morality in American politics.

Moral Questions and Levels of Morality

A moral code is essential to stable group life. This is an obvious truth, as old as civilization. Even children playing together have a code. Growing up is in one sense a process of accepting a more advanced code; and one mark of an adult is his ability to restrain his impulse to snatch, scratch, bite, or pick up his toys and go home when there are differences within the group. Some children don't grow up morally, and there are some juvenile carry-overs in all of us, but reasonable adherence to a moral code is the essential basis for the unity of a stable society.

The basis for the moral code of Western civilization is the Ten Commandments. At least from the Christian era on they have been the approved official standard of conduct. Even though it is a high standard not attained by all men at any time, or by any man at all times, the fact that it has survived is evidence that no lower standard is satisfactory in the advancing society of the Western World. Although the moral code was old and well tested when the Christian world inherited it from the Hebrew people, each generation laboriously and painfully rediscovers the validity of this ancient revealed truth, adding interpretations and explanations as have the generations which went before them. A good bit of this practice of elaborating or interpreting basic moral precepts is necessary, for circumstances of life change, and moral issues have a way of becoming complex.

Does the basic moral code govern the conduct of public officials and men in public life? All civilized men recognize that it must. The necessity is not challenged, and the reason is obvious. The code is the basis of group unity and stability, and the larger the group to be kept together as one, the more important it is that the code be observed by men in official position and by the group leaders. The state is the largest firmly organized group in Western society, and all who have anything to do with its affairs are under obligation to respect the code scrupulously. Nothing is more naïve than to think that minor peccadillos do not matter. One of the oldest phrases of moral rebuke is the "unjust judge." If officials are not faithful to the moral code, the law becomes unpredictable, justice loses its meaning, private interests replace the public interest in administration, uncertainty and resentment mount, the basis for loyalty fades, and disorder leads to chaos. Temporary moral failures do not produce immediate chaos, but corruption is a way of repudiating moral standards, and it is always a sign of weakness. Without public servants of integrity, governments cannot be strong for long.

Obviously not all of the Ten Commandments apply directly to public affairs. Some are concerned more pointedly with religion, health (mental as well as physical), and family life. But the sixth commandment (Thou shalt not kill), the eighth (Thou shalt not steal), and the ninth (Thou shalt not bear false witness) certainly do apply. The general public insistence that men in high position must also show respect for the moral code in its entirety is also subconscious recognition of the fact that the code is an essential unifying and stabilizing force. The rigid standards of the English royal family are a matter of political common sense in democratic Britain and are evidence of that nation's political maturity. The President of the United

States as chief of state also finds that the public expects him to follow extremely high standards of personal conduct.

A second question is closely related to the first. Is the moral code binding only within select groups, or is its jurisdiction as wide as society? The inclination of all peoples is to limit the coverage of their code. One must not steal from his family, but may raid his neighbors. He may not cheat friends, but strangers are fair game. Deal fairly with fellow citizens, but exploit foreigners. These are beguiling propositions which men have only slowly learned to resist. The progress of civilization has depended in part upon moral progress in recognizing that moral obligations are universal, and that they govern all relations of men with each other.

A third question gets closer to immediate difficulties in American life. Does the moral code also govern group conduct? Obviously many of the Ten Commandments apply only to individual actions, but if individuals can do through an organization what it is wrong for them to do as individuals, then the effectiveness of the moral code is destroyed and the unity of society is jeopardized. There can be no escape from the necessity of subjecting organized activities to the same moral restraints that are imposed upon individual efforts. The corporation, the trade association, the union, the farm organization, the party, and the government itself are all morally obligated—if the moral basis for the unity and stability of society is to be continued. A government, for example, which is ruthless in taking the lives of its own nationals necessarily must rely on police, secret police, and armed forces to maintain its position. To the extent that it repudiates the moral code, or abandons it through corruption, it cannot rely upon morals as a basis for national unity and stability. The traditional respect for life and liberty in the United States, and the traditional avoidance of armed force as a method of political action reflect the strength of the moral code as a force for loyalty and order. A nation of 150 millions without a garrison of troops, even a token force, is unimaginable and unimagined behind the Iron Curtain.

The Ten Commandments are the moral law underlying our moral code. But does this code, even if reasonably well respected, set high enough a standard for politics in the modern state? Unfortunately it does not. The essentially negative morality of Old Testament moral law—thou shalt not kill, thou shalt not steal, thou shalt not bear false witness, thou shalt not covet—does not provide sufficient restraint or sufficient guidance for men who have great political power in the positive state where public policies necessarily vest in public officials great discretion. As discretion goes beyond the law, so must moral standards go beyond simple negations.

If the public interest as the criterion by which to judge the exercise of authority is to be more than a vain phrase, men in authority must be imbued with a positive devotion to the welfare of their fellows which more nearly approaches the level of the great commandment—love the Lord and love one's neighbor as one's self (also a product of the most advanced Jewish doctrine which Christ drew by cross-examination from a Hebrew lawyer of his day). The famous story of the Good Samaritan was told to give meaning to this greatest commandment, and it makes several points inescapably clear. The obligation is universal; morality is not intra-national. Scrupulous respect for the formal requirements of the law and even the moral code are not enough. The essence of morality is a positive good will of sufficient strength to move men to act, guided by their best judgment, in the interests of the universal neighborhood of mankind. Only when men—at least their leaders—are committed to such a standard is it safe to go as far as modern governments must go in giving discretionary power to public officials.

This high standard, however, is not something which confronts the public official alone in public affairs. Every other powerful organization and every powerful person must face up to it. There are probably a dozen great organizations which are active in politics that could, by following a policy of ruthless disregard for the public interest, endanger the nation. Either collusion or ruthless conflict between two or more of such ruthless organizations would be almost certain to bring disaster. It would be almost impossible to act quickly enough to make a public policy of sufficient precision and feasibility to control the effects of such ruthless tendencies. If reasonable adherence to this highest of all standards cannot be expected, the only alternative is to return to a simpler economy and a more primitive political system. When the discretion of men who have power cannot be trusted, the only recourse is to limit it by law. This means laws and more laws, rules, regulations, red tape, and administrative rigidity, which in the end add up to loss of both social and economic efficiency and of individual freedom.

Even the golden rule is not enough; good will must go with it. Narrowly construed the golden rule becomes a policy of you scratch my back and I scratch yours. Broadly construed, if without good will, it tends to degenerate into a legalistic conflict over my rights and your duties. The weakness of the welfare state is not the services which it provides but the danger that the services given become so devoid of feeling as to be barren of satisfaction for all concerned—demanded but resented, given but begrudged. In a society in which more and more of the services that men provide for each other are furnished by vast and complex social, economic, and political organizations it is essential to retain something of the rich satisfactions which go with the direct mutual aid of man-to-man. Can this be done? Some may be doubtful; but the evidence indicates that the task is not impossible if it is faced directly.

III

MORALITY AND THE LEGISLATIVE SYSTEM:
REPRESENTATION

The Heart of Representative Government
In taking up specific questions of morality in politics, the
starting point is the legislative assembly and the legislative
process. The legislature is the heart of representative government. Without a representative assembly which has lawmaking power, representative government as we know it is impossible. Without an elected representative assembly, an
elected chief executive would be inevitably a dictator, although
an elected dictator. The central role of the representative assembly is a historic fact; it is the basic principle of the Constitution of the United States and of the forty-eight state constitutions; and it is logically inescapable.

The Congress, to use it as an example, is by design the center
of the government. It meets in the capitol; the Chief Executive
has to transact business, like a country lawyer, at his residence.
It is *the* law-making agency of the government; others participate rather extensively, but only the Congress is indispensable.

The parties, pressure groups, lobbyists, and administrative agencies contribute greatly to shaping public policy, but the approval of no one of them is required to make law. Not even the President, upon whom has fallen much of the responsibility for proposing public policy in recent years, is strictly essential. Acts of Congress may become law without his approval, or may be passed over his veto by a two-thirds vote in both houses.

More important than its lawmaking function, strictly defined, is the *way* in which Congress is intended to make law. It has fact-finding powers and can compel presentation of evidence and testimony germane to its proper inquiries.[1] It is a deliberative body to sift and weigh evidence as to the needs of the state, the desires of the public, and the feasibility of any proposed course of action. It is a representative body designed to reflect in its membership the opinion of the public and of all geographic sections of the country. It is a public body, meeting in public, publishing its proceedings, required to keep a journal and to publish it, and required to make a record of how members vote on certain matters (reconsideration of vetoed measures, and on demand of one-fifth of the members present).

In setting up the Congress as a representative, deliberative, public, lawmaking body, the men who wrote Article 1 of the Constitution were fully aware of their own legislative tradition and of the parliamentary tradition of England. They knew that a legislative assembly which is genuinely representative in character, which gets the facts, which weighs them rationally in public, which makes decisions after full discussion has great moral force and great moral leadership, and they expected the Congress to dominate the government. Through such a legislative process, a self-governing people can make decisions which are "right" in that they reflect the public's values and embody the best judgment of its representatives on the issues. In this way also they can develop the consensus so necessary for effectiveness in making and carrying through new public policies. Most important of all, only in this way can lawmakers gain the courage and moral force which are essential to a positive attack on difficult problems of public policy. Without this moral force public policy tends to be extremely conservative, even negative in character.

This is the essence of the legislative process in representative government. The Congress must be right rationally, that is in getting and weighing the facts, and in getting as close to the truth as reason can. It must be right representatively in applying to policies the criterion of the public interest. It must furthermore use its own deliberations to help the public to think through and debate the more fundamental issues, so that decisions will have, ultimately if not immediately, that genuine public support which is the secret of the vitality of representative government, and also the measure of its success.

"In republican government, the legislative authority necessarily predominates." [2] The men who designed the Government of the United States were so sure of this fact, and it was so well demonstrated in the state governments, and in the history of other republics which they had studied, that they went so far as to urge their fellow Americans to be on guard against it. They conceded that where there is an hereditary monarch "with numerous and extensive prerogatives" . . . "the executive department is very justly regarded as a source of danger . . . But in a representative republic, where the executive magistracy is carefully limited, both in the extent and the duration of its power; and where the legislative power is exercised by an assembly which is inspired, by a supposed influence over the people, with an intrepid confidence in its own strength; which is sufficiently numerous to feel all the passions which actuate a multitude, yet not so numerous as to be incapable of pursuing the objects of its passions, by means which reason prescribes; it is against the enterprising ambition of this department that the people ought to indulge all their jealousy and exhaust all their precautions." [3]

Nothing is clearer in *The Federalist* papers than the fact that the learned statesmen who launched the federal government under the new constitution expected the Congress to dominate the government, and to be the great source of initiative and leadership. The state legislatures were already completely dominating the state governments, and their dominance, although it might be modified, also was certainly expected to continue.

Not only the design of the government and the essential nature of popular assemblies, but also the extensions of legal powers have provided a base for leadership and authority. Although the course of constitutional interpretation has veered at times from stressing limitations to emphasizing powers, the trend and the net result of this changing perspective of the Supreme Court have been the enlargement of legislative power. State legislatures have lost to the Congress their hegemony in regulating the commerce and industry of the nation through a conveniently more realistic interpretation of the commerce clause. But the powers of both Congress and the state legislatures to act in economic matters have in fact been expanded, and the limitations, established by judicial interpretation, on the power to act have been beaten down, also by judicial interpretation. The battle of political scientists to establish a concept of the legislative power adequate for the needs of the nation has largely been won. The Congress stands supreme in a "constitution of powers" [4] replacing "what was once vaunted as a constitution of rights."

Legal Strength and Moral Weakness

In the light of the constitutional plans, expectations, and powers, why then has Congress failed so miserably to achieve the moral force and the moral leadership expected of it? And why have the state legislatures lost the moral strength and the leadership which they once had? Legislative leadership in the national government and the state rests with the chief executive. In times of great crisis this is to be expected. But it is also true at other times. The moral force and moral courage which should be the great asset of legislative bodies have somewhere and somehow disappeared. American legislative bodies are not at present known either for their courage or for their leadership in tackling tough questions. The great forum, potentially the greatest in the world, which Congress provides for debating the great issues of national policy that are of deep concern to the country and to the entire world, has given way to 150 side shows —the thirty-four standing committees, the special and select committees, and the hundred-and-thirty-odd subcommittees.[5] This "greatest show on earth" has almost completely lost its big top, and the important decisions are largely determined before action reaches the center ring. The state legislatures are much the same. American legislative bodies do not exercise legislative leadership on great questions of national or state policy, and they seldom clarify basic issues or educate the public by their debates. They have great legal power; but they lack moral force and functional effectiveness.

Evidence of Failure—Prestige

The evidence of failure to fulfill the great mission of legislative assemblies is painfully clear.[6] An item to start with is the low prestige of legislatures and legislators. Congress, which stands

highest of all among American assemblies, is an example. Whatever in fact their prestige rating may be, members of Congress
feel that it is low. The fact that they are politicians by definition
attaches a stigma to them as a group. Many of them, perhaps
those who are most conscientious and sensitive, have this impression thrust upon them by their legislative experience. The
propositions sometimes made to them and the requests for improper assistance reflect on their character. They are painfully aware of the newspaper polls and other surveys of the
prestige of public office which have been anything but compli-
mentary. While others forget, they recall the remark of Artemus
Ward, "I am no politician, and my other habits are good." [7]
They believe that legislative prestige is much lower than the
facts of life warrant, and ask rather pathetically, "Do you think
there is any way in which we could induce the people of a republic such as this to have a little higher regard for public office?" [8] The columnists confirm their fears with the dictum,
"certainly the situation is really very bad today . . . a large part
of the public has but contempt for most officeholders." [9]

This pessimistic view is not shared by all thoughtful students
of public life and public opinion, and it is agreed that the prestige rating is much lower in the abstract than is the standing
of particular individuals—senators, representatives and other officeholders. Justice Jackson observed to the Senate Committee
on Ethical Standards in Government:[10]

> I do not know that the public thinks as badly of men in public office
> as we sometimes think they do. They place a great deal of confidence
> in them . . . [and] . . . nearly all the ills they suffer . . . they ex-
> pect to be solved by the men in government.
> *Senator Humphrey.* That is for sure; maybe too much so.
> *Mr. Justice Jackson.* But I think it is a general part of the climate of
> opinion in the country over a long period of time. This is nothing that
> has happened within the last decade or generation. Service in govern-

ment has been held as a secondary occupation. For example, there was one public-opinion poll taken a few years ago—and I am not saying that public-opinion polls are always valid, but at least they give some trend or indication—where the mothers of American young people were asked whether or not they would consider it desirable for their boy or girl to go into public service, and over 80 per cent answered "No." As a matter of fact, better than 80 per cent. I am sure my mother would have answered the same thing.

Senator Humphrey. I am sure mine not only would, but has. What I am getting at is that apparently there must be some attitude on the negative side as to the merit or value of public service.

It is scant comfort to members of Congress to be assured by men who have had extensive business experience and who know the business world that Congressional standards of behavior compare very favorably with business standards.[11] Although they have real personal power, and they are subject to great pressure from many sources, they are suspected as a class—not respected.

Perhaps the formal deference and elaborate courtesy of members of the Senate or House in dealing with each other as colleagues can be explained as a ritual to compensate for lack of public deference. When it is almost a matter of habit to throw in a declaration of admiration and esteem or a fulsome compliment in addressing a fellow senator, even though he be a detested opponent, the atmosphere becomes slightly psychopathic. Traditional parliamentary gallantry seems to be a bit overdone in the present-day practice of Congress.

Although one should be on guard against accepting a few polls and general impressions without reservation, there can be little doubt that the prestige of Congress and of state legislatures is so low as to suggest failure in some way to achieve the great role for which they are designed.

Evidence of Failure—Negativism

A second evidence of legislative failure to fulfill its expected role is the negativism which characterizes legislative bodies. They are skillful in objection and obstruction, but inept in synthesis and construction. They have ways and means of defeating proposals for which there may be real need and substantial general support, but they find it difficult to add to public policy if there is very much organized opposition, no matter how urgent the issue. For example, the 1941 act to extend service of draftees beyond the one year specified in the 1940 law, a measure vital to permit the build-up of military strength, was very nearly emasculated by the isolationists in the Senate in the summer of 1941 and passed the House by only one vote. Congress has lost much of its sense of responsibility for initiating policy and for proposing a legislative program that is comprehensive, consistent, and adequate. This has come to be the task of the Chief Executive rather than of Congress. The President speaks up as to the public need. He formulates plans and takes responsibility for proposing integrated programs; and little happens legislatively until he does so. To use the vernacular, the President "sticks his neck out"; the Congress does not. Very seldom does new and positive legislation in a new field of policy originate in the Congress or owe its passage to legislative leadership.

The exceptions to this general practice are few and partial. Most notable is bonus legislation. Congress has the distinction of having demonstrated its ability to legislate in opposition to the wishes of every President since Wilson in providing bonuses to veterans.[12] Few other exceptions come to mind. Congress went ahead of the President in enacting the Defense Production Act of 1950, but this was by no means pioneer legislation. The impetus for the National Labor Relations Act of 1935 also seems to have come from Senator Wagner rather than the President; but the act was in essence an outgrowth of NRA experience.[13] Perhaps the chief example in recent times of Congressional initiative in new legislation is the stock-market investigations of the Senate Committee on Banking and Currency, 1932-34, which led to the Securities Act of 1933 and the Securities and Exchange Act of 1934. The exception confirms the rule. Normally Congress looks to the President for leadership in new steps of positive public policy, and it leaves entirely to the President responsibility for formulating an integrated and comprehensive legislative program. In its modern role the Congress can refine, revise, review, delay, and obstruct positive legislation, but except for so noble an objective as the bonus, or without so great a cataclysm as the economic crash of 1929 it is not able to mobilize its strength to the point of leadership.

Evidence of Failure—Friction and Frustration

Despite its abdication of legislative leadership, the Congress shows evidence of jealousy of the President to whom it has abdicated. The alleged conflict between the Congress-as-a-whole and the President is exaggerated, as will be shown later, by the way power is distributed through the organization and rules of the two houses. But the evidence of friction between the powers-that-be in the two houses and the President is unmistakable. Despite repeated deliberate efforts on the part of the President to avoid this friction, no President in recent years has long been successful. Presidents Harding and Truman came from the Senate to the Presidency with the idea of "restoring" good relations, but soon found themselves facing the same resentment as had their predecessors, Wilson and Roosevelt, who were ex-governors, and thoroughly familiar with the hedgehog tendency of legislative bodies to put their best quills forward in dealing with the executive. The President's "honeymoon" period in dealing with Congress seldom lasts beyond his first months in office. When they get down seriously to the business of putting through a legislative program the friction begins. Because of Mr. Roosevelt's legislative successes, it is easy to forget his difficulties; but the New Deal was a constant battle between President and committee chairmen.

The legislative asperity is evident also in relations with lower ranks of the administration, department heads, bureau chiefs, and even lowly division directors. Congress passes the laws, authorizes the programs, appropriates the money, makes very persuasive suggestions to the President for key appointments, and the Senate confirms appointments, but it nevertheless regards administration as a whole with deep suspicion. They are "bureaucrats," accused of twisting the law to their own ends, and charged at the same time with apathy and excessive zeal. This stereotype is not limited to the misfits and chronic gripers. It tends to be general; leading members of the Congress express much the same views.

In questioning Judge Learned Hand, Senator Aiken, recognized for his integrity and public spirit, said:

> I would like to point out what I consider to be one of the major ailments of Government and see if you have any suggestion on that. Congress passes legislation and necessarily cannot legislate in detail, so they authorize the agency concerned with the legislation to promulgate rules and regulations for putting it into effect, and it frequently happens that the agency concerned will promulgate such rules and regulations that completely controvert or contravene—I do not know the legal word for that—the act of the Congress. And then we sometimes pass legislation and the agencies have got away from the practice which was originally set up of asking the Attorney General for an interpretation when the meaning of the law is in doubt. Each has its own solicitor's department, and the solicitor hired by the de-

partment head is supposed to bring to the department head such interpretation of the law as he wants.

In some cases that has happened. Sometimes the solicitor's interpretation is directly contrary to the intent of the Congress. Have you any suggestion as to how we can get away from that, because it is pretty common practice? [14]

The reply of the famous jurist is of interest because it brings out the difference between legislative and judicial views of administrators.

Judge Hand. Do you find that very often the regulations in your judgment or in the judgment of any of you conflict with the act?
Senator Aiken. Yes.
Judge Hand. That has not been much my experience.[15]

Some of the causes of friction are considered in the discussion of morality and immorality in the legislative system, which comes later; but whatever may be the causes, the suspicion and asperity which are apparent in legislative attitudes toward administrators are unmistakable evidence of legislative frustration, and of discontent with the legislature's failure to achieve a satisfactory role in governing.

Evidence of Failure—Non-Legislative Activities
Striking evidence of failure to fulfill its legislative mission is the fact that non-legislative activities have come to occupy more than half the time of members of Congress. Some estimates put the time so spent at 80 per cent of the total, and conservative estimates put it at 50 to 60 per cent of the total.[16] These activities also absorb at least one-half of the time of the staff of members of Congress.

Senator Kefauver says [17] that the "errand boy" work, the function of serving as a "Washington representative" for particular constituents is a "terrific burden" that "is sapping the ability of individual members to give the thought and study necesary to contribute to the solution of national problems confronting the Congress. Collectively it gnaws away at the entire legislative function."

The most important errand that a "Washington representative" does for his constituents is to serve as a lobbyist with administrative agencies of the government. This is euphemistically called the "reference function." A member of Congress may simply introduce clients by letter, by telephone or by a personal visit to administrative agencies. He may go farther and vouch for them as a character reference, and ask fair consideration of their case. Or he may go all out and try to get them what they want—a loan, a contract, surplus property, a subsidy payment, a commission in the armed services or a discharge from the service. In this role the members of Congress are administrative lobbyists who excel all others of this numerous company in the pressure which they can and do bring on the administrative agencies of the government.

The universal testimony of members, not challenged by anyone, is that the burden of this Washington-representative function is well-nigh intolerable. Why then does it continue? Members explain it on several grounds. It brings to their attention complaints from which can be winnowed some evidence of administrative failure. It keeps them in touch with constituents— at least those who want the Washington representative's help in getting something. But most important of all, members of the Congress feel that they must do this lobbying to get re-elected. Although they obviously got into office without it, once elected they all feel compelled to busy themselves running errands for importunate constituents.

There is a curious emotionalism in the attitude of legislators toward their reference function. Whenever this function is questioned, and they are speaking for the record, they grit their teeth and stoutly defend the right of the constituent to demand and the duty of the legislator to supply such special services. The tone and manner suggest to the observer, however, that "Methinks, he doth protest too much." If they were not just a little ashamed of being so deeply involved in this avowedly burdensome and sometimes noisome business, would the members of Congress be quite so defensive?

In his 1945 testimony before the La Follette-Monroney Committee on the Organization of Congress, Representative Robert Ramspeck attacked the problem with characteristic honesty and apparently a straight face.[18]

> All of us like to do things for our constituents. We like to be able to go to the Post Office Department and get a rural route extended, or the city delivery route extended a block. We like to go to the Federal Works Agency and get a project for our district or for our State. We like to help our constituents solve their problems in the matter of priorities with the O.P.A. But we cannot do those things and do an intelligent job of legislating under present conditions.
>
> Therefore I am suggesting, Mr. Chairman, for the consideration of this committee, that we go back to the job that the Constitution gave us, the legislative job. I am suggesting that we adopt a constitutional amendment which would prohibit a Member of Congress, or Senator, from contacting the executive branch of the Government except in regard to legislation.
>
> That we reduce the House of Representatives by half and provide for the election by the people of a Representative who would represent them before the executive branch of the Government, to assume all this other business that, through lapse of time, has become part of the job which we are undertaking to do and which we cannot do, in my judgment, without sacrificing the time necessary, under present-day conditions, to properly consider the legislative matters facing this Congress.
>
> Now, there are any number of legislative problems facing us right in this session that a Member could devote many weeks and even months of careful study to, if he did nothing else, with profit to him-

self and the country. But you are not going to be able to do it if you have to do these other things. . . .

I think that is the only real solution that there is to this problem. For the past two and one-half years I have been the Democratic whip in the House. Perhaps I ought not to say this, but, without being critical of anybody, I know that the Members of the House are finding great difficulty in giving sufficient time to legislative matters because of the constant and pressing demand from their constituents to deal with matters in the executive branch of the Government. . . .

Mr. Ramspeck's remedy was too drastic for the committee, and the problem may not admit of any simple solution, but it is unmistakable evidence of one thing—Congress is not fulfilling its designed role, the role which is recognized to be its prime mission. As Congress is now organized and as it now proceeds through its legislative business, members believe, participation in the legislative process is not a means of communicating with the public or a basis for asking public support.

Evidence of Failure—Committee Particularism

It has long been recognized that most of the work of American legislative bodies is done in committees—some of their best work and some of their worst. This characteristic has both good and bad features. A feature which reflects the weakness of the Congress, for example, to fulfill adequately its primary legislative mission and to find satisfaction in it is the preoccupation of the standing committees with administrative details. It is as if, frustrated with their inability to establish a broadly controlling public policy for the-government-as-a-whole through action as a whole Congress, many of the members, as individuals, compensate by desperate efforts in the committees to control petty details in the many parts of the administration. This tendency is an important cause of legislative weakness as well as a compensation for it; for there is not time for Congress to put its attention on many questions. If it chooses to concentrate on details selected at random at the whim of individual members, the basic questions of policy will suffer correspondingly for lack of attention.[19]

The departments and agencies of the executive branch are divided among the committees of the House and Senate which take a proprietary interest in the agencies that are allotted to their jurisdiction. Normally every administrative department, bureau, and division of the government must make its peace with at least four committees—House and Senate subcommittees of the two appropriations committees, and one standing committee in each house on other legislative matters. Secretaries of departments, assistant secretaries, bureau chiefs, heads of divisions, and other administrative officials appear before House appropriations subcommittees and later before the Senate appropriations subcommittee to "justify," that is, explain and defend, their estimates of the need for funds submitted in the President's budget. In the course of their cross-examination any question of interest to any member of the subcommittee may be raised and explored at length. The decisions of the subcommittees are so influential in determining the action of the full committee on appropriations and of the whole House or Senate that administrators are constrained to give great weight to the wishes of the subcommittee members. Experienced administrators are careful to respect "understandings" with the committees even though they are not written into the appropriation acts, and have no legal authority. The task of administrators is complicated by the fact that the law itself may not be precise, by the necessity of deferring to the wishes of four different committees which not infrequently disagree in their views of public policy, and by the demands of individual committee members that certain specific action be taken.

In addition to their four normal committee contacts, administrators are subject to investigation by the Committees on Expenditures of the House and Senate, and by other special and select committees of Congress.

Committee examination of administrators on questions of budget or legislative policy can be, and frequently is, penetrating, systematic, balanced, and fair, but every administrator who has had much experience in appearing before committees can recall instances, all too numerous, in which the examination has passed over important basic questions to relatively trivial details, or has been motivated chiefly by the animus of a particular member with a personal grievance. Even when considered as a whole, a standing committee of the House or Senate tends to reflect a particular point of view and a special interest. It is atypical rather than typical in its complexion and almost never representative of the whole house. The committees thus tend to be instruments of localism and particularism, which skew public policy into the hands of the most aggressive and best-organized special interests rather than hold it strictly to the values of the general public.

Evidence of Failure—Corruption Without Discipline

The extent of corruption is never exactly measured, for frequency cannot be measured by publicity. Interest in any subject is both cumulative and cyclical. It builds up for a time, then wanes, and the publicity also fades. One of the oldest phenomena of local politics is the manufactured crime wave. In the words of Louis Brownlow, "Any city editor can make a crime wave any time he pleases by simply taking the crime news scattered throughout the paper and putting it all together and blowing up the headline. I know that because I have had it done to me when I was running police departments, and I know it because when I was a city editor I have done it to police departments. I have had experience on both sides." [20] It must be noted that men of unquestioned integrity and judgment who have been observing legislatures carefully over the longest period of time tend to agree that they are less corrupt than they used to be. They believe that present standards of conduct are higher than formerly and that they are better observed.

Drawing on fifty years of experience as a journalist, city administrator, and student of government at all levels, Mr. Brownlow, the dean of American professional administrators, concludes: [21]

> In 1904, when I came to Washington as a correspondent and entered the Press Gallery, I knew quite well some of the gentlemen who sat outside of the door in the corridors at the House end and Senate end of the capitol with railroad passes in their pockets to give to any Senator or a friend of a Senator or anybody who was introduced by the Senator. . . .
>
> At that time it did not seem to be very much of a lapse from ethics to accept a railroad pass. I was a newspaperman; and, of course, no newspaperman ever paid his way on the railroads. . . .
>
> So one sees that the general custom, the general public opinion affects these things. But we have improved, I think, a great deal in the fifty years that I have been actively looking at the conduct of public officials . . . Our conduct is greatly improved. We have made our standards higher and the lapses are fewer, corruption is taken less as a matter of course.

Robert Ramspeck, thinking back over forty years to earlier days in Washington, told the Senate Subcommittee on Ethical Standards in Government,[22]

My own personal reaction to the Washington of today as compared to the Washington of 1911 is that if there is any difference it was a less moral city in 1911 than it is today. We had open red-light districts. We had numerous saloons. We had more drunkenness, I would say, and I think particularly it is true that the moral standards of the Members of Congress today are higher than they were then, that is, as to their personal conduct. They work much harder, they are here longer during the year, and there is less personal drinking and things of that sort.

At this point in the testimony, Senator Neely interrupted to ask a question.[23]

In view of that statement, then, you must conclude that the law is much more strictly enforced today than it was in 1911 because in recent years there have been more Members of Congress sent to the penitentiary than were ever sent there in any previous period of similar length.

Mr. Ramspeck. Yes, sir; I think there is stricter enforcement of the law, Senator Neely. Furthermore, there are more opportunities to do wrong today in the Government than there were in 1911. The stakes are higher. The spread of the operations of the Government have been so extensive that the pressures are greater than they were in those days. The economic pressures are greater, and that, I am sure you will agree, has something to do with whether people do right or wrong.

Testimony of this sort may be accepted as at least persuasive. But Senator Neely's question brings out sharply the unpleasant fact that corruption exists in the Congress. This cannot be denied, nor can the fact that the House and Senate have done little or nothing about it. Any corruption is too much corruption, and the standards of conduct are too low for the needs of the times. This, too, is generally accepted. Just as Senators were more shocked by the absence of strong student disapproval of the basketball scandals ("shading points" or throwing games for gamblers), so the public is justified in being more concerned over the failure of House and Senate to do something about corruption and improper practices among its members than it is concerned over the corruption itself. When a legislative body vigilantly disciplines conduct which imperils its integrity as a representative assembly, it gives convincing evidence that violations are not general. But when it fails to discipline its members for conduct which is improper, corrupt, or illegal, the public has no choice but to make the inference that such conduct may be quite general. How general no one can tell; but why are members so hesitant to act?

The Constitution makes each house of Congress the "Judge of the Elections, Returns, and Qualifications of its own Members," and authorizes each house to "determine the Rules of its Proceedings, punish its members for disorderly Behavior, and, with the concurrence of two-thirds, expel a Member." [24] In the past fifty years these powers have been used in only a few instances, and no instance comes to mind in which either house has punished its members since the nineteen-twenties.[25] Criticized for what were then considered large expenditures ($195,000) in the primary campaign of 1918 against Henry Ford in Michigan, Senator Newberry was convicted of violating the Federal Corrupt Practices Act, but the conviction was reversed in the Supreme Court. His seating was contested but he was admitted. In subsequent elections a number of his supporters were defeated; influenced by this trend, he resigned his seat in November, 1922.[26]

Senator Frank L. Smith, of Illinois, was denied a seat in 1926 because of his campaign financing. He spent what were then considered large sums ($458,782), of which $203,000 was received from officers of Illinois public utilities while Mr. Smith was a member of the state regulatory body, the Illinois Commerce Commission.[27] William S. Vare, of Pennsylvania, was also denied the Senate seat to which he was elected in 1926 because of fraud, corruption, and excessive expenditures ($785,000) in his primary campaign.[28] Since the nineteen-twenties improper or illegal conduct which has been made public has not been grounds for punishment by the Congress.

Senator Hiram Bingham, Republican of Connecticut (now chairman of President Truman's Loyalty Review Board), was censured formally by resolution of the Senate, introduced by Senator Norris, and passed 54 to 22 on November 4, 1929.[29] The resolution condemned the action of the learned Senator for having placed upon the rolls of the Senate a professional lobbyist, Charles L. Eyanson, assistant to the President of the Connecticut Manufacturers Association, and for having taken Mr. Eyanson into the meetings and executive sessions of the majority members of the Senate Finance Committee at work upon the new tariff bill. As amended and as passed the resolution absolved the Senator of "corrupt motives," but not of improper conduct. Although official discipline went no further, the censure must have been felt. A Republican Senator was condemned by a Republican Senate, and the Republicans who voted were evenly divided, with 22 favoring and 22 opposing the resolution. Even the colleagues who defended him in the four-hour debate on the floor did not approve or condone his action, which had first been checked by criticism of fellow Republicans on the Finance Committee. The censure was reported to be the first in twenty-seven years,[30] and no similar disciplinary action is recalled in the subsequent years.[31] One clear resolution of censure in a half-century suggests either that members are scrupulous or that the Senate does not take its responsibility for self-discipline very seriously.

Representative John M. Coffee of Washington, who accepted

a $2,500 "campaign contribution" from a war contractor in mid-term (1941) after helping him to get a contract, was investigated by the Mead Committee, but no action was taken by the Committee or by the House.[32] Representative Eugene Cox, Democrat of Georgia, was found by the Federal Communications Commission to have accepted a retainer from a broadcasting station in 1941 for services rendered in Washington in connection with the station's dealing with the FCC—an apparent violation of Section 113 of the criminal code.[33] The violation was disclosed to the Commission with documentary evidence and sworn testimony in the course of its routine procedures. Representative Cox, who was (and still is) the ranking member of the powerful Rules Committee, was not disciplined by the House in any way, but was made the chairman of a select committee, established by a resolution which he introduced, which conducted a punitive investigation of the FCC in 1943. The investigation was notoriously unfair in its methods and was in essence a propaganda campaign against the Communications Commission. Representative Cox eventually resigned from the investigating committee under pressure, but the pressure came from adverse public reaction, not from the House. Speaker Rayburn and Majority Leader McCormack, who praised Mr. Cox while accepting his resignation, deserve less credit than the *Washington Post*, which spoke bluntly in asking that he be relieved.

James M. Curley, a leading figure in Boston Democratic politics for a generation, was indicted in September 1943, while serving in the 78th Congress, for using the mails to defraud.[34] He was convicted, after a jury trial in January, 1946, and sentenced a month later, February 18, 1946. After unsuccessful appeals he began to serve his sentence in the Federal Penitentiary in the summer of 1947. President Truman commuted his sentence (6 to 18 months) to five months on November 26, 1947. Between indictment and the commutation of his sentence, Mr. Curley completed his term in the 78th Congress, was re-elected to the 79th Congress and served out his entire term there. (He was elected in November, 1946, to be Mayor of Boston with a plurality of 50,000 votes.) At no time during either the 78th or 79th Congress was Mr. Curley disciplined by the House of Representatives (by Massachusetts authorities, or by the public). He continued in Congress for almost a year after conviction until the expiration of his term. He was more successful in completing his term in Congress than he was in serving out his prison term.

Representative Andrew Jackson May, Democrat of Kentucky, was elected to the House in 1930 and through seniority became Chairman of the House Committee on Military Affairs.[35] In that position he intervened with the War Department in all sorts of matters: to get a man released from the Army after six weeks of service, to have a friend's son brought back from the Pacific, to influence a court martial, to award the "E" where it was not earned, to get war contracts for his friends, and to influence the renegotiation of contracts. In the course of such enthusiastic discharge of his "reference" function, Representative May became so involved with the now notorious Garssons that his apparently improper activities came to the attention of the Mead War Investigating Committee, and eventually got into the courts. He was convicted of bribery and conspiracy in July, 1947, and was sentenced to a prison term. Representative May was not disciplined by the House; but despite the pleas of Senators Barkley and Chandler for his re-election, he lost his seat at the polls in 1946. Majority Leader McCormack in a public statement during the campaign said, "I consider your re-election essential to the best interests of your people and the welfare of the nation"; [36] apparently his constituents did not think so.

In 1948 J. Parnell Thomas, Republican of New Jersey and Chairman of the House Committee on Un-American Activities, was indicted for conspiracy to defraud the Government through salary kick-backs from persons on his own staff and the staff of the Committee on Un-American Activities. When the case came to trial in November, 1949, after delays of almost a year, Mr. Thomas changed his plea from not guilty to *nolo contendere* and threw himself upon the mercy of the court. He was sentenced to 6-18 months in prison and fined $10,000. He submitted his resignation December 9, 1949, to be effective January 2, 1950, the day before the opening of the new session of Congress. Mr. Thomas was relieved of the Chairmanship of the House Committee by the elections of 1948 which returned a Democratic majority to the House of Representatives, but he was not disciplined by the House in any way.[37]

In 1951 Representative Walter E. Brehm, Republican, Ohio, was convicted of receiving salary kick-backs from his own House staff and was fined $5,000.[38] He has continued to sit in the House as a member in good standing. There is no positive evidence in recent years that the House considers conviction of crime a disqualification for the high office of serving in the Congress.

The Senate record of handling possible disciplinary cases which have been forced upon its attention in recent years is similarly brief.

When Senator Albert B. Chandler's free swimming pool, constructed by a war contractor, became an issue in the Kentucky Democratic primary campaign in 1942, the Truman War Investigating Committee looked into the charges through its chief investigator, Matthew J. Connelly.[39] It did so at the request of Senator Chandler who was then a member of the committee. The prompt report of the committee cleared the "happy" Senator of using his influence in behalf of the war contractor in question; and a parallel report of the War Production Board found no misuse of war materials which were then under priority regulations. Neither the committee nor the WPB commented on the propriety of a Senator's accepting a swimming pool from a contractor who has business with the government. The Senate found nothing to justify disciplinary action.

Senator Theodore G. Bilbo, Democrat of Mississippi, a much rougher diamond, was less successful in clearing his name after his successful 1946 campaign for re-election.[40] He was charged with two different improper actions—encouraging and provoking terrorism and intimidation to prevent Negro citizens from voting in the primary, and accepting gifts, valuable services, and money from war contractors in a number of ingenious ways. As the subsequent investigation revealed, he got a lake, a church, a parsonage, and two "dream houses," as well as a swimming pool, with the assistance of war contractors and other generous donors. Senator Bilbo was not seated pending investigation of the charges. The Special Committee to Investigate Senatorial Campaign Expenditures, under the chairmanship of Allen J. Ellender, a fellow Democrat from Louisiana with somewhat similar views on the race issue, exonerated Bilbo of campaign terrorism despite persuasive evidence to the contrary received by the committee in public hearings in Jackson, Mississippi, one of the most improbable places in the world to expect to receive such testimony.

The report of the War Investigating Committee, prepared by a subcommittee headed by Senator Mead, was a different story. After a more extensive investigation, to which there was much less local opposition, the committee found,[41] "Senator Bilbo's acceptance of expensive gifts and donations of personal property and the acceptances of improvements to real estate, provided by contractors who have profited out of their work for the Government in the war effort, to be an illegal practice in violation of existing Federal statutes," and it concluded that "the evidence . . . clearly indicates that Senator Bilbo improperly used his high office as United States Senator for his personal gain in his dealings with war contractors." No action, except for these reports, was taken by the Senate. After failing to be seated at the opening of Congress Senator Bilbo returned to Mississippi for a series of operations, and died in August, 1947.

A recent instance of potential disciplinary action by the Senate is the 1950 election in Maryland of Republican Senator John Marshall Butler which was investigated by the Subcommittee on Privileges and Elections of the Committee on Rules and Administration. The committee's investigation disclosed clear violation of the Maryland election laws by Senator Butler's campaign manager to whom he had given full authority and a free hand. The manager was indicted; he pleaded guilty, and was fined. The committee also found clear violation of the accounting requirements of the Federal Corrupt Practices Act and possible or probable violations of other provisions of the act, "shocking abuse of the spirit and intent of the First Amendment to the Constitution" (defamation under the guise of freedom of the press), violations of the Federal and State laws requiring disclosure of sponsors of campaign publications, and ignoring of the law by the Senator and his campaign manager. The unanimous report of the subcommittee (three Democrats and two Republicans), which was reported favorably to the Senate by the Committee on Rules and Administration, did not recommend any disciplinary action toward

Senator Butler. It chose to overlook the 1950 campaign and to look to the future. The committee suggested revision of the Senate rules covering the contesting of elections to make clear the intent of the Senate in future campaigns to punish such actions as occurred in Maryland in 1950.[42]

The committee report treats the "defamatory nature of the campaign of John Marshall Butler," and the "nature and extent of activities and influence of non-residents of Maryland in the senatorial campaign" as perhaps more serious than the clear violations of the law. Hence its recommendations that standards be established where they are not now clear. One of the principal non-residents involved in these activities, McCarthy of Wisconsin, himself a member of the Committee on Rules and Administration, somewhat scornfully has "noted that the members of the subcommittee . . . suffered from a bad case of jitters over the 'outsiders' who took a hand in the Maryland Senatorial campaign."[43] A few days after the committee reported, Senator Benton, apparently without jitters, introduced a resolution directing the Committee on Rules and Administration further to investigate the participation of McCarthy in the Butler election "to determine whether or not it should initiate action with a view toward the expulsion from the Senate of . . . Senator Joseph R. McCarthy."[44] In January, 1952, when the Gillette subcommittee (of the Committee on Rules), to which the resolution was referred for investigation, began to consider the voluminous data prepared by committee investigators, a move was reported to replace the Republican members with Senators more friendly to the accused.[45] This maneuver was partially successful. Senator Margaret Chase Smith, of Maine, accepted a new subcommittee assignment, but Senator Robert Hendrickson of New Jersey stuck to his guns.[46]

It was expected that the subcommittee would take some time to reach a decision.

Several points stand out in the matter of House and Senate discipline: (1) Both houses have acted chiefly when issues have been forced upon them by publicity or other outside pressure, and punishment has been meager. Since the barring of two Senators and the formal censure of one in the twenties, no actual punishment has been inflicted. (2) No member has been expelled or disciplined in any way for receiving money, gifts, services, swimming pools, lakes or anything else from contractors or other persons doing business with the government. (3) No member has been expelled for violation of the law even when indicted, tried, and convicted of crime. (4) The impulse in the nineteen twenties to safeguard the electoral process through the disciplinary power of the Senate has apparently passed away. The implication is that according to Congressional standards anything goes, not only everything the law allows, but also what it does not allow.

These standards of discipline are not the characteristics of a body that has a high morale, is confident of its mission, and proud of its integrity. Despite the fine words of members about the nobility of the representative function of Congress, actions of members speak louder than words, and the trend of behavior points to the conclusion that Congress lacks the morale to defend its own integrity. The famed "club spirit" works only to defend the members, not the club.

If anyone thinks that there is something inherent in a legislative body which makes it impossible to impose self-discipline, let him note the Congress itself. In protecting themselves, individual members of both the House and Senate are consistent and vigilant in enforcing strict rules. Section 19 of the

Senate rules has the following provisions which are strictly enforced:[47]

> Sec. 2. No Senator in debate shall, directly or indirectly, by any form of words impute to another Senator or to other Senators any conduct or motive unworthy or unbecoming a Senator.
>
> Sec. 4. If any Senator, in speaking or otherwise, transgresses the rules of the Senate, the Presiding Officer shall, or any Senator may, call him to order; and when a Senator shall be called to order he shall sit down, and not proceed without leave of the Senate which, if granted, shall be upon motion that he be allowed to proceed in order, which motion shall be determined without debate.

In protesting against the current interpretation of this rule which permits the aggrieved member to determine whether a violation has occurred, Senator Lehman said to the Senate Committee investigating the organization and operation of Congress,[48]

> . . . it seems inconceivable to me that the framers of rule 19 intended the use to which it has lately been put—namely, to permit any Member of the Senate to be the independent judge of what is and what is not a reflection and imputation of conduct or motives unworthy or unbecoming a Senator."

Later the following discussion between the Committee Chairman, Senator McClellan, and Senator Lehman occurred:[49]

> *Senator Lehman.* . . . You may recall that there have been several instances in the two years during which time I have been in the Senate, when a man has been taken off his feet by another Member of the Senate, because he felt that he had been aggrieved. In two instances that I know of, the point of order was raised with the Chair, that the Chair should interpret whether in fact anything had been said or done which would reflect on a fellow Senator.
>
> The Vice President in a ruling last year said that he was bound by precedent and by the strict interpretation of the rule, and that it was not within his jurisdiction to make any ruling as to relevancy, as to whether or not————
>
> *The Chairman.* In other words, as it is now, any time a Senator thinks

that he has occasion for offense, all he has to do is to raise a point of order?

Senator Lehman. That is right.

The Chairman. Then the Senator who has the floor is compelled to take his seat, and he cannot further proceed until someone makes a motion that he be permitted to proceed in order, and that motion is carried. Now, as I understand it, you would have the Chair rule, first, when a Member raises a point of order, whether the language used or the conduct was such as to reflect upon the Member?

The House has a similar rule against a member's impugning the motives of a colleague. A member who is called to order for violating the rule must stand silent until the chair has ruled. An appeal may be taken from the ruling of the chair. These rules are strictly enforced. There can be no reasonable doubt that the two houses can discipline their members and enforce strict rules, if the members choose to do so.

The failure of Congress to achieve its designed, expected, and proper role in making the basic public policy of the nation is matched also by the state legislatures. Despite differences in composition and organization, they exhibit similar shortcomings. American legislatures have great constitutional power but little or no moral authority. They are feared but not respected. They are at the very center of governmental power but lack prestige. In an age which requires positive and constructive action they distinguish themselves by negation. Instead of the fruits of fulfillment, they taste the bitterness of frustration. Why should these things be?

The explanation is a double one. Some of the causes lie in the men themselves, men who are perhaps rather typical of American life. The other causes lie in the institutional setting in which these men have to work, specifically in the organization, the rules, the procedures, and the traditions of the legislative bodies. The latter will be considered first.

The only justifications that a legislative assembly has for being what it is—a group of men met collectively to make policy—are that it is representative and responsible, and that it is right. It must be representative and responsible in the sense that it is chosen by the public, reflects the public's more important views, values, and interests with some degree of proportionality, and acts for the public interest as a whole. It must be right in the sense that it comes closer to reality and makes decisions which over the course of time give greater satisfaction to the total public than other types of governmental authorities can do.

Representation—Distortion of the Principle
The representative quality is the starting point. In this respect both Congress and most of the state legislatures have a handicap. One chamber of the bicameral bodies gives much greater weight in the chamber to the people of some areas than to others. Representation is not equal but unequal. In the Senate each state has two Senators. New York with 15,000,000 souls has two Senators, and so does Nevada with 158,000. The represented strength of men and women of Nevada is almost 100 times greater in the Senate than the strength of New Yorkers. The people of the ten smallest states collectively are represented seventeen times as heavily as the people of the ten largest states. Representation of territory (the states) rather than of population skews the representative principle, for the states are unequal in area and density of population. Equal representation of states in the Senate was originally intended to protect the small states from the large states; but it has never been needed for this purpose, for on the important issues

the interests of the large and small states have not been in conflict, and opinion has not divided along those lines.

The effect of equal representation of the once sovereign states has been to exaggerate sectionalism in national affairs, and to increase the power of blocs, for example the silver bloc of Senators from the mountain states, and the cotton bloc of the South. Senator Paul Douglas called attention to these facts in the cloture debate of March, 1949.[50]

> . . . a majority of the Senate is now elected by 19 per cent of the population, while the remaining 81 per cent of the population are represented by a minority in the Senate.
>
> Let me emphasize that point again. One-fifth of the population already controls the Senate, even on those matters which are decided by a simple majority vote of the Senate, while the remaining four-fifths of the population are represented by a minority, even in cases where a simple majority of votes is required.
>
> . . . It may be well to show these results on a sectional basis. Let us take the twenty-four States of the South Atlantic, East South Central, West South Central and Mountain regions. The Senators from these regions form exactly half the total membership of this body. But the population of these regions in 1940 was only 45,100,000 or 35 per cent of the population of the country.
>
> In other words, sections of the country with 35 per cent of the population now elect as many Senators as the Northern, Midwestern, and Pacific States that have 65 per cent of the population. The people who live in these regions, therefore, now have approximately twice as much per capita representation in the Senate as those who live in the more populous States.
>
> I digress here for a moment to say that the eight Mountain States, with a total population of only a little more than four million, have sixteen seats in the United States Senate. Eight States, with a population of only 4,000,000, have sixteen seats, whereas my own State of Illinois, with a total population twice as great as all of these eight States together has only two seats. The eight larger States have a total population of 60,000,000, and yet they have only the same representation as the eight Mountain States with a population of only 4,000,000. I hope my friends from the Mountain States will excuse me if I bring this out. . . .

. . . They have great political power in the Senate, because they have sixteen votes. Personally they are as fine a group of men as could possibly be assembled. They are lovable. They are open-hearted. They are personally generous. They are generally progressive in their views. But they work pretty hard for their States. They want to see large Federal appropriations for public works, for irrigation, and for other purposes. They are interested in a tariff on wool, in a tariff on sugar, and in high prices for silver. I think on occasion they have carried on flirtations with those who are interested in the prices of cotton and tobacco.

This may be hard to accept, but it is the literal truth. If we of the large industrial States did not pay the cost of the tariffs on sugar and on wool; if we did not pay high prices for silver; and if we did not pour our money into public works, a large proportion of the population of the Mountain States would either have to leave that region or go on relief. The Mountain States are greatly indebted to the rest of the country. . . .

Nor is this all. We of the twenty-four States of the North, the Midwest, and the Pacific coast pay 80 per cent or four-fifths of the personal-income taxes of the Government while the remaining twenty-four States pay only 20 per cent or one-fifth of the total. The two States of New York and Illinois alone pay approximately a quarter of the entire income taxes of the country or more than all twenty-four of the States of the South Atlantic, West, and East South Central, and the Mountain regions combined. . . . Moreover, we of the large industrial States of the North and Midwest are open-handed in the appropriations which we make for the people of the South and the Mountain States. We alone are giving in excess of a billion and a half dollars in the form of Federal aid to the States. The South and the Mountain States are getting more than their proportionate per capita share in this. . . .

It is much the same with public works. We of the North and Middle West somehow never get much of these appropriations. When the pie is passed around we get only a thin slice. But we gladly pour billions into protecting the Southern and Western States from floods, into harnessing the waters of the Tennessee and the Columbia Rivers for the benefit of the people of those regions, into power projects in Texas, Arkansas, and the Mountain States, into the arid deserts of New Mexico, Colorado, Arizona, and into the valleys of California. I am pushing for the development of the Missouri Valley, although my own State does not stand to benefit directly by a single penny because of it. I mention all this to show that those of us from the North and Midwest who regard ourselves as liberals and progressives are trying to put the national interest first and that we are trying to help the people of other regions who need our help. We are taxing ourselves to help these regions because we believe it will help the United States of America. I regret to say that though I have listened for years, I have failed to hear any appreciable recognition of this fact from the spokesmen of those regions who are at the receiving end of this help.

Similarly, we progressive Democrats of the North and West have been generous in the organization of the Senate. Of the fifteen committees of this body, all but one, and that the least important nationally, the Committee on the District of Columbia, are headed by Southerners or Senators from the Mountain States, namely eight from the South and six from the Mountain States. We of the North, the Midwest, and the Pacific coast regions who win the national elections for the Democratic Party come to the Senate to find ourselves treated as poor relations, and almost as interlopers, and prevented from defending either the legitimate interests of our sections or advancing the interests of the country as a whole.

I have said enough to indicate that even under our present system of majority voting we of the North and the Midwest are the suppressed classes and second-class citizens in the Senate and in the Nation. We pay the taxes and what we do decides whether we win or lose the elections. But after winning an election, we find it almost impossible to get anything for ourselves or for the Nation. We do not ask for position as individuals, but we do want to further the welfare of the people of the United States, most of whom live in our regions.

Since the Constitution of the United States specifically provides that "no state, without its consent, shall be deprived of its equal suffrage in the Senate," unequal representation in the Senate is destined to continue. It cannot be escaped. Time will mitigate the grosser inequalities, however, through the industrialization and growth of population in the South and West; and eventually this trend may moderate the violence of sectional differences in the Senate.

The situation in the states is much worse. Although there

have never been local governments with sovereign powers to be defended within the states, the principle of unequal representation is also entrenched in the legislative assemblies of the states. This occurs in a number of ways, and the effect is always the same—to give rural voters disproportionate weight, sometimes grossly disproportionate strength in at least one house of the legislature. State constitutions which give each county equal representation in the upper house tend to make it a chamber which a rural minority dominates. In New Jersey, for example, the four largest counties which have more than one-half of the people of the state have only four votes out of twenty-one in the Senate, and the eight most populous counties, with four-fifths of the state's population, have only eight out of twenty-one votes.[51] Polk County, Iowa (Des Moines), with a population of 195,835, has one Senator and so also does Mohaska County, with a population of 26,485. Silver Bow County, Montana (Butte), containing 53,207 people has one state Senator, and so does Petroleum County which contains only 1,083. The chosen Senators from the rural counties are a solid majority, although they speak for only one-fifth of all Jersey men, a smaller group than Hudson County alone.[52]

States which give at least one vote to each town or township in the lower house make that chamber the preserve of the rural voters. Hartford, Connecticut, with a population of 177,000, has two votes in the lower house of its state, and so does the town of Colebrook with a population of a few hundreds. Allegheny County, Pennsylvania (Pittsburgh), with a population of 1,400,000, has twenty-seven representatives in the lower house, while thirty-six rural counties, with a population of only 1,200,000, have thirty-six representatives. Denver County, Colorado, has a ratio of 21,500 people for each representative in the lower chamber, while Bacca County has only 6,207 people for each representative. In Wisconsin there is a population of 67,447 people per urban assembly district and a population of only 15,827 per rural assembly district. Echols County, Georgia, with a population of only 3,000, has one representative in the lower house, while Fulton County (Atlanta), with a population of 393,000, has only three representatives.

A third basis for disproportionate representation is a limitation upon the representation from urban areas applied to one or both houses. In New York, for example, no county may have more than one-third of the Senators. There are also other legal devices to protect the control of rural politicians in state legislation—all of them products of nineteenth-century ingenuity.[53] The basic inequity of these devices, as originally conceived, has been greatly enlarged by the shift of population from country to city living in the past fifty years.

State constitutions which attempt to provide for equal representation have been nullified and are being nullified illegally by the refusal to reapportion the state legislature. Residents in many metropolitan centers find themselves discriminated against in both houses of the state legislature. Chicago is perhaps most abused. Cook County has more than half of the Illinois population, but only 37 per cent of the votes in either house. Other centers in a similar fix are Wilmington, Delaware; Baltimore, Maryland; and Portland, Oregon. In Illinois, where representation is supposed to be proportionate in both houses, the down-state politicians have simply ignored the clear constitutional requirement to reapportion the state after each decennial census. There has been no reapportionment since 1901, a deliberate and illegal violation of the Constitution, but one for which no judicial remedy has been found. Missouri and Michigan also have stopped reapportioning with the census of 1900. Kentucky last reapportioned in 1893, Mississippi in 1892,

Connecticut in 1870, and Tennessee in 1834.[54] Disproportionate political power continues in the hands of those who benefit from violating the Constitution, and they have continued to
nullify it. Is there any way except revolution by which the urban residents of Illinois may secure their constitutional right
to equal representation in the state legislature? If there is another remedy, it has not yet been discovered.

One would suppose that these nineteenth-century inequities
would have been corrected by constitutional amendments or in
the drafting of new constitutions after their inequitable effects
were aggravated so greatly by the industrial and urban evolution. But this has not occurred. Constitutional processes have
been used to prevent changes in the character of the legislatures. Constitutional conventions have been denied jurisdiction
over this subject when authorized (as in New Jersey in 1948)
or the constitutional conventions have been so constituted as to
maintain the *status quo*. The written constitutions of the states
have thus been used to deny equal representation to people
who live in the larger cities, particularly the metropolitan
centers, and to continue rural politicians in control of the
legislative power.

St. Louis, with a population of 850,000, has no more votes in
the state Senate than eighteen rural counties with a population
less than one-fifth as large.[55] The half of California's population living in San Francisco and Los Angeles fill only 5 per
cent of the seats in the state Senate. The metropolitan centers
of Cleveland, Cincinnati, Toledo, and Youngstown have to face
the fact that rural counties containing a third of Ohio's population control the state legislature. People who live in metropolitan cities throughout the country are under-represented in
state legislatures.

This situation is intolerable from the rational point of view and from the ethical point of view. Legislative power based upon grossly unequal representation prevents majority rule and establishes minority rule—a direct challenge to the basic principle of democratic government. Legislatures so constituted are relying on legalism for their authority. They have no more moral force than hereditary monarchies. Where minorities continue in control of legislative power through their refusal to comply with reapportionment requirements their power is in effect illegal and arbitrary. Eventually the courts must recognize the situation and take some action.[56] But the courts will not act until they are forced to; and until urban residents organize and prepare to fight for their rights in some way, nothing is likely to happen.

The evil consequences of this situation are serious and far reaching. State legislatures have been so apathetic in recognizing industrial and urban problems and so negative in doing anything about them that they have allowed the function of regulating the economy to pass almost entirely into the hands of the national government. Some of the transfer was necessary because of the national character of the industrial system. But many problems could have been dealt with if state legislatures had chosen to act.

One state legislator asks the question bluntly,[57] "What is the outcome in terms of practical legislation?" And his answer is specifically illuminating. "Our state [Oregon], as an example, has a rigid milk-control law which discriminates heavily against urban consumers by forbidding grocers to sell grade 'A' at low prices. Again the legislature declined to take any positive steps toward slum clearance in the cities, but on the other hand, it created a potato commission with authority to levy an impost on every sack, regardless of boosting the price to consumers. Destitute children, again, fared far worse when it came to appropriations than did rural roads. And, to cite one more indignity, automobile license fees were doubled on lighter-weight passenger sedans, a city dweller's type, at the same time that tolls went down for a 34,000-pound truck and trailer." If the centralization of power that has occurred since the advent of the New Deal is excessive, the system of arbitrary government by rural minorities in urban states is a major contributing cause.

The disproportionate power of rural representatives in state legislatures is also a major cause of personal corruption. The over-weighted legislators are inherently vulnerable, for they have votes which can be used to defeat measures which may little concern their own constituents but which are of great concern to the urban or industrial sections of the state. These votes have great market value, and they can frequently be bought in one way or another. Hence the alliance so frequently observed between conservative business interests, which are located in urban sections of a state, and the rural politicians. One group has money; the other has votes.

The disproportionate power of rural politicians contributes greatly to pork-barrel politics. If they are a majority of one house of the legislature, they can very nearly demand what they want, and get it, in public works, highways, contracts, and jobs. They have to be appeased. They are also in a position to engage in blackmail. At every session of many state legislatures, measures are introduced which are not meant to pass, but which move along in the legislative mill until their sponsors are bought off in one way or another. The interests (usually business interests) that would be injured if such bills should pass know what they are expected to do and come across.

Great power brings its temptations inevitably, and the temptations of irresponsible power are well-nigh irresistible. The power of representatives of a minority of a state's population to pass legislation, or to block it, is the most dangerous sort of irresponsible power.

The fabulous Arthur H. Samish of California ("I am the legislature"), a man of many clients who is known to have received nearly $2,000,000 over a period of six years from a single client-industry—the brewers of his state—to be spent in legislative politics, cannot be explained entirely by the irresponsible power of rural representatives; but that power is a contributing factor to their corruption. In "explaining" to the Kefauver Committee why so many large checks were drawn to "cash" during general election periods, the following exchange between Mr. Samish and the Committee took place:[58]

Question. And where does the money go, sir?
Answer. It is expended.
Question. It is expended?
Answer. (Nodding affirmatively.)
Question. And what does that mean?
Answer. Well, it is expended in connection with campaigns.
Question. And who gets it?
Answer. The cash is handled through me.
Question. You get the cash, then?
Answer. Yes.
Question. And what do you do with the cash?
Answer. We spend it. Make contributions and distributions. . . .
Question. Well, sir, we are not arguing policy with you. We are trying to find out where the money went, physically; whose hands it got into.
Answer. Well, it comes into mine.
Question. And then where does it go from yours?
Answer. It is given in contributions.
Question. To whom?
Answer. To different campaigns.

Question. Name one.

Answer. Well, I don't keep a record of that. I would be glad to see if—to see if I can find it for you. . . .

Question. Now you have the money in your hand; you have $10,000; you are going to give it to the campaign committee. How do you do it?

Answer. I handle it. I have been doing it for a great many years.

Question. Do you handle it in cash?

Answer. Well, we pay bills sometimes. Sometimes we may handle it in cash.

Question. What is wrong with writing a little check to the campaign committee?

Answer. I tell you what I decided after this situation: I told Mr. Hoertkorn [his bookkeeper], "For your information, starting March 1, [1951] everything in that fund is going to be by check."

The Chairman. May I ask a question at that point? Mr. Samish, just looking here at one month—for instance in May of 1950—you have "contributions $10,000," "$10,000," "$10,000," "$10,000"— four of them definitely marked "contributions" there; others here, "liquor," and somebody is a trustee, and "Louis Lurie Company"—I guess that is printing. But anyway, there is $40,000 in "contributions" that I assume you handle by paying some bills or giving to the candidates, or whatever it may be.

Question. Is there a distinction between "cash" and "contributions"?

The Chairman. Is that the same thing?

Answer. "Cash" and "contributions" are the same thing.

Question. Who decides whether it is going to be a contribution or cash?

Answer. All of our contributions, with rare exceptions—once in a while we may make a check out if I don't happen to be around, or for what reason I don't know. But I would say 95 per cent of it is in cash.

The evil effects of disproportionate, arbitrary power in state legislatures do not end there, but are compounded in the Congress of the United States by improper apportionment of seats in the House of Representatives, an impropriety which is unconstitutional, but which goes uncontrolled. The Congress itself divides the representatives in the House among the states; but each state legislature determines the size and shape of congressional districts in which its representatives are elected, and this power is abused to distort representation in the House. In general, rural congressional districts tend to be smaller in population than urban districts, thus exaggerating the rural vote. Sometimes the distortion is extreme. The smallest congressional district in Illinois in 1946, for example, had only one-eighth of the population of the largest district, for the districts had not been changed since 1901 despite the changes in population. In Ohio the smallest district has less than one-fourth of the population of the largest district. In almost one-third of the states (which have more than one representative) the smallest district has less than half of the population of the largest.[59] This method of stealing votes is fairly easy. A state legislature merely has to do nothing while its metropolitan centers grow.

When a state legislature acts to redraw the congressional district boundaries to take care of a changed apportionment by Congress, it can deliberately distort the representative principle in districts of peculiar size and shape. This practice of gerrymandering,[60] as every schoolboy knows, got its name from the Massachusetts Act of February 11, 1812, signed by Governor Elbridge Gerry which created a district resembling a salamander in shape. ("It's not a salamander; it's a gerrymander.") The venerable practice is still in vogue. Queer-shaped districts are drawn by the party in control of the state legislature to exaggerate its own strength in Congress and the well-proved method is to dilute the votes of the opposition with safe majorities of one's own party. Massachusetts is an example of how the gerrymander works. Although state-wide elections more often than not go Democratic, the Republicans (except in 1932) continually elect a majority of the state's Representatives to Congress.[61] The urban citizen is always the loser. The exaggerated strength of the rural politicians in the state legislature gives them an almost certain veto in both houses, and when they control both, they can do what they please.

Congress has the power to control these abuses, if it chooses, by establishing standards in the apportionment law governing the size and shape of districts and the limits of tolerance for discrepancies in population. But it has never enforced such standards vigilantly, and after 1911 it has ceased to put effective standards in the apportionment act.[62] A vicious circle is in evidence. Exaggerated voting strength in state legislatures, out of all proportion to population, leads to both perpetuation of the inequity in the state and its extension to the Congress, which then in turn fails to control the corrupting influence at its source. It is a wicked system.

The effect on Democratic-Republican party competition is noticeable. Outside of the Solid South the Republicans tend to poll more votes in the country and the Democrats in the city. The Democratic governor and Republican legislatures have come to be a typical combination in industrial states. New York's famous Governor Alfred E. Smith called attention to the immediate effect of this system quite bluntly:[63] ". . . when I campaigned through this State, I campaigned against as good men as the Republican Party could put up, and we talked these issues; and each time that I won, I was inaugurated, and the next day the Republican Speaker was elected, and then they came down to talk to me about their platform—a platform that had been thrown out of the window, repudiated, cast aside by the electorate of the State. That is what happens under an unfair apportionment."

Although not so obvious, the longer range effects are more serious. The situation encourages a minority party to hang on to power to which it has no moral right—and frequently no legal right. Instead of making a rational appeal for majority support, and so rebuilding its strength, it must resort to more and more unscrupulous means to maintain its hold. Although it becomes adept in the wiles of a governing minority, how can it retain its moral force, and how can it escape the sickening spread of corruption which is inherent in the very structure of its power? Will not any political group which relies on constitutionalism, legalism, and the gerrymander, and which also violates the most fundamental constitutional principles and directives, destroy its own power in a democratic society?

Representation—Abandonment of the Principle

Although Congress and the state legislatures are handicapped at the outset by the distortion of the representative principle in their composition, it is less serious in its consequences than the abandonment of the representative principles within the legislative bodies. The internal organization and procedures of American legislative assemblies almost destroy their representative character. In many respects the legislative process is only a caricature of representative government.

Rejection of the representative principle has come about in a number of ways. Most legislative work is done, and the features of legislative measures are largely determined, in committees. In Congress, for example, the center of gravity is in the thirty-four standing committees of the House and Senate. These committees are not representative committees in the sense that in their composition they reflect the make-up of the houses. They are atypical rather than typical. They are essentially and deliberately biased rather than balanced, for Representatives and Senators generally seek membership on committees in which they or their best-organized constituents have a strong economic interest. Initial interest in the subject will grow as they continue on the committee year after year. The committees thus tend to take on the character of specialists concerned with special interest groups—as specialized and as biased in perspective and values as the particular executive departments and as the lobbies with which they deal.

The thirteen members of the Senate Committee on Agriculture and Forestry, for example, are all from strongly agricultural states. Ten of the thirteen members of the Senate Committee on Interior and Insular Affairs are from the Western states in which Interior activities are concentrated; only three are from the states that pay the bills, who might conceivably ask what is the national interest, over and above the sectional interest, in Interior projects? The Senate Committees on Banking and Currency, and Works and Public Welfare are less extreme in their specialized perspective, perhaps necessarily so, since the Senate in representing states rather than population over-represents agriculture and under-represents industry. But these committees also have majorities of 8-5 favoring the states where finance and industry are predominant.

In the House of Representatives, where representation is supposed to be in proportion to population, the specialized bias of standing committees is less pronounced, although still a distinct feature. Twenty-four of the thirty members of the House Committee on Agriculture are from agricultural states. Although Representatives from the West are relatively scarce in the House, since Nevada and Wyoming have only one representative each, and seven others have only two representatives, they nevertheless manage to get a majority on the Committee on Interior and Insular Affairs, with the help of the Pacific Coast (14-13). House Committees on Banking and Currency and Education and Labor have substantial majorities from the regions where finance and industry are strongest (17-10 and 15-9).[64]

The representative principle is further rejected by the character, power, and methods of committee chairmen in the Congress. First of all they gain their position by reason of seniority, *i.e.*, longest continuous service on the committee. The exceptions to this rule are so infrequent as to be collectors' items. One a decade is a high average, and the textbooks have to go back to 1921 for a good example.[65] Committee chairmen thus come from the most decidedly partisan political areas where one-party majorities are pronounced and continued. The chairman is even less likely to reflect the sentiment of the House and of the country than is his committee. When the Republicans are in power the rural areas of the North and East furnish the chairmen, and when the Democrats are in power the Solid South has the lion's share, supplemented by a few chairmen elected by Democratic city machines.

The chairmen of standing committees in the 82nd Congress are a vivid example of this unrepresentative rule. Western states have six chairmanships; and the Southern states have eight. That leaves only one standing committee, the relatively less important Committee on the District of Columbia, chaired by Senator Neely of West Virginia, a border state. Fourteen of fifteen chairmanships fall to two regions. There are no chairmen from the Pacific Coast, Middle West, or Northeastern states.

In the House of Representatives the South again has the lion's share, eleven out of nineteen chairmanships. Western states have one, Middle Western states four, Northeastern states three, and the Pacific Coast none.

If the chairmanships are combined, the score for the Congress as a whole is: South   20

West   7

Middle West 4
Northeast   3
Pacific Coast 0

These chairmen have great power. They select and determine the order of matters to be taken up by the committees,
have large control over the personnel and assignment of subcommittees, and conduct hearings and meetings of the full
committee. They also direct the committee's staff, and they or
their subcommittee chairmen report legislative measures to the
whole house. The latter function is extremely important—as the
capstone to the total array of powers. The chairman has almost
a veto over legislation. He cannot force his committee to support a bill, but he can in effect prevent his committee from taking favorable action. He may decline to hold hearings, put off
committee consideration, or even defer reporting a measure
that has committee approval. In the words of a member of the
House of Representatives,[66] "Of course the chairman of a committee cannot report a bill without the consent of a majority
of the committee, but under the unwritten, and, I believe, the
unbroken, rule no majority has ever reported a bill without
the consent of the chairman. On the floor the bill is absolutely
in his hands.

"It is obvious that the power to say that legislation shall not
be considered is the power to legislate. It is the negative power
which lends real significance to these chairmanships. This negative or obstructive power rests in the hands of a few men
and may be exerted at any of the various stages of the bill's
progress toward final passage."

The seniority principle dominates the entire committee as
well as the chairmanship. Strict protocol is observed in all
things. Ranking members have precedence over members jun-

ior to them (in their party) in such things as picking subcommittee assignments. Even seating at the committee table is governed by seniority. A well-polished brass name plate, firmly screwed down, protects each member's position with reference to the head of the table. By waiting patiently for his turn a member is sure eventually of great power—personal power. As he moves up the table his prestige and perquisites increase. As the ranking minority member he has great power, and as chairman he becomes a potentate in everything but name. Huey Long must have been inspired by the United States Senate when he coined the slogan "every man a King." The seniority system is not a matter of rules but of conventions. It is nevertheless firmly entrenched. A newcomer cannot afford to challenge the system and an old timer does not want to.

Seniority is the primary influence also in selecting party and house officers. Henry Clay in 1811 and William Pennington in 1859 were chosen Speaker of the House as first-term representatives, but that is a thing of the past. Since 1896 the prior service of men chosen Speakers has averaged more than twenty-two years.[67] Other party officers, floor leader, and whip are also commonly men of long service. Although the floor leader is normally in line for the position of Speaker, the long-time chairman of an important standing committee is sometimes chosen. To be elected a party officer, a man must have had long service and must have gained recognition. Almost the only road to recognition is the committee chairmanship. Thus seniority limits the choice initially to two or three men, from whom the caucus makes its choice on the basis of other factors.

The Rules Committee of the House of Representatives, which is in effect the "governing committee" of the House, is perhaps even less representative than many of the other standing committees. For the past twenty years a solid segment of this committee has had little sympathy for the New Deal, the Fair Deal or the rank and file of the House. It is a small committee of twelve members, and the fortuitous factor of personality plays a large part in its decisions—decisions which vitally affect the course of legislation and the organization of power in the House. Almost all important legislation is considered under a special rule which determines how debate shall proceed and when a vote shall be taken. The Rules Committee sometimes refuses to report bills and resolutions entirely, or it may amend them as a price of permitting them to come to the floor. For example, the Rules Committee for many months in 1951 held up legislation which would authorize shipment of wheat to relieve famine in India, and forced revision of the bill before letting it come to a vote.[68] The twenty-one-day discharge rule of the 81st Congress, which allowed courageous standing-committee chairmen to bring measures to the floor if the Rules Committee failed to act, stimulated the Rules Committee. For example, "They let the housing bill out, and for the first time in five years, the individual Members of the House had an opportunity to vote on the merits of the legislation." [69] But it did not greatly change the power of the Rules Committee. The Committee may also block measures which committee chairmen are trying to get considered on the normal calendar. The Rules Committee can be overridden by a petition of 218 members to bring a bill to the floor, but this process is so laborious as to bar its use except on rare occasions.

An unrepresentative committee with such arbitrary power probably could not exist except for two things. One is the fact that it is the channel through which amendments in the basic rules of the House come before that body. The second is the skillful and sophisticated use of its powers. By performing negative services, by blocking measures which may have public support, but are unpalatable to the powers-that-be in the House, by winning friends through favors, and by gauging carefully the lengths to which it can go without stirring up opposition that would defeat it, the committee is able to maintain its position even though it is completely unrepresentative.[70] The House has come to depend upon the committee to control the legislative traffic and has allowed the traffic cop to become the governing committee, perhaps on the theory that an arbitrary governor on the legislative engine is better than none.

The unrepresentativeness of power as it is exercised within the Congress is not a new discovery. This system has been a matter of caustic comment by outsiders for sixty-five years. Insiders find it best to say little. Even a few injudicious comments by members of the Congress who have not yet climbed the ladder can discredit them with the powers-that-be; and once the ladder is climbed the system doesn't seem so bad. Even so courageous a group as the Douglas Committee on Ethical Standards in Government found it necessary to avoid comment on the seniority system, which destroys the very basis for the moral force of Congress.

How representative can representative government be when the legislative assembly which is at the heart of representative government is unrepresentative in its internal organization and procedures? At best it is a gross distortion.

IV

MORALITY AND THE LEGISLATIVE SYSTEM: RESPONSIBILITY AND REASON

If the organization, conventions, rules, and procedures of the Congress have distorted the principle of *representation*, it can be said that they have flatly rejected the principle of *responsibility*. In neither the House nor the Senate does a party majority effectively hold the men who have power responsible for what they do. For all intents and purposes, the powers-that-be are potentates with life tenure, not subject to discipline, not required to carry out the wishes of a majority, not called to account, and not recalled from office while they continue in the Congress, and while their party continues in the majority.

The Principle of Responsibility Rejected
The chairman dominates the committee and neither the committee members nor the party members in his chamber control him. The traditional deference for the chairman allows him to convert his position to one of personal power and to turn its

perquisites to his own ends. The appointment of "professional" staffs for committees following the Legislative Reorganization Act of 1946 is generally thought to be a great reform, despite the fact that not all staffs are as "professional" as they might be. Little has been said about the practice of some chairmen, however, who make the committee employees a personal staff rather than a committee staff. The tendency and the tradition are to let the chairman get by with anything. Like the monarch of old, his only restraint is his conscience. Some monarchs had a conscience, and so do some chairmen. But there is no system of responsibility.

The committees (dominated by their chairmen) dominate the Congress. The houses have no effective procedures to call them to account, and no way to make sure that the committee action reflects the wishes of a party majority. The majority has no systematic procedures for instructing committees as to priorities or basic policy, and it has no way of compelling committees to act. Measures which the Senate committees choose to report can be amended (except conference-committee reports) on the floor in the Senate where the small size and the freedom of debate make such action possible. It is so difficult to revise complex modern legislation on the floor without wrecking it, however, that radical revision is seldom attempted, except to emasculate a bill. In the House of Representatives, where most important legislation is considered under a special rule, the Rules Committee decides how much debate and what opportunities for amendment on the floor there shall be. A committee chairman who makes a good deal with the Rules Committee is thus able to put his bill through the House without great difficulty. Under a "closed" rule, which is sometimes used in tax legislation, only amendments approved by the standing committee may be made on the floor.

The only recourse of the House to escape the dictation of a standing committee or its chairman is to get 218 signatures, a majority of the total membership, on a petition discharging a measure from the committee. This permits the House to act, but does not discipline the chairman or his committee. So laborious is this process that it is seldom used.

In the 81st Congress the House was hailed for its "liberal" rule which permitted the "chairman of a standing committee to call for House consideration a bill favorably reported by his committee, if the Rules Committee reported adversely, or failed to report within twenty-one days—calendar days—on any public bill or joint resolution referred to it." [1] Eight measures were brought to the floor in this way during the 81st Congress, and the threat of its use persuaded the Rules Committee to act in other cases.[2] The 82nd Congress eliminated this rule.

The houses of Congress also lack a system for holding party officers of the houses responsible. The caucus, although a mixed blessing, is a means by which the rank and file of the (party) members can act together, and a means by which party leaders could be forced to justify decisions. It has ceased to be used for these purposes, however, in recent years, and its principal function is to assign power through organization of the Congress at the beginning of a new session. It has ceased to be a means of continuous party government, or of enforcing responsibility.

As long as their party remains in the majority, committee chairmen and party officials continue in office, and they return to office when their party returns to power. There is no two-term tradition, no constitutional amendment to prevent three, four, five, or six terms, and no recall procedure. It is a rule of American law that no administrative official has a property right in his office; but it does not affect the legislative branch. In effect, committee chairmen have a valuable property in their offices, and all members similarly have a corresponding right to their position on the seniority escalator. At present there are no more securely vested interests in American life than these powerful offices.

The Rational Principle Challenged

Representativeness, responsibility, and rationality are the bases for the moral authority of legislative bodies. If the Congress as it now functions has twisted the principle of representation into a caricature, and has rejected the principle of collective responsibility until it lacks even the reality of a fiction, what is the status of the principle of reason? Perhaps it is so well established as to give legislative action moral force after all.

The function of Congress to discover, establish, and disseminate the truth by rational means is also under serious internal attack. Congress has power to investigate, now well established in American constitutional law. The legislative reforms of 1946, furthermore, tried to strengthen the fact-finding function by better staffing of committees, by enlarging the legislative reference staff of the Library of Congress, and (in part) by providing an administrative assistant for Senators. But the conduct of certain committee "investigations" and the practice of certain members in making reckless, irresponsible, or untrue statements, relying on the cloak of constitutional immunity from suit to protect them from legal attack, have jeopardized the integrity of the fact-finding process.

Committee investigations have been criticized for a long time. Woodrow Wilson in 1885 wrote of the "irksome, ungracious investigations" which "can violently disturb but cannot often fathom the waters of the sea in which the bigger fish of the civil service swim and feed." [3] Walter Lippmann in 1922 referred to "that legalized atrocity, the congressional investigation, where Congressmen, starved of their legitimate food for thought, go on a wild and feverish manhunt, and do not stop at cannibalism." [4] President Calvin Coolidge in 1924, in protesting against the abuse of committee powers said, "Under a procedure of this kind, the constitutional guaranty against unwarranted search and seizure breaks down, the prohibition against what amounts to a Government charge of criminal action without formal presentment of a grand jury is evaded, the rules of evidence which have been adopted for protection of the innocent are ignored, the department becomes the victim of vague, unformulated, and indefinite charges, and instead of a government of law, we have a government of lawlessness." [5]

Although investigating committees have done some of the best work of Congress (for example, the Truman Committee on the Conduct of the National Defense Program), other committees and some committeemen have behaved so badly, judged by the normal standards of fairness and faithfulness to the facts, that they have tended to impeach the integrity of committees in getting at the truth. The careless investigations, reckless charges, and avid publicity of the early Dies Committee on Un-American Activities created the presumption that the chairman was more interested in attacking the New Deal than in getting at the root of the problem of espionage. The Cox Committee attack on the FCC was perhaps the most extreme example of committee procedures designed to disseminate derogatory charges, not to investigate the facts. Few committees have gone so far as these two, but deviations from conventional standards of accuracy and fair play have been numerous enough to demonstrate the existence of a real problem. Even in the less spectacular committees, unrestrained members at times betray evidence of a sovereign complex, or use the hearing to conduct a personal fight. "Far to often," says Marquis Childs, a highly respected Washington columnist,[6] "I have seen conscientious and honest civil servants treated when they came before the committees of Congress as though they were culprits in the dock. The very fact that they have a Government job, which they are far more often than not attempting to carry out conscientiously, seems in the minds of some Congressmen to incriminate them." There is something anomalous about the situation when members of the Congress, at the very center of authority in the Government of the United States, browbeat witnesses who are citizens of the United States, and insult men who are the Government's employees. As lawyers in private practice they do not so treat their clients, and as employers they must be more courteous to their kitchen help—if they wish to have a cook. The anomaly is plain to the witness and to the observer, but less apparent to the committee member.[7]

No one denies the value of legislative investigations when they are well conducted, or challenges the importance of maintaining investigating powers unimpaired. It is conceded also that most committees try to get and weigh the facts, and that most committee members presumably try to be fair in cross-examining witnesses. Yet there have been so many exceptions to this presumptive rule of reasonableness that committee actions are widely, severely, and incisively criticized by the bar (both practitioners and learned members), by professional students of government, by the press, by the general public, and, last but not least, by many distinguished members of Congress. The gist of these criticisms is that [8] "investigating committees . . . can assume the aspects of a trial without the safeguards to the individual of regular court proceedings; that legislators appear in the role of judges and combine the functions of prosecuting and judging which should be separated; that as a result of the publicity of committee hearings witnesses may be exposed to such penalties as dismissal from their jobs, loss of pension payments, character assassination, or injury to their reputations; that exposure through public hearings can be substituted, in certain types of cases, for regulation by law, enforced by the courts; that this process of control by exposure before an investigating committee is not subject to special rules of procedure laid down by Congress; that the legal rights of individuals, guaranteed by the Bill of Rights, are in practice abridged by congressional investigations; and that conformity to prevailing ideas is enforced by fear of censure."

The reputation of Congress as a rational body for getting at the truth is also jeopardized by conduct of individual members on the floor. Accusations with full publicity but meager data are now so well known as to have provoked widespread public criticism. The smear has long been a familiar tactic of heated campaigns where it appears in furtive forms. But wholesale, unchallenged defamation of character by remarks on the floor of the Senate or "extended" in the *Congressional Record* is a new development. It must be recognized that the situation is made ripe for such tactics by the coincidence of Soviet Russia's militarism and aggressive foreign policy, the communist efforts to infiltrate American politics, and the general anxiety resulting from constant publicity given to even flimsy information or speculation about Russia, the "Kremlin," and communism. Some committees have contributed to this anxiety complex by publicizing charges in hearings rather than proved conclusions in committee reports; but the general tendency of press, radio, and television (perhaps it is unconscious) to play up "news" on Russia, communism, and the threat of war is probably more largely responsible. Considering the fact that there has never been a time when there was so little reliable information about so large a portion of the world, the "news" coverage of Russia and her satellites is phenomenal.[9] If the communist countries had to pay for this publicity it would exhaust their dollar exchange very quickly.

It is not so much the danger of war (which although indeterminable, most Americans accept) as it is the inflated publicity which contributes to the anxious state of mind. The anxious state in turn creates a market for more "think pieces," new confessions of ex-communists, and additional counter-spy memoirs. This background of news policy paves the way for the communist smear. If the communist label can be pinned on an opponent even briefly, although it may not be made to stick, it will hurt him. The hungry press-radio-television facilities will suck up the charge and broadcast it immediately, protected indirectly by the Senator's immunity from suit.[10] Denials, refutation, and the evidence may never catch up with the original accusation. Circumstances have combined to give the communist smear such bite that it is not strange that some men have not scrupled to use it; and the Senate, with its traditions of unlimited debate, and without a rule of relevancy to make sure that remarks are germane, is the ideal forum for the smearer. In the unduly discouraged view of one Senator, "Now there is no restraint at all . . . They can say anything they like and there is nothing anybody can do about it." [11]

The views of Congressional critics of the abuse of immunity are reflected in the remarks of Senator Lester C. Hunt on the subject.[12]

> This unusual prerogative of immunity, conferring protection against arrest or civil suit, is one of the most jealously guarded of Congress' rights and privileges. It was lifted from the English law and placed

by the founding fathers in our Constitution with, apparently, little debate . . . the immunity afforded Members of Congress was designed to allow criticism of the Executive without fear of retaliation. It was plainly their intention that the Congress be protected not from its constituents but from the executive branch of the Government.

It was also part of the intention of the Constitutional Convention that the doctrine of privilege should be valid only within the Halls of Congress. The framers of the Constitution would be surprised and appalled if they knew that, as construed today, it is applicable to speeches which are never made before Congress but which are written or adapted by Members as extensions of imaginary remarks and circulated throughout the country in the *Congressional Record*. They would also be shocked to learn that it has been extended to committee reports and to testimony in committee hearings.

Such broad interpretation of the term "immunity" has led to three flagrant and, in my view, intolerable abuses. The first of these is that, under the aegis of the immunity privilege, unscrupulous Congressmen can impute unworthy or unpatriotic motives to any department of Government or any member of an administration, by innuendo or as an outright accusation, without offering any evidence in support of such charges. An apparent error of judgment on the part of a public figure may be attributed to motives of treason. The accusation may be utterly without foundation and the accused's purposes may be of the highest, but the doubt which is cast on the Government departments concerned not only lowers public confidence in those departments but also in time undermines the people's faith in our form of government.

Still another abuse of the immunity principle is that practiced by the Congressman who uses it in building up his own political personality. When a Member of Congress, either with or without intent to injure, makes an accusation against another person, the tactic pays off in three ways. It makes of him, as a Member of Congress, a man to be feared. It disgraces his opponent. And it gives him publicity that he does not deserve but which is of paramount usefulness in furthering his personal ambitions. This is done at the expense of a person who has no direct recourse against the defamer.

Thus we come to the third abuse of the immunity privilege, that involving a basic violation of the accused party's constitutional rights. This works in two ways, for not only is the ordinary citizen usually denied the right to defend himself against his more privileged accuser, but he is in fact placed in double jeopardy. He is tried in committee and subcommittee, in the newspapers and over the radio. Then, if an iota of evidence against him is found, he is again tried in a court of law; a manifest violation of the due-process clause of our Constitution.

Senator Margaret Chase Smith challenged the abuse of the Senatorial discretion in matters of speech more pointedly, but also with a touch of despair in her famous "declaration of conscience," which six other Republican Senators also signed:[18]

STATEMENT OF SEVEN REPUBLICAN SENATORS

1. We are Republicans. But we are Americans first. It is as Americans that we express our concern with the growing confusion that threatens the security and stability of our country. Democrats and Republicans alike have contributed to that confusion.

2. The Democratic administration has initially created the confusion by its lack of effective leadership, by its contradictory grave warnings and optimistic assurances, by its complacency to the threat of communism here at home, by its oversensitiveness to rightful criticism, by its petty bitterness against its critics.

3. Certain elements of the Republican Party have materially added to this confusion in the hopes of riding the Republican Party to victory through the selfish political exploitation of fear, bigotry, ignorance, and intolerance. There are enough mistakes of the Democrats for Republicans to criticize constructively without resorting to political smears.

4. To this extent, Democrats and Republicans alike have unwittingly, but undeniably, played directly into the Communist design of "confuse, divide, and conquer."

5. It is high time that we stopped thinking politically as Republicans and Democrats about elections and started thinking patriotically as Americans about national security based on individual freedom. It is high time that we all stopped being tools and victims of totalitarian techniques—techniques that, if continued here unchecked, will surely end what we have come to cherish as the American way of life.

> *Margaret Chase Smith*, MAINE.
> *Charles W. Tobey*, NEW HAMPSHIRE.
> *George D. Aiken*, VERMONT.
> *Wayne L. Morse*, OREGON.
> *Irving M. Ives*, NEW YORK.
> *Edward J. Thye*, MINNESOTA.
> *Robert C. Hendrickson*, NEW JERSEY.

The Roman Catholic Bishops of the United States in their November, 1951, statement commented tersely on the moral standards which must govern political speeches whether or not there is immunity from civil suit. "Dishonesty, slander, detraction and defamation of character are as truly transgressions of God's commandments when resorted to by men in political life as they are for all other men." [14]

Ethics of the Filibuster

No review of ethical weaknesses of the legislative system dares pass over the Senate filibuster—the power of even a small group of Senators to prevent measures from coming to a vote, even though a majority of the Senate desires to make a decision. By speaking in turn at length, a few men can hold the Senate floor indefinitely. The Senate has only two ways of closing debate, by unanimous consent, and by the cloture rule. The latter permits sixteen Senators to petition to close debate; if on the second calendar day following, the Senate approves cloture by a favorable vote of sixty-four Senators, two-thirds of the entire membership, debate is limited to one hour for each Senator and a vote is taken when all who wish to speak have done so. Until the 81st Congress, only a two-thirds vote of those voting, i.e., as few as thirty-two Senators or two-thirds of a quorum, was required to close debate; but even so the requirement was so onerous that it was not effective in permitting the Senate to act. In only four instances out of nineteen attempts since 1917 when the cloture rule was adopted have measures been brought to a vote under the rule, and no cloture action has been successful in the past quarter-century.

There was a joker in the old rule, as it had been interpreted in recent years, which made it possible for even a small but skillful and determined minority to prevent cloture entirely. That is, the cloture procedure did not apply to procedural motions including motions to consider a legislative bill. A filibuster could thus begin before a measure was before the Senate and could prevent its being *considered*.[15] In an alleged liberalization of the rule, adopted March 17, 1949, the 81st Congress made it applicable to a "motion, or other matter pending before the Senate" as well as to a legislative "measure." But this "liberalization" was at the cost of two further concessions to minority power: the requirement that two-thirds of all Senators "duly chosen and sworn" must vote to close debate; and the specific exemption from the cloture rule of any proposal to change the standing rules of the Senate. As a result cloture may now be applied to get a bill before the Senate, as well as to get a decision on it, but so large a majority is required to close debate that it will seldom be possible to do so, and debate cannot be closed except by unanimous consent on proposals to modify the cloture rule itself.

Both the Senate and the House have devices by which a small minority may prevent the majority from making a decision. The Senate rules give small groups the power to block action by talk. The House gives its Rules Committee (any coalition of seven members of the twelve-man committee) power to block action by silence. Both are effective, and both are arbitrary. The filibuster and the rules-committee veto are an expression of personal power which the internal organization, rules, and traditions of Congress vest in individual men. They squarely challenge the basic principles of representative, responsible, reasonable government.

The System of Personal Power—Why Does It Exist?
Conditions in state legislatures differ in details from Congress.
But in the basic weaknesses of Congress they are no better.
They are not more responsible; generally they are less representative, and rational public discussion of basic issues is even
less in evidence. Tricks, trades and the trivia of organizational
and procedural rules are the life blood of the legislative process
—not evidence, reason, analysis, and public discussion. Deals,
not debate, dominate the legislative forum.

How can this be? How could it have come about? Why is it
tolerated? The answer is long and involved, but some explanations are evident.

The over-representation of rural populations, established
when the cities contained a minority of the population, is an
anachronism in the urban industrial nation of today. Rural politicians are hanging on to their disproportionate, and to that
degree irresponsible, power. They are hanging on to it deter-
minedly. Their veto on public policy has not yet been seriously
threatened, and they give every evidence of continuing to
make a very good thing of it. Their rationalization is that they
are defending the rural public; but the general public doesn't
really have a chance to decide whether it wants to be so defended. Rural politicians and rural political machines have a
commercial asset of great value which they will not let go
without a fight. The issue of fair representation is never put
up to the rank and file of Americans.

The pattern of internal legislative organization and procedures which has grown up over the years has produced what is
essentially a system of personal power, of assured and certain
personal power for men who will conform to the pattern. It uses
both the carrot and the stick to force legislators to go along. It

gives some rewards soon and more later to the faithful, and punishes those who revolt.

Revolt is impossible for one man and difficult even for a substantial group. In the Congress, for example, the Senate is continuously organized, and newcomers are always less than a third of the members. They are in no position to start a revolution, and time quiets the inclination to do so. The reputed "club spirit" in Congress is a political reality, which has to be experienced to be understood. The "club" has about as much sympathy for a man who challenges its sacred ways as a gang of boys playing in the street has for the queer kid who doesn't belong. The frequency with which the more progressive members of the Congress find it necessary to protest that they are not reformers, not self-righteous, and not different from the rest of the crowd is evidence of the real strength of the urge to conform. One Representative spoke for a lot of Congressmen when he said, "I do not want the public to get the impression that I am a crusader, because I am not. I am just like the rest of you." [16] Such remarks appear in the *Record* and printed hearings very frequently, and always when reforms are being considered. The eagerness to be one of the gang is pathetic.

The personal character of power in the Congressional "club" is illustrated by the institution of "Senatorial courtesy" in the Senate. Under this tradition the Senate does not give its consent to Presidential appointments for which its approval is required, if a Senator of the majority party in the state in which the executive or judicial offices are located objects to the appointment, and invokes the unwritten rule of Senatorial courtesy. But to invoke the rule a Senator must object not on principle to the quality of the appointments. It does him no good to challenge the nominations on their merits. He must utter the ritualistic objection that the appointments are "personally obnoxious." If he puts his protest on this personal basis the traditional rule operates, the committee does not report the nominations favorably, and the appointments are not approved.

Even if a Senator's real objection to persons nominated by the President is on what he believes to be the merits of the case, he must put his claim for Senate support on a personal basis. This was demonstrated again by the Senate in 1951 when it refused to confirm two of President Truman's appointments to the Federal bench in Illinois. In sending the names to the Senate the President had ignored suggestions of Senator Paul Douglas of Illinois. (His Illinois colleague was Republican.) Senator Douglas felt that the two men passed over were much better qualified for judicial posts than the men the President had named, reportedly on the recommendation of former Senator Lucas. Mr. Douglas then polled the bar associations of Chicago and Cook County to ascertain their views. The Illinois Bar Association was also polled, according to reports, at the suggestion of the Chairman of the Judiciary Committee. All three bar associations by substantial majorities rated the Douglas slate much higher than the Truman nominees. The President was reported to have told his press conference, when queried, that the bar does not make the appointments, and he declined to withdraw the two names at issue. It was clear that Senator Douglas, a man of good will, had no personal feelings against the challenged nominees and did not wish to attack them, although he believed they did not measure up to the proper standards for Federal judges. In advance of the hearings, the action of the Judiciary Committee on the nominations was uncertain. Would it support the administration or would it support a Senator who had obviously incurred the President's ill will? Senator McCarran, Chairman of the Judiciary Committee, gave some rather strong hints as to what must be done by a Senator to secure committee support. He was reported by the press as saying, "Assuming that Senator Douglas comes before the Committee and makes his objection in a vigorous manner, I'm with him." [17] The Chairman then went on to make it clear that his position was based solely on respect for Senatorial privilege, and that he was perhaps even less impressed by the bar-association judgments than was President Truman.

Senator Douglas did appear before the Judiciary Committee at each of the hearings on the two challenged nominations, and did protest vigorously that the "manner and method" of each nomination was "personally obnoxious," and hence the nomination itself was personally obnoxious. This sufficed to block action.[18] The rule of Senatorial courtesy applied, and the Committee did not report the nominations to the Senate. Several months later, perhaps under administration pressure, the nominations were brought before the Senate. Senator Douglas objected again that the manner and method of the nominations were personally obnoxious, and the Senate by voice vote refused to confirm the President's nominees.[19] The controlling consideration was not the quality of the nominations but the personal privilege of a Senator.

Mr. Truman doubtless recalls a similar situation in 1938 in which President Roosevelt nominated for a judicial appointment in Virginia a man who was not among those recommended by Virginia Senators Glass and Byrd. The Senators declared the nomination "personally obnoxious," although they did not question the qualifications of the nominee. The Senate refused to confirm the appointment, and among those voting not to confirm was Senator Truman.[20]

The House of Representatives has to organize and adopt its rules at the beginning of each new Congress. This it does as its first official acts. New members are naturally and necessarily guided by the old timers who have been re-elected. Once the House is organized and the rules adopted, the system of personal power is fixed for another two years. It has been forty years since there was successful revolt from within the House to change the rules. The twenty-one-day discharge rule of the 81st Congress was a product of Presidential leadership, as were also the efforts to curb the Senate filibuster. Has the Congress lost its power to reform itself? All evidence available indicates that some outside pressure from the President or an aroused public is necessary to bring about change.

When the author was a war-time civil servant in the Bureau of the Budget during World War II, he was invited, with a colleague, to the office of an able and progressive Representative (now a Senator), who had some time before introduced a resolution which would make a minor but important change in the House rules, and which the Rules Committee had refused to report. After a very pleasant conversation he came to the point. Would the civil servants ask Harold Smith (the Director of the Budget) to ask the President, to ask the Speaker, to ask the Rules Committee, to please report the resolution to the House? That was, it appeared, the only way in which the House might have a chance to vote on the rule. It has always been a source of great regret to the author that despite the willingness of the civil servants to "ask Harold Smith," the Rules Committee did not report out the resolution.

The System of Personal Power—What Does It Cost?

The costs of this system of personal power are imponderable but enormous. Most serious is the constitutional cost—the undermining of the constitutional principles of representation, responsibility, and rationality. Congress, although it is a legislative assembly, is not really a collective body with the pride and moral force of men who have battled their way rationally to basic agreement on important issues. It is a collection of individuals. Personal power plays so large a part in so many decisions that the men who make them are denied the satisfaction which a genuine group judgment gives to men who are not only a majority of the chamber, but know that they are acting for a majority of the public and in the interests of the entire country. The system of personal power is a blow at constitutional foundations.

Corrosion of Personal Integrity

The functional costs of the present system, the loss of effectiveness in fulfilling the legislative job, were reviewed earlier in this chapter. But the corrupting effect of the system upon individuals must also be reckoned as a cost. Members of Congress as a whole, and probably state legislators also, are a better than average group of Americans—intelligent, hard working, well meaning. But the legislative system forces them almost inexorably to become lobbyists, particularists who are the servants of or indebted to special interests, ambitious for personal power, anxious to feel the public pulse rather than eager to educate the public mind. The system makes it easy to devote their energies to special interests, and makes it difficult to serve the general public interest.

A member of the Congress has almost no choice. He is under constant pressure to do favors for constituents, particularly those with an economic interest. He can easily become a specialist in the affairs of his committee or committees, making friends among the interested pressure groups, and establishing his contacts with officials of administrative agencies under the jurisdiction of his committees. He will have some influence in this realm of special interests very quickly, and eventually great power. This power will come to him not because he speaks for a great number of people, or because he has great vision to understand the needs of the nation, or because he commands the respect and admiration of his colleagues. The power inheres in his person—in the status and position he will acquire by seniority if he goes along with the system. The system itself is a corrosive influence upon personal integrity.

If the duly elected representative of the public should determine that he will avoid this course, and will serve the public interest exclusively, he faces great handicaps. Broad policy is not discussed on the floor of either house, only specific bills in final form for passage, after a committee has spent months working on them. The debate tends to be upon details, perhaps important details, but technical, not upon the underlying issues. (The decision to go ahead with the legislation in question is actually made for the legislative chamber by the standing committees.) At this level of discussion the nonspecialist finds it difficult to follow what goes on. It is very difficult to gain recognition in this way.

Once a Senator or Representative has accepted the inevitable and resigned himself to making the most of his personal power, he finds himself in a difficult moral position. It becomes easier and easier to identify the public interest with special interests, and more and more difficult to keep his broad public perspective. As his position strengthens, continued exercise of personal power tends to make even the most conscientious legislator less careful in exercising his power only for public ends. Irresponsible personal power is inevitably corrupting in its influence, and a system of personal power is essentially immoral.

Undermining the Party System

The idealistic Representative or Senator who wishes to participate in hammering out the party's broad legislative program and in explaining it to the public is completely stymied. The party itself is hardly recognizable as such within the legislative process. Within the halls of Congress, decisions are made by powerful individuals and by shifting coalitions of blocs, which resemble the splinter parties of France in their sharp bargaining and extremism. But these shifting groups, instead of standing out clearly under their own names and standing up proudly for their declared principles, maneuver obscurely under the Democratic and Republican party labels, exploiting the labels and the parties for their own ends.

If there is a legislative program, it is an "Administration" program, not a program prepared by men elected as members of the majority party or by trusted leaders of the majority. The individual representative has no chance to help create such a program and no opportunity to appeal to the general public by supporting, defending, and explaining such a program. If a legislator is to have a choice between a career as a lobbyist for special interests and a defender of the public interest, he needs a party program on which he can make his stand in the halls of Congress and in the election campaigns. Without such a program he is impossibly handicapped in going to the public at election time. For a choice between principle and particularism or personalities, principle must at least be identifiable.

Confusing the Public

The failure of the Democratic and Republican members of the Congress to develop recognizable legislative programs, identified with responsible party leaders, is a blow at public understanding on which self-government is based. Without such a program the public is bound to be baffled by the intricacies and obscurities of the legislative process. Even the experts who make a living reporting the activities of Congress find it difficult to follow more than a part of what is going on. If a party program of the majority existed, and if there were recognized and responsible leaders of the party, issues could be sharpened and dramatized in debate, the widening circles of comment in the press and via radio and television broadcasts would continue the process of popular education, and the public would find it possible to understand and follow the discussion of basic issues.

Some people doubt that popular understanding of issues of public policy is possible. This view ought not to be accepted. The difficulty is not in the fundamental issues, but in the present failure of American politics to focus on them consistently, and to dramatize them. The tendency of critics has been to hold the parties at fault, and to say that if party discipline were stronger, the legislative process would be better. This is true enough, but it puts the cart before the horse. Although the influence of parties and legislative assemblies upon each other is reciprocal, the greatest single source of difficulty lies in the internal organization of legislative assemblies. If representative assemblies do not bring out into the open issues of principle and program, if representatives do not select responsible men in their assemblies to take the lead in defending and enacting their programs, if there is not responsible party life within legislative assemblies, it is very difficult to develop healthy party life outside the legislature. The starting point in making parties mean something is among the men who have the power to govern. The legislative assembly should be the generic center of party life.

It may be useful to contrast the great game of politics with baseball, the national pastime. Baseball baffles foreigners, but millions of Americans understand it well and know the fine points of the game. They are competent judges of good and bad play and can appraise the strategy of managers. Despite its intricacy, it is an ideal sport for spectators. The play goes with the ball; there is one center of action. It is always clear who is responsible at any stage, and each of the repeated crises in the game builds up to a climax and is dramatized. With each batter a new dramatic contest begins, and suspense hangs on each pitch. Will it be a ball or a strike? Will the batter let it go, or will he swing? If he connects, will he get on base with a single, double, or triple? Will he hit into a double play, or will he clear the bases with a home run? The game is intricate, but it is understood and greatly enjoyed by millions.

Why is it so well understood? First, because the action is always centered and always clear. Second, because it is stylized and dramatized, hence describable. Third, because expert observers educate others by discussing the play. Some of these experts are amateurs, but there is also an army of professional sports writers, columnists, and commentators who call attention to the finer points, bring to mind comparable situations in other games, supply quantities of statistics, and review the game. A baseball fan can go to the park, listen to a play-by-play radio report, or watch the game on the television screen. The next morning, over his coffee (if his wife permits) he can read the full-length story in his newspaper, get the statistical summary, note the comments of his favorite sports columnist, and possibly find some reference to it in a story on league standings, or in a feature story on players, teams, or managers. By this time the fan is prepared to discuss the game in great detail and with great wisdom. It is easy. He has the interest, the data, and even the fine phrases with which to make his points. He knows what he is talking about and can hold his own in any discussion.

Intrinsically the *basic issues* of public policy are such that they could be made as understandable as baseball, and the legislative forum could sharpen them, dramatize them, explain them, and start in motion the widening circles of expert comment which contribute so greatly to general understanding. Politics is just as interesting to the public as any game, and there is a similar large army of political writers who turn out their daily stories on what happens. But consider how much more difficult is their task than that of the sports writers. In Congress, for example, the play is not centered on the floor of the houses. It is proceeding obscurely in more than thirty committees. Who has the ball? No one knows. The teams are not even well defined, and no one knows the pitcher for the day's game. There is no schedule of contests and no fixed end of the season. No one can quite be sure what is happening, and the build-up to crises is confused. If Congress should deliberately try to make its actions as confusing to the public as possible, would it need to make any changes in present organization, rules, and procedures? Probably not. In the course of time Congress has thrown away its great function of leading public thinking and discussion and of molding public opinion through its own central deliberation. A birthright has been tossed aside and both Congress and the public suffer.

Without a legislative program and recognized legislative leaders, political parties tend to be periodic campaign organizations held together by hope of gain or personal loyalties and relying on tradition for general support. Without a party program for which elected representatives are known to stand there is nothing to discuss in the election campaign except personalities. The so-called platform adopted by national conventions as the prelude to the nomination of a candidate has no official status, and would not get by the SEC if it were a stock prospectus. It is a campaign document prepared by an irresponsible *ad hoc* committee in a back room. The Presidential candidate may take the platform seriously, he may repudiate it, or he may forget about it, but the first attitude is the least frequent. Congressmen are not bound by this platform, which only a few as individuals may have had anything to do with, and the general public has only the vaguest notion of it. The absence of a program, even a modest one, prepared by responsible leaders who have authority, leaves the parties without a real basis for a national competitive appeal, and invites them to rely upon personalities and emotionalism. A high cost of present Congressional organization and procedure is the adverse effect upon the party system.

Sterilizing National Leadership

A further cost to the public is the failure of Congress to develop national political leaders. It develops sectional champions, and advocates of particular interests or industries. But it does not test and prove men as national leaders. There are labor Senators, farm Senators, and a variety of industrial specialists, but where in positions of legislative authority are the men of proved vision and devotion to the general public interest? They have no real chance to develop. The efforts of Senator Taft to broaden his interests and to associate himself with a wider variety of legislation have been handicapped. The Republican Policy Committee, of which he is chairman, has been a disappointment, and the standing committees on Finance, and on Labor and Public Welfare have remained the chief outlet for his activity. Only one successful Presidential candidate since McKinley has made his reputation in Congress—Warren G. Harding. McKinley had also served as Governor of Ohio. Mr. Truman won recognition as a Senator investigating the national defense program, but moved to the Presidency from the Vice Presidency. As a proving ground for men of Presidential caliber the Congress is a failure. The governorship of a state is much better. It may even be argued that long experience in the Congress unfits men for the Presidency.

Fiscal Costs

Those who prefer to reckon all costs in dollars and cents should consider the fiscal costs of the present legislative system. With tax policy, credit policy, and expenditure policies in the hands of separate and highly autonomous committees; with each of these committees (and their subcommittees) tending toward specialist points of view; and without any legislative cabinet to guide or integrate the work of these committees the idea of a "legislative budget" written into the Legislative Reorganization Act of 1946 is laughable. "In practice, many of the fiscal reforms embodied in the Act have been virtually ignored, or have failed to work." [21] Nothing could be more natural. Without a system of responsible leadership in the Congress, neither house has the capacity to develop or put through an integrated fiscal program. There is nothing wrong about the notion of considering estimated revenues and fixing a total ceiling on appropriations before appropriating funds for individual programs. (The President follows such a procedure in making up the executive budget.) But until the Congress is organized so that it has responsible leadership with both authority and a truly national perspective, procedures alone, no matter how logical, are futile.

The committee system is so designed that it gives maximum weight to the special interests that press for federal expenditures of all sorts. Is it strange that rivers-and-harbors bills go through year after year despite the universal belief that most of the projects cannot be justified on grounds of *national* need? Is it surprising that agricultural subsidies, which began when farm prices were depressed, continue when farm prices are high and when the original justification is gone? Is it unexpected that veterans' benefits are an ever-expanding charge on the federal treasury? If the need for every expenditure, no matter how noble or worthy its purpose, is determined separately by the standing committee or subcommittee which has jurisdiction, no good thing will be denied, and the definition of "good" will be generous. The present irresponsible organization of Congress is inherently inflationary. Committee members may cut specific items, which they do not like, very sharply; but it is not demonstrable that their effect on the total expenditure program over the years is very restrictive. Cuts in appropriations frequently control or even cripple approved and authorized programs; but Congress seldom cancels a program or withdraws the authorization to spend. Economy drives on the floor of the House or Senate may be more than the myth that Representative Cannon called them,[22] but they seldom achieve substantial results. Everyone would like to have economy—reduced expenditures and lower taxes; but no one wants to start with his own pet projects, and Congress, as it is now organized, does not have the capacity to take the comprehensive view in fiscal matters, or even to determine priorities rationally.

Three Basic Reforms

The basic remedy for the internal weakness of legislative bodies in the American system of representative government is so simple that it is usually overlooked. It is a moderate remedy in that it is well within the power of legislative bodies themselves. It does not require Constitutional amendments or even legislation. It is a conservative remedy in that it is consistent with the basic principles of representation, responsibility, and reason which are fundamental in the American Constitution. The remedy is radical only in that it cuts squarely across present organization, rules, and procedures—all of which are largely the creation of the legislative chambers themselves, and may be changed by them.

Congress, for example, needs to do three things to recapture its important role, regain its self-respect, and fulfill its mission. (1) It needs a legislative cabinet in each house, with the majority leader as its chief, to consolidate functions of existing majority party machinery in that house. (2) Each house needs to transact more of its important business on the floor and to make its deliberations the central forum for the discussion of national policy. (3) Each house needs to make its committees and chairmen representative and responsible. Reform need not end with these steps, nor would it, for they are basic, and other beneficial changes would be sure to follow. But unless changes center on fundamental correctives of this sort, they are futile. The commendable changes brought about by the Legislative Reorganization Act of 1946 have been disappointing chiefly because they dealt with secondary rather than primary weaknesses of Congress, the unrepresentative and irresponsible personal power of powerful individuals.

A Legislative Cabinet

In many ways creation of a legislative cabinet in the House and Senate would require few changes. The powers it needs are already vested in a few individuals and a few committees: the Majority Leader and party Whip, the party Policy Committees and Steering Committees, the party Committee on Committees, the Rules Committee (in the House of Representatives), and the chairmen of the standing committees. The new features of a legislative cabinet would be two. The powerful individual leaders would be brought together into a group, and they would be publicly responsible as a group for leadership within the Congress. The concentration of power in a few people would not be substantially greater than at present, but their responsibility would be collective, and their power would be as chosen leaders of the majority, not the result of personal status.

The choice of such a cabinet should not be difficult procedurally. The natural way is for the majority to choose its most trusted leader in the party caucus, and for the chosen leader to present his cabinet slate to the caucus for approval. The cabinet as a whole would assign party members to committees; and committee chairmen and members would be officially appointed by majority vote of the whole chamber as at present. The minority party in each house would naturally have its "shadow" cabinet composed in much the same way and similarly responsible to the minority party, but not officially responsible to the whole house for the legislative program. Co-operation between the House and Senate cabinets would be necessary and would be much easier than House-Senate co-operation under the present organization. Perhaps a joint House-Senate cabinet would evolve. The existence of legislative cabinets in House and Senate would also make for more effective co-operation between President and Congress; for the Majority Leader in each house could speak for the cabinet, and the cabinet for the house in a way that cannot be done now. At the same time the Majority Leader would be in a much stronger position to negotiate with the President on matters of party policy than he is now; for as the head of a cabinet responsible to the party majority he would have a foundation of honest support that he now lacks. Or he would have to modify his program to make sure of his support. Or if he objected to that in principle, he would have to resign his leadership and let someone else take the responsibility. The authority of the leader and of members of the cabinet would be greater than under present arrangements, but their power would be representative and responsible, and hence they would have less personal discretion than do the committee chairmen today.

If the President and the majority in the House and Senate saw eye to eye they would be able to work more effectively together. (The rank and file of the party has usually been closer to the President in viewpoint than many of the standing committee chairmen.) But where the majority in Congress differed with the Administration, they would by acting together through the legislative cabinet be able to develop their own program and to act positively, and thus make their legislative leadership felt in the government. The fatal weakness of legislators today is that if they do not accept the President's program (or the Governor's program in the states), they have no program at all. They are not able to work together as a *group* in making a comprehensive policy and an integrated program. This weakness throws the legislature back into its negative role of blocking action or whittling away at proposals they do not like.

Primary duties of the legislative cabinet would be to make

up the committees, to prepare the legislative agenda determining priorities among bills, and to make sure of reasonable consistency in the various parts of the legislative program. Many of the basic issues of policy could and should be discussed on the floor of the House and Senate and settled along general lines before bills are referred to committees. It has been noted that under the Legislative Reorganization Act of 1946 Congress tried to achieve a more consistent fiscal policy through a joint Budget Committee, "ceilings" on appropriations, and a consolidated appropriation bill. But without a legislative cabinet these requirements were swept aside by the Congress as mechanical gestures. The processes of enacting substantive legislation, appropriation bills, and revenue acts continue their separate ways.

There are other important fields as well in which questions of policy necessarily fall to the jurisdiction of several standing committees, and an over-all cabinet is essential to secure consistent decision and to unify policy. Such fields, for example, as foreign affairs, national defense, and natural-resource problems.

Under the leadership of a legislative cabinet better use could be made of discussions on the floor in making basic decisions and to create general understanding of the broad issues of public policy. The process would also tend to develop national leaders within the Congress—men recognized for their vision, acumen, and integrity. In public affairs it is useful to identify men with policies and to thresh out the issues in a forum where there is the give and take of fair debate among equals, where allegations or arguments may be challenged immediately, and where the tradition is one of rational discussion.

More Representative Committees

Despite the fact that with a legislative cabinet much more business could and should be done on the floor, the standing committees will inevitably continue to do a large part of the work of Congress. They ought to be more representative, to have a more balanced membership, and to more nearly reflect the sentiments of the whole House and Senate. To that end, not more than half of the members of a standing committee should be specially interested parties. That is, for example, not more than half of the members of the House Committee on Agriculture should be from dominantly agricultural districts. The other half or two-thirds should be from urban districts and from mixed urban-rural districts. Similarly the Senate Committee on Interior and Insular Affairs should represent the nation as a whole, not merely the "Western" states; and the committee on Labor and Public Welfare should represent rural as well as urban areas. The rules of the two houses should require the committees to be representative and there might well be some rotation of committee members.

Responsibility and Competence vs. Seniority

The party leader in choosing committee chairmen will properly and inevitably give great weight to experience and demonstrated capacity. But the seniority rule must be discarded. Not until Congress gets away from this corrupting principle will it regain its moral stature.

Committees would be obligated to develop legislation in keeping with basic decisions made by the legislative cabinet and by the whole house. A recalcitrant chairman would have to be replaced, and a committee that disregarded basic instructions would have to persuade the legislative cabinet to accept the change before reporting back to the House or Senate. At the same time, the fact that broad policy was settled by the majority would make it easier for the standing committees to prepare good legislation. Their concentration upon ways and means, upon techniques, and upon the all-important details (that sometimes determine the success of policies) would be entirely proper. Well-considered, well-prepared, realistic legislation is one of the important ingredients of good government.

The remedy of a legislative cabinet, greater use of the whole House and Senate, and standing committees which are representative and responsible might have many variations in details. For example, would the Speaker become the party chief in the House of Representatives, or would the Speaker be an honored elder statesman acting as an impartial chairman and leaving the leadership function to the floor leader? How would the majority in either house enforce its control of the legislative cabinet? On what issues would a defeated cabinet have to resign, and when could it adjust its program and continue in office? A good many questions as to how such a system would work could not be answered in advance. But despite variations in details and undoubted problems that would arise, it is clear that the simple remedies here suggested are quite possible, and that they would work.[23]

Many observers of American government including some American politicians, have thought that eventually the country must come to a parliamentary form of government with executive functions vested in the leaders of the Congress. This would be a revolutionary change, inconsistent with the trends of institutional development in American politics and American life generally. It is an unwarranted gamble which should not be attempted. A legislative cabinet is an entirely different matter. It requires no constitutional or legal change, and it is entirely consistent with our separation of powers and with a strong and independent executive. It is, moreover, an essential step without which Congress cannot achieve its proper role in representative government.

What are the prospects for reform? Dismal at best. Personal power is entrenched in the present system. The choice is between great personal power for individual legislators and great strength for the legislature. If Congressmen wish to fulfill their collective function they must work collectively, and they must establish a rational system of responsible group action. The powers-that-be will not give up the system in which they are entrenched without a fight. There are no signs of such a fight within the Congress today. The present system will continue until there is sufficient outside pressure to force action. The pressure will have to come from the President and the public, and neither will be aroused until the situation becomes intolerable. Congress will resent criticism and fight back against critics whether in the government or out. But the longer the existing system continues the more unsatisfactory it will become. As outside criticism slowly mounts, courageous members of Congress will also protest. A scandal or a crisis may be a stimulus to action, and if the stimulus is followed by the election of a new Congress in which there are many new members and only small party majorities, decisive first steps could be taken. There is no prospect of early change.

Unfair Representation—How Much Will People Stand?
The remedy for under-representation of urban Americans in state legislatures is plain but not simple. It has had little effect so far for the U. S. Conference of Mayors to point out that the three-fifths of America residing in cities produces three-fourths

of the wealth, pay nine-tenths of all taxes (federal, state, and local), and elect only one-fourth of the state legislators.[24] But it is essential to make the facts clear to the public, and all political representatives of the public have an obligation to do so. Historically moral indignation is the first step toward reform, and political leadership in arousing that indignation is long overdue.

First of all, urban Americans are entitled to their legal representation under the law. There is no excuse for the failure to observe constitutional requirements to reapportion legislative bodies; and the gerrymander has been laughed at too long. These practices undermine representative government, and the fact that urban politicians have done nothing about them is damning evidence of their present incapacity for real leadership.

Next in point of attack is the idea that eighteenth-century notions in nineteenth-century constitutions which discriminate against city citizens of the United States of America should be continued. Nothing could be more fantastic, and nothing in fact has been more subversive of strong, vital, self-government. It is not strange that state government has been moribund. It is constitutionally corrupt at its very core in providing for minority rule, without even protection for majority rights. It cannot be justified by citing Thomas Jefferson; and no sins which can be charged against city dwellers can compare in sheer wickedness with the brazen abuse of their political powers by the rural politicians of America, who will not allow the men, women and children who live in metropolitan centers to have equal representation in state legislatures.

How can the evils be remedied? Although moral indignation is an essential first step, it is not enough. Organized political action will be required, and a political battle probably cannot be avoided. But there are no grounds for despair. Urban citizens have the capacity to force the issue if they put their minds and their hearts into it. With a little ingenuity and persistence they can use the representative strength which they still have to force an honest deal in the state capitol. Even where a minority in the legislature they are large enough a minority to carry the day for so good a cause; they will attract support eventually even from rural sections. Americans do believe in fair play.

Minority tactics which have been used so well to block legislative action can be used also to force constitutional revisions. Reform cannot be had without some unpleasantness. So far city men and women have been soft politically. Toughness and good leadership are needed. It is just a matter of time until a competent leader who is a real patriot takes up the cudgels. Victory will come in one state, and then the tide will swell to overwhelm the archaic inequities in the others. But the problem will not solve itself. Men will always have to work and fight for their rights. How much worse will the situation become before men will act?

V

THE EXECUTIVE

Although the legislative process is the heart of representative government, and the architects of the federal government expected the Congress to be the great central dominating body of American political life, the record of legislative assemblies has been disappointing in comparison with the achievements of both the judiciary and the executive. In the nineteenth century, judicial review of both legislative and administrative acts became a unique American contribution to the art of government, and for more than a century and a half the persistent and continued development of the role of the independent, elected executive has been the dominant feature of American public affairs. The Presidency as it stands today is a great political institution, perhaps the most notable product of our politics; and the governors of the states have also evolved steadily, from weak beginnings, to become the central pivot of state affairs. City government is distinguished by two types of executives, the strong mayor, and the city manager, the latter a deliberate and successful invention.

Executive Institutions

There is no doubt that the framers of the Constitution intended to create in the President a strong and stable executive. Their purpose was conscious and their effort deliberate. The chief executives of the states, however, became strong despite an intent on the part of the framers of the early state constitutions that the governors should not be strong.

What is the explanation? There are doubtless many contributing causes. One is obviously the failure of legislative bodies to fulfill their mission, and the correspondingly greater pressure on executive (and judicial) institutions. The growth of the executive is in part compensatory, to carry a greater share of the total responsibility of government which irresponsible legislative assemblies have shirked. It may be also that the total configuration of American life, economic and social as well as political, is such that it has nurtured executive concepts, attitudes, and skills. The "executive" is a common and more or less standard article in business, civic, educational, and ecclesiastical circles. While Americans are notoriously awkward, even inept, in committee work, it seems that executive talent can be found in every sizable group of people. In the team work and team play which are so pervasive in the highly organized and yet individualistic life of America, executive leadership is a key element.

The most striking fact about the executive in American theory and practice is the high standard of responsible behavior which tends to govern executive conduct. The executive has become strong and also responsible—perhaps strong because he has demonstrated his responsibility. Successful business corporations survive the weaknesses of size and impersonality (which Adam Smith demonstrated to be fatal) in large part because they command the services of executives who are dedicated to the corporate enterprise. Governors of American states have steadily grown in power and influence beyond their legal authority, in part, because they have demonstrated their effective concern with the public interest, in comparison with legislative bodies. The President of the United States has great power, but he has great responsibility far exceeding his legal authority. The American Presidency has been characterized by an active sense of responsibility to the nation. The people of France dare not establish a strong unitary executive lest the president or prime minister make himself a dictator. Latin-American countries which have copied our Presidency have had constant difficulties with dictatorship. In sharp contrast to these tendencies abroad, no President of the United States has ever shown the slightest interest in making himself a dictator, or in seeking irresponsible personal power. The Presidents have varied in ability; some have had greater capacity than others; but all have been challenged by the great responsibilities of the office, and nearly all have risen to the challenge.

The Paradox of President and Congress

The President and Congress present a paradox. The Congress, by nature a collective body which can fulfill its institutional function only by rationally integrated group action, has moved far toward a system of personal power for individual Representatives and Senators. The President is a sharp contrast. Although the Constitution vests power in the person of the President, he has moved steadily toward institutionalizing and depersonalizing his power. That is, as the responsible head of the executive branch of government, he has become the focal point for the experience of the government in action, and a spokesman for the administration, and administrators, as a whole. He is in a sense voluntarily and consciously subject to the discipline of his subordinates who would push him or pull him in many different directions, in accordance with their special interests; and his task is to discover and clarify the wise course of action in the national interest among the varied and frequently conflicting internal pressures of his administration. This internal discipline is potentially and essentially a rational discipline (subordinates do not have authority over the chief executive) and it forces the President to try to find a common ground of agreement, a middle-of-the-road program, which best meets the needs of the administration as a whole.

The President's function as an elected representative of the public complements and reinforces his dedication to the public interest. He (with the Vice President) is the elected representative of the nation. Senators represent states, and members of the House represent districts, but the President's constituency is all the people throughout the land. The Presidents of the United States have always been conscious of this constituency and have tended to act with a high sense of responsibility to the general public.

Moral Force of the President
The great strength of the Presidency is its moral force based upon its moral-rational foundation. The moral force of the Chief Executive far exceeds his legal powers. It is based on the presumption that has been built up over the years that the President is faithful to the public interest, and on the success of the President in demonstrating day-by-day that he is in fact pursuing the national interest. The President has in reality based his power on the representative, responsible, and ra-

tional foundations of authority (which the Congress has neglected or repudiated), and it is this moral foundation which gives him great authority.

The President has in fact very little independent power given to him directly by the Constitution. In most of his duties as the chief of the executive branch he is in charge of administrative organizations created by Congress, carrying on activities authorized by Congress, manned by personnel authorized by Congress, financed with funds appropriated by Congress, and following procedures prescribed by law. The President's discretion in directing administrative officials must be exercised within the limits of law enacted by Congress. Congress has allowed the President little or no discretion in directing certain parts of the national administration, the "independent" commissions. The volume of business handled by the national administration makes it physically impossible for the President to direct administrative action in individual cases. Even if he should attempt to do so, he could give his attention to only a few items. His power of direction and supervision, therefore, must be exercised chiefly through broad policies, general standards, and comprehensive programs. Since he can give direct attention to relatively few matters, these tend to be the issues which he believes to be of greatest importance.

In the field of foreign relations and as Commander-in-Chief of the armed forces, the President derives authority to act directly from the Constitution, but here also he has become increasingly the agent of Congress. Congress must act to authorize military, financial, and technical assistance to foreign powers, to provide sinews for the diplomacy of "cold war," to create a military establishment, and (in so doing) to determine the limits of defense policy.

Nearly all of the President's important appointments must be confirmed by the Senate, and even his removal power, which the courts have held to be inherent in his executive function, may be limited by the Congress in those very important fields of administrative regulation where Congress has established "quasi-judicial" regulatory commissions.

The President's constitutional powers have been essential to the development of the office, but the President's constitutional position in our scheme of government far transcends his legal powers. He has moral force and moral authority, which are an essential element in our government. The President's leadership in legislation is today indispensable. Without it, the centrifugal forces which play upon both Congress and the administration would tear the government apart. The dangerous tendency to make important decisions separately without regard to their effect upon the total program would be unrestrained. Decisions dictated by the demands of organized groups would produce impossible conflict and confusion in subsequent administration. Until the time comes when Congress develops its own internal leadership of a national character, the entire government must depend upon the President for unifying leadership. Anything which threatens the strength and stability of the Presidency in national affairs jeopardizes the security of the republic. If the President seems too strong, it is because Congress is too weak.

It is easy to forget that the President's leadership rests largely upon his moral force. He cannot coerce Congress. The governors of the states have to do a good bit of "dealing," trading, and bargaining with legislators to get their programs approved, and the patronage and perquisites that they dispense are very useful in the process. The President, however, can't buy very much support with his patronage. There isn't much of it over which he has real discretion. The traditional positions

—postmasterships, collectors of customs and internal revenue, U. S. Marshals, U. S. Attorneys, and judgeships—are claimed by Senators and Representatives as a matter of right, and any attempt to use these positions to buy support makes more enemies than friends. The President's leadership in public policy depends not upon his legal power or his patronage, but upon his ability to persuade the Congress that he is right and that he has the country behind him. Congress accepts this kind of leadership, sometimes reluctantly, even unhappily, but it has to go along eventually. This was Roosevelt's strength. The honeymoon of the New Deal was short. Most of the time FDR was dealing with the same incongruous combination of Southern Democrats, Northern metropolitan machines, and famished Western interests that have plagued the Fair Deal. But in his battles with Congress, he concentrated on issues one after the other, and when it appeared that he had the public with him on an issue, he won.

Obligations of the Chief Executive: The Public Interest

The first and primary obligation of the President is to be faithful to the public interest, as distinguished from all of the personal interests, group interests, and special interests that play upon him. A second obligation is to keep his personal integrity above suspicion, even in small matters, as an earnest of his moral discrimination in great issues of policy. A third obligation is to set the moral tone as chief executive for the entire administration. His own decisions and attitudes largely determine the morale and the standards of officials throughout the government. His words and actions have consequences beyond their immediate effects. A fourth obligation (partly moral and partly political) is to get results, to see that the government meets the pragmatic tests of at least moderate success in dealing with great national problems—unemployment, war, diplomacy, depression, inflation, and human dignity and freedom. The President is the man to whom the country looks for decision in national crises, and for action in hammering out solutions to national problems. Members of Congress can be passive, or even negative, and most of them can get away with it. But the President cannot. He is expected to produce. He is responsible.

The President's obligation to stand by the interest of the whole public is his paramount obligation. He may not do anything that impeaches his integrity in this respect without destroying himself and weakening his office. He will suffer for any deviation from this high standard. This is the unforgivable sin in the constitutional law which is growing up around the Presidency. Other weaknesses or failures are regrettable, but secondary and forgivable. The public is a tolerant but jealous mistress. The President must love no one else.

This means, of course, that the President must be scrupulous in his personal affairs. He must not exploit his power or his position for his personal advantage. He must avoid even minor improprieties, for if he lacks discrimination and a sense of what is right in small matters, the presumption must be that his judgment cannot be trusted in large questions.

"Court-house politics" in the White House entourage inevitably hurts the President and the Presidency. There is no doubt that President Truman has suffered from the petty improprieties of persons on his staff. The words "deep freeze" and "mink coat" have taken on new and unfavorable connotations in American parlance, which reflect both the high standards which the public sets for the Chief Executive, and its chagrin that all who are associated with him are not immaculate. Free entertainment from commercial sources may be all right for the assistant to a corporation president, but it seems out of place for an aide to the President of the United States when it is supplied by an RFC borrower. Speculation in commodities is a normal activity for some men in private life, but is it proper for an army medical officer who is the President's physician? These matters concern the public and must concern the President, for they can jeopardize the moral position which is the basis for his leadership.

The need for a fine sense of propriety and good taste in the White House is further reinforced by the fact that the President is Chief of State. He is the symbolic head of the nation as well as the active leader in legislation, and a functioning chief executive.

Conflicting Standards of Presidential Behavior

A fair-minded person must have a great deal of sympathy for the President in his multi-functional office; for some of his various functions set up conflicting standards for his conduct, and it does not get him out of his dilemmas to know that the basic requirement of loyalty to the public interest runs through them all. In his role as Chief of State, the President must be dignified, restrained, correct, full of human kindness, and free from any evidences of pettiness or partisan feeling. He can reconcile these requirements with his character as Commander-in-Chief and his constitutional function of sending and receiving ambassadors. But he is also chief legislative leader and party leader. In this capacity he must put through a legislative program. During the Roosevelt years it came to be expected that the President would be the principal advocate and defender of this legislative program. How then can he avoid political controversy which is unbecoming to the formal head of the nation, who in this exalted role should be above the heat of political battles? The public expects of the President respect for the dignity of his high office, but has not yet come to demand due deference to it on the part of other politicians. Personal attacks on the President from the Senate floor are tolerated, yet when he replies in kind he loses his dignity and also some of his standing and prestige. To escape this dilemma he must ignore attacks upon him or reply with such a quick and clever thrust to some vital weakness of his opponent that his own dignity remains unruffled. The standards are such that the President is subject to censure even when he shows irritation in his regular press conferences, an ordeal which most private citizens would never go into more than once.

Only a genius of superhuman restraint can fulfill all of these requirements. Not many such will be nominated and elected to the Presidency. Some way of avoiding the conflicting demands of the office without destroying its multi-functional character must be found. But until it is found all Presidents will have a rough time.

Probably the President will have to accept the fact that his least vital role, that of Chief of State, must set the tone of his public statements and public appearances. These rigid requirements are normally relaxed when the President is in the midst of a formal presidential campaign. But at other times he will have to be circumspect.

Relieving the President

One way out of the present dilemma is for the heads of executive departments and agencies to shoulder a much larger share of the responsibility for explaining and defending the administration's program. It is entirely proper for them to do so as the political heads of departments who are the President's chosen assistants and who are publicly responsible for important parts of the administration. The late Secretary Harold Ickes was outstanding in Mr. Roosevelt's cabinet chiefly because of the forthright way in which he addressed himself to this political duty. He was willing and able to defend his department and did not have to run to the President for protection. Federal Security Administrator Oscar Ewing similarly is to be commended for speaking out boldly on the issue of health insurance. He may be right, or he may be wrong, or partly right and partly wrong on the substance of the issue, but he is clearly correct and conscientious in shouldering the burden of public discussion.

When the House and Senate develop a more representative and responsible internal organization, it is quite probable that responsible leaders there will also take a larger part in the public discussion which is necessary to thresh out public policy that will be feasible and will have adequate support. To the extent that responsible leaders of the Congress are in accord with the administration they can relieve the President and his associates of a considerable part of the burden of exposition. To the extent that they disagree, a more responsible leadership in Congress will make it necessary for the President and his department heads to be more systematic and thorough in their discussion of issues.

Fair Play

There is no reason why the Congress should wait for internal reorganization to give the administration protection from irresponsible or unfair attacks from Congress itself. If it is proper for the rules of the House and Senate to prohibit any member from even questioning the motives of fellow members in their remarks on the floor, it is no more than decent to accord the President and the heads of executive departments some protection under the rules from irresponsible and unsupported charges. Charges of incompetence, impropriety, or unfaithfulness to the public interest should be in order when supported by evidence. It is the duty of Congress to investigate such questions, and through the impeachment process, to remove the President, or any other "civil officer" who is guilty of "Treason, Bribery, or other High Crimes and Misdemeanors." The latter phrase is broad enough to cover misbehavior of many sorts, including willful abuse of discretion contrary to the public interest. Evidence of misconduct should be presented and considered by the appropriate committee with such additional investigation as may be necessary. If the committee finds that there are grounds for impeachment, the House of Representatives should be requested to act in presenting a bill of impeachment for trial by the Senate.

It is also within the power of Congress to establish a special tribunal to consider charges against public officials and to remove officials, even judges, for conduct in violation of the constitutional standards of "good behavior." [1] This would relieve Congress of any considerable burden, particularly in dealing with minor officials. If there is evidence of misconduct Congress should act, but it should make a determination or provide for such a determination. It should not allow unsupported charges against administrators to be repeated without evidence and without any determination as to their probable validity. Such charges should be contrary to the rules, subject to challenge on a point of order, and ruled out of order by the chair. A simple rule of this sort would make it easier for legislators to act who object to abuse of legislative privileges, as did the signers of the "Declaration of Conscience." [2] It would be a practical, enforceable rule.

It would also be reasonable under the rules to confer upon the heads of departments who are attacked on the floor of either house an early opportunity to reply in the same forum. This is no more than fair play. Until legislative officials are willing to defend as well as attack the administrative officers of the government, it is less than decent not to accord administrators the right of self-defense.

The Senate Subcommittee on Ethics in Government noted that these measures would "enhance the dignity, the usefulness, the integrity and the moral leadership of the Congress." It gave them its approval in principle and recommended early action to make appropriate changes in the rules of the House and Senate. [3]

All of these steps would help to reduce the burden on the multi-functional office of President. But until the political heads of departments and responsible leaders in the Congress become more active and more effective in advocating policies and defending their administration, the President will continue to carry an impossible burden.

New Hazards

The trend of public policy has tended to increase the moral hazards of the Presidential office. When only industrial or entrepreneurial interests were highly organized, powerful, and aggressive, the President knew from what quarter to expect threats to the public interest. But now that labor and agriculture are also highly organized, powerful, and aggressive, the task of making sure of the public interest is more difficult.

Both labor and agriculture received large assistance from the

Government, under the leadership of President Roosevelt, in acquiring their present strength. In the space of twenty years they have gone from poverty to prosperity, from feebleness to organizational strength, and from political frustration to great power. The very success of public policy has created new problems for the President. If he had to be on guard in the old days against undue concession to "the interests," he now has to watch an enlarged number of more varied interests. The prolonged depression in agriculture between the two world wars tended to make the "poor farmer" a sacred cow. Anything that could be done for him was obviously in the public interest. Labor also got the rough end of the stick in pre-New Deal America. The labor force was largely unorganized, and unions usually found that management could turn to the law for aid while they could not. The injunction seemed to work only one way in labor disputes. The plight of labor in the depression confirmed the sympathy of liberals in politics for labor, and the liberal position became fixed as one of supporting organized labor. The Wagner Act changed the picture, and the Taft-Hartley law has not turned the clock back.

The President's problem of defending the public interest is greatly complicated as a result of these changes. All of the major interests in the economy identify their own purposes with public welfare (and they are partly right). But they have neither the mental habits of making sure that their objectives and methods are in fact consistent with public welfare, nor a developed sense of public responsibility. They are also aggressive. In this situation there is open no simple course of raising up the weak or enriching the poor among the segments of the economy. Appeasing any one interest at the expense of the others may be a betrayal of the public interest, and yielding to the demands of all would almost certainly lead to disaster. Yet these organized interests also tend to dominate geographic sections of the country which are combined in national elections to determine who shall be President. Every candidate for the Presidency tries for a winning combination of sections through an appeal to their dominant economic interests. He will be tempted to make deals with all organized groups that may add up to appeasement of organized demands all along the line. Can a candidate do this and preserve his role as prime defender of the national interest? And if the President violates that fundamental obligation of his office, will he not quickly destroy the strength and usefulness of the Presidency? If that should happen, with Congress in its present state, responsible representative government as we know it in the United States would be in real peril.

Moral Sense and Political Sense: The Truman Administration
Fair-minded observers respect President Truman's courage and apparent devotion to the public interest on the important issues. He has faced the big problems squarely. He could have ducked the problem of an adequate national defense organization at the end of World War II, but he tackled it head on and, despite bitter opposition from the Navy and some sophisticated feet dragging by its Secretary, he did "bull through" to the first stage of what may eventually develop into an adequate solution of the problem. He could have hedged on FEPC, but he realized the basic moral importance of this issue in a society which is either democratic or it is nothing. Despite his painful legislative defeats on civil-rights questions he has helped to make the public aware of the importance of the issue, at some cost to himself. On the health-insurance question the President must have been tempted to pass over it and avoid another

headache. But he met the problem squarely. On the major issues the record seems to show conscious effort to fulfill his moral obligation to look out for the public interest.

Any analysis of the moral sense of a President, however, is complicated by being involved with his political sense and his economic sense. It may be that Mr. Truman made mistakes in handling the problem of Army-Navy unification. Perhaps he could have achieved more for civil rights by asking for less or moving on one objective at a time. Possibly the health-insurance scheme proposed is not the best step to take next in improving public health. It may be that the Fair Deal program as a whole is too much like the sack which Santa Claus carries over his shoulder; it has something in it for everybody. It may not be enough of a practicable schedule with priorities and target dates carefully fixed. Even so, it is dishonest only if it is a deliberate attempt to catch votes with promises known to be impossible of fulfillment, and not taken seriously by the promiser. The evidence belies this interpretation. If Mr. Truman did not expect to win on his issues, he apparently expected to build them up sufficiently to bring eventual victory closer. The more probable explanation is not lack of moral sense (on the big issues), but lack of political sense. Despite the President's reputation as a politician it would seem that this is where he is weakest. He has seemed to be direct, forthright, and courageous as a political leader, but the nuances of tone, emphasis, and timing are beyond him. The probable explanation is that he has only average political sense and skill and perhaps only average comprehension of the finer points of the substantive issues with which he deals.

If President Truman's moral armor has chinks in it, they are not in his positions on the big issues of public policy or in his purposes. He is vulnerable in other things where his standards have a primitive cast. Perhaps this grows out of Missouri politics or his training in the Senate. It may well be that long experience in the Senate unfits any man for the Presidency. One of the most revealing bits of General Vaughan's testimony before the Hoey Committee was his description of his duties as military aide and administrative assistant to the President. In doing favors for people who importuned the White House, he was carrying on the "reference function" which is so large a part of the work of members of Congress and of their staff. The General told the Senate Committee, "My duties at the White House . . . were a continuation of my duties, the same duties, practically the same duties as I had here in Senator Truman's office." [4] But matters which seem small in the Senate, or in Missouri, loom larger in the White House.

A vulnerable point is the President's public attitude toward the improprieties of his personal staff which have come to light. No matter what his private position may be, he has publicly defended and continued the associates who have embarrassed him, and they have lacked the good grace to get out from under his feet.[5] The President has been more considerate of them than they of him. The effect upon the morale, the attitudes, and the standards of the administration is inevitably depressing. It is not enough for the President of the United States to be against sin in general; he must also oppose it in particular, if he wants key officials and civil servants to be scrupulous. Actions speak louder than words. The obligations of the Presidency permit no conflicting loyalties, even to his friends.

The public record of the President's attitudes toward misconduct in the executive agencies and departments is also vulnerable. The impulse to defend his administrators first and to check up later apparently has been irresistible, and certainly embarrassing. The President did not react to direct reports from members of the Senate that all was not well with RFC, but later he resented public criticism of the RFC and its board of directors, and called "asinine" a report of the Fulbright subcommittee which reviewed the extensive evidence of improper influence leading to abuse of discretion by the board members.[6] Still later he scrapped the board and put in a new administrator to clean house.

Senator John J. Williams challenged the integrity of the Bureau of Internal Revenue in 1948, and, as he accumulated data, began in 1950 to give the Commissioner of Internal Revenue convincing evidence of misconduct in one regional collector's office after another.[7] The Commissioner, a former assistant to the President, had to be prodded to act by the Senator's public revelation of his evidence. In the efforts of Senator Williams there is evident no attempt to smear the administration. The responsible official, a direct appointee of the President, was given opportunity privately to act on the evidence, but he did not act. Instead, after an interval, he resigned and a new Commissioner was appointed in August, 1951, to clean up the Bureau. The Secretary of the Treasury and the President had public notice that the Bureau was under attack, but delayed remedial action and allowed the initiative to remain with Senator Williams, investigating committees, and the press. The score on March 18, 1952, then stood: eight of sixty-four collectors of Internal Revenue dismissed or resigned under pressure, three of these indicted with two of them convicted, and 166 other bureau employees dismissed or forced to resign.[8] (Disciplinary dismissals of thirty-five to forty a year in this bureau of 57,000 employees are normal.)

When scandal involved the Department of Justice in the summer and autumn of 1951 the President again found himself on the defensive, and had to remove Assistant Secretary Caudle after the King Subcommittee of the House Committee on Ways and Means had developed the facts in the case, and less than a month after he had written Mr. Caudle an approving letter.[9]

When the *St. Louis Post Dispatch* reported in July, 1951, the apparent involvement of William M. Boyle, the Democratic National Committee Chairman, in the sale of political influence, the President's impulse to stand by his friends and subordinates again was too strong to be resisted. Mr. Truman publicly maintained his confidence in Mr. Boyle, even after the Senate Investigations Subcommittee began to dig into the story. But in October Mr. Boyle resigned and a new Chairman of the Democratic National Committee took his place, full of enthusiasm for good government.[10]

It is not unreasonable to argue that the President showed lack of moral sense in his handling of these delinquencies in his official family, although no one has suggested that he gained personally by his actions, and it is obvious that he lost heavily —politically. A certain lack of objectivity on the part of the President in his executive judgment of his key officials is apparent. Bias of any sort that keeps a responsible official from deciding public questions on their merits is a moral weakness, and determining the adequacy of official conduct is such a question.

More obvious and perhaps much greater, however, were the administrative naïveté and the lack of political judgment. Friends of the administration gave the President more than enough evidence of weak spots to arouse his sense of executive responsibility, if he had recognized them as friends and considered the evidence objectively. The first lesson in over-prompt defense of unfaithful friends could have been enough to teach caution. One rotten apple in a barrel puts a prudent greengrocer on his guard. The failure to recognize the situation, to appreciate its seriousness, and to act are serious defects in a Chief Executive.

Political Responsibility Repudiated

The most serious outcome of the scandals of 1951 is not the delinquencies themselves, nor the delay in corrective action, but a new doctrine that the President and his heads of departments are not responsible for what has happened. This is a most dangerous heresy, and if it were to be accepted, it would undermine American political stability. The Presidency has come to be the one clearly and consciously responsible office in national affairs. Although the President's leadership in legislation is a product of constitutional history, his responsibility as Chief Executive was written into the Constitutional document itself in 1787 and has never been challenged so boldly before. The heads of departments in which bribery, corruption, impropriety, and incompetence have been revealed have assumed the attitude of not being at fault, in fact, an attitude of hardly being concerned at all. The Secretary of the Treasury has not resigned and the Attorney General's resignation was delayed until April 3, 1952. The President is reported to have asserted flatly in December, 1951, that department heads are not responsible for the breakdown of integrity in their departments.[11] If they are not responsible, who is responsible?

It is the function of department heads to be politically responsible for the success or failure of their departments. They get credit for success and blame for failure. It has always been their function, and the President has recently and unmistakably strengthened and clarified this function by Executive Reorganization Plans in the spring of 1950, which transferred to five department heads, from subordinate officials, powers which had previously been vested in the latter by law.[12] This is consistent with the clear and proper policy of the administration to strengthen the line of authority and command and to make it unmistakably clear from the Chief Executive through department and agency heads to the most junior official in the administration. Both President Roosevelt and President Truman have seen the importance of this principle to effective and responsible administration and have very properly sought to give effect to it. This step was also a principal recommendation of the Hoover Commission on Organization of the Executive Branch of Government. It is well publicized and well understood by every student of government and by every experienced official, including the President.

One may concede that Secretary of the Treasury Snyder did not know personally that the Collectors of Internal Revenue in St. Louis, San Francisco, Philadelphia, New York, or Boston (and men under them) were unfaithful to their duties or were receiving gifts, favors, or bribes, or were blackmailing taxpayers. But he had the authority, the organization, the procedure, the staff and the duty to know. He could have known. He should have known. Senator Williams has repeatedly insisted that the evidence of misconduct was available to the Commissioner of Internal Revenue, to the Secretary of the Treasury, and to the President, that it was down in black and white in the reports of the Bureau's own auditors and investigators. In fact, Senator Williams used this information in forcing the administration to act.[13] He tried to interest the Commissioner and failed. He tried to interest the Secretary and failed. But when he tried to interest the Senate and put the information in the *Congressional Record*, the administration came to life. Even if the President and heads of departments had not had evidence thrust upon them, they would still be responsible for the administration. That is the essence of their function. It is ridiculous for any executive to attempt to escape responsibility for his own organization; and in the executive branch of the government of the United States, the idea that an executive can do so is subversive.

Responsibility and Reality

The attempt to assert in 1951 that the President and the political heads of departments are not officially responsible for the administration is an anomaly. Normally Presidents have sought to find ways and means to make their official responsibility effective in their day-to-day work. The public has tended to hold Presidents responsible for the success or failure of entire national policy, while Congress has been reluctant or unwilling to give the President the means to make good on his public responsibilities.

Since the national administration began to grow at the end of the Progressive era and the beginning of the First World War, the Presidents have found that they lacked authority, staff, and institutional arrangements to do their job, and to live up to their broad responsibilities. This deficiency became more pronounced as acute economic and military problems forced the government into a greatly expanded program. Both Presidents Hoover and Roosevelt recognized that the national administration was not so organized in fact that the President could direct and supervise the work of the government. It was a sprawling organic structure of "over 100 separately organized establishments." [14] The President's Committee on Administrative Management, the famous Brownlow Committee, was concerned with this problem in the period 1936-39, and the Hoover

Commission on Organization of the Executive Branch of Government again in 1948-50. These committees also identified and documented the President's need for authority and professional staff assistance, and the similar needs of department heads.[15]

Staff Assistance to Executives

Since 1937 there have been some notable developments which have helped to make it possible for the President and his political heads of departments to make good on their responsibilities. The most striking change has been the creation of a professional staff in the Executive Office of the President (a new concept) to help him with the heavy load of executive responsibilities. The Executive Office now contains personal secretaries and clerks (the old White House staff), administrative and other assistants (a new professional staff), and important staff organizations, e.g., the Bureau of the Budget, the Council of Economic Advisers, the National Security Council, the National Security Resources Board, and the Office of Defense Mobilization. Although the organization and staffing of the Executive Office necessarily change from time to time (they are still in an experimental phase of development), the fact is now established that there must be some such professional group if the President is to be Chief Executive in more than name. It is possible to criticize the personnel of the Executive Office, or its organization. But informed persons do not challenge the need for such an executive staff. It is in accord with American organizational experience generally, and the President would today be a figurehead without it.

The problem now is to apply the same principle of unified staff assistance at the next lower level in the principal departments and agencies. The Secretary of the Interior, the Secretary of Agriculture, the Secretary of Commerce, the Secretary of Defense, the Federal Security Administration, and the other heads of departments and agencies cannot direct and control the powerful bureaus and services of their departments without a unified professional staff. Without it they are the captives of their bureau chiefs, unable to keep up with the volume of business, and baffled by the technicalities of the multitudinous activities of the government.

Historically the first step in providing staff assistance for department heads occurred in legal matters. Agency heads now generally have a solicitor, general counsel, or other legal officer to advise them on day-to-day legal matters, which are numerous. Many legal officers also have come to give advice on questions of policy more generally. Considerable progress has been made also in equipping department heads to deal with "business management" or housekeeping activities, i.e., budget, accounts, records, personnel, organizational planning, and similar matters which are a problem in every large organization. But progress has been least (in fact very slight) in providing a program staff prepared to analyze the endless substantive questions that confront department heads, and able to give sound advice quickly in these matters. It must be recognized that the operating bureaus and services of the government are specialized agencies with their own particular programs and objectives. Many of the bureaus have a peculiar clientele, an organized pressure group behind them, and one or more committees of the Congress looking over their shoulders. The clientele, the lobby, and the committees all seek to exert as much control as they can over the Bureau. In this situation the Secretary, or head of the department, is in no position to throw himself upon the tender mercies of his bureau chiefs. Their zeal, competence, and earnestness of purpose may be taken for granted, but their perspective and values are shaped more by the particular interests of their own area of operation than by the national interest.

Even if the head of a department should be willing to be guided exclusively by the advice of his bureau chiefs, he would find it impossible to do so. The bureau chiefs would frequently disagree. If, for example, the Secretary of the Interior were to give free rein to the Bureau of Reclamation, an agency which has a splendid record in protecting the public interest in the conservation and utilization of resources, he might find himself flooding national park sites, destroying game preserves, and liquidating the salmon industry of the Pacific Northwest, not deliberately but inadvertently. Or he might find himself in control of reservoirs that were rapidly silting up from the erosion of improperly managed watersheds. Or he might find that he had displaced large numbers of Indian Americans from their ranches and cattle ranges without making provisions for resettlement on newly reclaimed and irrigated lands. If his attention to these questions should be delayed until they forced themselves upon him, it would be too late to find a satisfactory solution. Compromise would not do. Such difficulties must be foreseen and possible conflicts in values reconciled by working together from the beginning. For such leadership a Secretary needs the assistance of a highly competent professional staff with a broader perspective than that of any one bureau, no matter how important its program may be.

Congress has supported the development of the Executive Office of the President, but it has been slow to recognize the need for comparable assistance (on a smaller scale) at the departmental level. When, for example, the Secretary of the Interior asked for funds to establish a small program staff in Interior, he met stubborn resistance year after year. Some members of the Congress blandly advised the Secretary that the bureau chiefs could give him all the help he needed. It is hard to believe that this reluctance is entirely administrative naïveté. The head of a department is in a sense competing with the lobbies and the committees of Congress for control of his bureaus, and the committees are not very enthusiastic about strengthening Secretarial control. If the tendencies of the more extreme committees were unchecked, they would produce a kind of bastard parliamentary government which would be neither unified nor responsible. The need for strong departmental leadership has not yet been met.

In 1950 the President and Congress vested in five department heads[16] the substantive statutory authority of their departments, which in many instances had been given directly to subordinate officials by Act of Congress. This was a logical step toward making department heads real executives. But alone it is a gesture. Without adequate staff, the Secretary is in no stronger position than before.

The Concept of Political Leadership

It must be conceded that one difficulty in strengthening management at the departmental level has been the attitude of the department heads themselves. For the most part the members of the President's cabinet and the other agency heads have not been eager to shoulder the burdens and endure the headaches that inevitably go with political responsibility. For many years, and particularly during Mr. Roosevelt's administration, they have tended to let the President handle the big political problems and to let their bureau chiefs take the heat on the hot issues that come up in day-to-day administration. It is easy for them to fall into this pattern, and difficult not to. The committees of Congress also prefer it; they prefer to deal with bureau chiefs and division heads, and even junior officials. Since the Secretary of a department normally has lacked the staff to penetrate the mysteries of the bureaus and to keep in close touch with their operations, he will frequently be ignorant of issues until they break, and he will lack the staff assistance to prepare himself to discuss the issues. It then becomes easy for him to step aside and let a bureau chief shoulder the burden of threshing out differences with a committee of Congress—a political function, even though the bureau chief is intended to be a professional administrator.

Part of the difficulty is in the concept. The idea is not yet fully established in American government that it is the duty of the political head of a department to be active in carrying the political responsibility for his department in fact as well as in principle and law. Political department heads are by nature the expendibles in national administration, and as such it is properly their function to speak up on all administrative matters of political importance and to be actively responsible to the President, to the Congress, and to the public for the work of their departments. When things go well they are entitled to full credit, and when things go badly they must take the blame.

The President's position as chief of state makes it desirable for him to maintain a certain amount of aloofness from political controversies except those involving fundamental issues. The range and volume of his duties as chief executive allow him only limited time for the affairs of any one department. If he is forced to "run with the ball" on every play, he becomes politically exhausted, sacrifices some of his standing with the public, and also loses the sharpness of judgment needed for his quarterback role. The fact that the President serves for a fixed term of office and is the chief stabilizing element in the government makes it functionally necessary for him to avoid these hazards.

The President must work through his team—the political heads of departments and agencies, and they must take their function of political leadership seriously.

The virtuosity of FDR obscured this point for thirteen years. Too large a number of department heads leaned on the President's political strength; he was not able to lean on them. Harold Ickes stands out as the exception. Although without administrative experience in office, he had the "instinctive acceptance of responsibility" [17] which is essential for effectiveness in an executive position, and he made it his point to be responsible for his departments—Interior, the Public Works Administration, the Petroleum Administration, and the Solid Fuels Administration—to the best of his ability. Consequently he grew in his position from obscurity to a first-rank political figure. His policy of making every fight involving his department his own fight was commendable, and in line with the constitutional necessities of the national government. If any one in the department was under attack, he came to his defense. But he was equally zealous in setting standards and enforcing discipline. He made it his business to set a high standard of integrity and of faithfulness to the public interest. Until the responsible attitude of an Ickes becomes the rule instead of the exception among agency heads, the chain of responsibility will be weak in the national administration.

Department heads also tend to throw too much of the political burden on their bureau chiefs. For the most part most of the latter are intended to be (and all of them should be) professional administrators, career men who are thoroughly competent. The public cannot afford to have its work in inexpert and inexperienced hands. Theory and the trend of practice agree on this point. When department heads allow these men to take the heat on controversial matters, which are by definition political matters, they thrust them into an impossible position. They jeopardize the professional character of the bureau chief by forcing him to represent the department in political controversies. Participation in political battles endangers the professional administrator's career status. Even though successful, he will accumulate so many political enemies that sooner or later he will have to go. The price of experience, expertness, and permanence in a civil service is either total abstinence or at the most very modest participation in political controversy. Until department heads become regularly active as the executives publicly responsible to the President, the Congress, and the public for their agencies, bureau chiefs will continue to have incompatible duties.

The Missing Keystone

The weakness of political leadership at the departmental level is related to the nature of the national civil service. It is essentially a body of highly competent specialists. There is, of course, much routine work and much clerical work. This is necessarily true in any large organization, and it is particularly true in government where records are important. But the service gets its character from the experienced, skillful and learned men and women who are expert in the multitudinous and varied activities of the government. The term specialist is not used invidiously. By and large these men have breadth as well as depth of knowledge; they have some insight into politics and a grasp of administration, as well as a mastery of their profession or peculiar calling. In its ranks of professional specialists, the national civil service is probably superior to any other national bureaucracy.

The professional competence has risen steadily over the years and noticeably since the middle nineteen-thirties, when the importance of good public administration to the nation began to be more generally recognized. Improved methods of selection have also helped to increase and maintain the quality of the civil service. The old discriminations against educated men and women which were contained in pre-war civil service examinations are not so restrictive as they once were, and the effort to get a fair share of the talent of each generation into the national administration is becoming more earnest and systematic. Progressively improved salary scales since 1944 have also helped to make the civil service more attractive. Salaries to career men in the regular civil service now go as high as $14,000.

One all-important element is missing, however, from the national civil service. In the goodly company of specialists which constitute the service, one group is almost entirely lacking. These are the "generalists," men who are specialists in the art of knitting together the work of other specialists, civil servants who are expert in integrating the activities of other experts. In this sense they are administrators. They have the intellectual power to comprehend successive technical problems, with the advice of subject-matter specialists; they understand the economic and political setting in which they work; and they are articulate and skillful in dealing with people. There are men of this sort in the civil service, but there are not enough of them; they are not developed systematically enough; and they are not placed high enough in the administrative structure.

The national administration needs and does not now have permanent positions for career administrators in the line of command between the political heads of departments and the bureau chiefs to handle substantive questions of policy and administration. Career positions for professional civil servants have been created to handle organic problems of budgeting, accounting, personnel, office services, organizational planning and the like. This is a recognizable trend, and the pattern is to put these activities in the charge of an executive officer or an administrative assistant secretary who is not a party man but a professional civil servant. The trend is good, so far as it goes, but it stops short of meeting the still greater need of a professional subordinate and staff upon whom the Secretary can rely for wise counsel and follow-up action in handling the substantive issues of policy. The Secretary of a cabinet department is today better equipped to deal with the secondary questions than the primary questions. To deal with the latter he has to improvise his own management team after he takes the oath of office, and he has to scratch around for competent persons to man it. By the time he has a smoothly working staff he is normally nearing the end of his official life span. In the meantime he has been a neophyte in an unfamiliar and complex situation dealing with experts to whom it is an old game.

The failure to have high departmental positions (as distinguished from bureau positions) within the career service handicaps the entire civil service as well as the Secretary. It makes for a bureau perspective rather than a departmental or government-wide point of view. It weakens the emphasis upon good management and civil-service discipline. It cuts off the career ladder at the bureau level, depriving civil servants of opportunity for advancement to professional positions at the departmental level. It is no substitute to put career men in political positions of Assistant Secretary and Secretary; for to accept these appointments they must step out of character, and take on the burdens of the political executive. This dooms them to impermanence, and the civil service to loss of continuity and loss of professional sophistication in its supervision. A civil service needs sophisticated supervision at the departmental level just as much as an infantry company needs its top sergeant in addition to a commissioned officer in command. If an army is expected to be no better than its "non-coms," it is unreasonable to expect a national civil service to be at its best without professional supervision at the highest level.

To state this need is not to make an argument for displacing the political heads of departments with career men. Both political and professional leadership are required, and the latter must be subordinate. The experts must be on tap not on top. This is axiomatic in responsible government.

For many years there has been public debate as to how the needed (but not created) positions in the higher civil service should be filled. The principal cleavage is between those who favor some sort of "officer corps" and those who oppose it. Nearly all of the ideas advanced are good; that is, they could work. But discussion of them is academic until the permanent civil-service positions at the departmental level are created. There are at least three ways in which such positions could be established. There is the concept of the general manager, prevalent in business, that could be adapted to the government services. There is the somewhat similar pattern of the under-secretary, a non-party career man, which the British have used successfully.[18] Various departments have quietly experimented with an official who, starting as a business manager, has taken on some of the functions of a general manager or permanent under secretary. But no such office has been formally established. There is also a third plan which the Department of the Interior has developed in embryonic form, a "program director" and modest staff concerned with substantive questions, paired with the Administrative Assistant Secretary who is concerned with organic questions. The Secretary of the Interior can turn to one or the other, or to both of these two men and to the Solicitor for briefing, advice, or follow-up action on any item of departmental business that may arise. Their commitment is to the department rather than the bureaus, and they stand outside of the bureau structure.

When civil service positions of this sort are created generally in executive departments and agencies they can be filled in a number of ways. Almost any systematic procedures will do. It is not necessary and probably not desirable to set up a separate officer corps for them. But that idea could be used if the doors of admission to it were kept open from many sources and at many levels. The important thing is to be systematic in discovering and developing men who have capacity for this executive-integrating function. They should be identified and trained through their successive assignments for increasing, and ultimately the highest, responsibilities. Qualities of character and intellect will emerge clearly in this process and it will not be too difficult to spot the outstanding men who are qualified for the highest positions when they fall vacant.

It will be important to recruit men from many sources. The federal government is absorbing a modest number of highly competent college-trained men through its examinations for junior management assistants and junior professional assistants. Some of these are men of great promise for ultimate general executive work. Many civil servants who start their career as technicians and professional specialists also prove to have the breadth of mind and interest and the strength of character and personality to become real leaders in administration. Social scientists, physical scientists, engineers, lawyers, and others have become successful administrators in the national government. American specialists are trained more broadly than their European brethren, and large numbers of them build their professional training on the foundation of a good liberal education. It is only natural, in consequence, that professionally trained men in this country have wide development possibilities that their foreign counterparts lack. Although the majority of men prepared for the highest administrative positions will have to be developed within the civil service, entering early in life, some lateral recruitment from outside the government in later years is possible and probably desirable if it is done systematically and with scrupulous care to make sure that the basis of selection is real capacity. Business, the professions, and academic life have all supplied men to the national administration who have been able to adapt themselves to the new environment and make definite contributions. Lateral recruitment must always be limited, but when it is not excessive it is a way of introducing new blood that every civil service needs, no matter how good it is.

All of these questions of policy can be worked out pragmatically, in the characteristic American way, once the keystone of the civil service arch is fitted into place. The important thing now is to set up permanent administrative positions at the departmental level. This is the missing keystone.

Responsibility and the Span of Control

Although men differ greatly, it is a truism that each has a limited span of attention. Similarly an executive has a limited span of control. The essence of the executive role is to work with and through other men; but an executive can deal effectively with only a limited number. The exact number varies with the man, his associates and subordinates, and the nature of their tasks. If the organization is such that an executive is forced to exceed his span of control in dealing directly with subordinates his effectiveness and the organization's effectiveness suffer. All of the subordinates get less supervisory attention than they require, and if a few take a great deal of time, others get none at all. As the span of control is further exceeded the executive loses control of his subordinates, teamwork breaks down, and the organization falls apart.

The necessity of respecting the executive's span of control is accepted in all organizations, except, perhaps, the Government of the United States. Army doctrine rigidly limits a commanding officer's subordinates to a small number (the optimum number is three); he works through them no matter how vast his command. Business corporations are elaborately equipped with vice presidents, general managers, and department heads, to keep business within the president's span of control. Universities have numerous deans, provosts, and vice presidents, to strengthen the president's influence over the heads of the teaching departments. These arrangements are normal in American life for all executives except the President of the United States, and he is held responsible for a government so organized as to show no respect whatever for his span of control.

The Brownlow Committee on Administrative Management in 1937 noted that there were more than "one hundred separately organized establishments" including a dozen independent commissions—"a new and headless 'fourth branch' of the Government." The committee recommended that this sprawling enterprise be reorganized to bring all activities within the general supervision of the heads of twelve executive departments of cabinet rank. The Congress refused to permit this change and President Roosevelt had to be content with an organization of ten executive departments, three executive "agencies," the veterans administration, the TVA, numerous other small organizations, and twelve independent commissions. Problems of national defense and World War II quickly enlarged this structure into a vastly complicated mechanism, with a new crop of alphabetical agencies added—WPB, OPA, OWI, FEA, NWLB, ODT, OCD, OWM, WMC, WSA, SWPC—to name only a few.

Emergency defense and war agencies were dismantled rapidly after the war, but Congress and President Truman both realized that the national administration needed a thorough overhauling. The Hoover Commission was set up to survey the situation and make recommendations. It found that in the national administration in 1949 there were fifty-two agencies reporting to the President plus nine important "independent commissions" engaged in economic regulation over which the President had little authority, although the public tends to hold him generally responsible, since he appoints the members and may remove them for cause. Since then, the Korean War and the partial mobilization have produced a further growth of new activities and organizations in the government. Since the Hoover Commission presented its recommendations there have been a number of changes by the President under the authority of law and also by Acts of Congress. These improvements, however, have not materially reduced the numbers of departments and agencies which the President must try to supervise directly. In 1952 there were still nine executive departments, including the triple-headed Department of Defense, five executive "agencies," five "administrations," two "authorities," seven boards, eighteen "commissions," two "corporations," and enough additional miscellaneous units to bring the number of separate organizations to fifty-six.[19] As the Hoover Commission said,[20] "It is almost impossible to comprehend the organization and management problems of the Federal Government . . . The sheer size, complexity and geographical dispersion of its operations almost stagger the imagination. As a result of depression, war, new needs for defense, and our great responsibilities abroad, the Federal Government has become the largest enterprise on earth." The President's responsibility for agencies which report directly to him or for which he has some responsibility still far exceeds any reasonable span of control.

Responsibility in Fact

In twenty years the national administration has changed greatly. Beginning with Franklin Delano Roosevelt, the Presidents have faced, and their successors will face, problems radically different from those of their thirty predecessors. The government has a long way to go to catch up in its organization, civil service, and management practices before it will be possible for the President to have in fact the control over the administration that earlier Presidents had.

The problem of administrative reform is not insoluble. Size is not an insuperable obstacle. No magic will be required in the remedies, but the corrective action will have to be more fundamental and drastic than the measures recently taken and recently proposed. The Hoover Commission did a good job, but lacked imagination, pulled some of its punches, and more or less assumed the world of 1920, not that of 1950. The first new President who is either administratively sophisticated or well advised will certainly demand prompt and fundamental changes to restore him to the position of Chief Executive, in fact as well as name.

The means of progress are conservative and well tested. The only radicalism required is willingness to apply known principles to a known problem. The creative measures must include concentration within the executive departments of nearly all executive agencies. Probably a few new departments will be needed, but they should not be many. Eventually the "independent commissions" will also have to be brought under the general supervision of the heads of executive departments. The scheme suggested by the Brownlow Committee in 1937 is still the best way of doing so. These steps will make it immediately urgent to strengthen both political and administrative leadership at the departmental level, as has been suggested above.

There is an alternative way of moving toward a realistic span of control that could be followed. It would be possible to add a new echelon of executive authority and responsibility under the President and above the departments. Instead of enlarging the departments by drawing all other executive agencies into them and so changing their character, departments and agencies could be grouped together in clusters under executives in the new echelon.

These men would be political officials, publicly responsible, and would have the assistance of a strong professional staff composed largely but not exclusively, of career men. Under professional leadership, these new "executive secretaries" would necessarily and properly concentrate on broad policy, the integration of program, and maintenance of standards. The appeal of this solution of the span-of-control problem rests on the argument of experience that when the functions and size of an organization are greatly increased it is easier to regain its over-all unity by adding new echelons at the top than by enlarging the constituent operating units at the bottom. When the Army increased in World War II from its prewar strength of less than 200,000 to 10,000,000 men, it was only natural to create new commands and new ranks of generals to fill them. The alternative of making over the contingent regiments, divisions, corps, and field armies was obviously difficult, probably undesirable, and perhaps impossible. The problem of organizing civil administration is not completely analogous, but there are comparable difficulties in regaining organizational unity through enlarging and making over such old and traditional organizations as the executive departments.

These changes, however, are in the future. Under the present circumstances, how far can the public go in holding a President responsible as Chief Executive for the efficiency and integrity of his administration? A fair-minded public will make some allowance for administrative realities. The alternatives are also important. In a national election, what are the prospects of a party whose Presidents have given evidence of devotion to the public interest on the big questions of policy even though they have fallen short in maintaining standards of efficiency, as did Mr. Roosevelt, or in maintaining standards of integrity, as did Mr. Truman? If its nominee must compete against a candidate whose devotion to the public interest is equally well established, it will lose support. But its nominee will normally be preferred over a candidate whose faithfulness to the public interest (as distinguished from particular interests) is not established. The candidate of the Democratic Party has a tremendous advantage in 1952 in being able to point to the record of twenty years of constructive legislation and of progressive public policy clearly in the public interest which his party has sponsored, torn with dissension though it is. Perhaps the problem of a Republican candidate is to convince the country that he and his party are not the captive of a single interest, and that they are genuinely loyal to the public interest on the big questions of policy. Although politics has its paradoxes, it is still difficult to believe in the possibility of establishing an upper-class party in a country which refuses to have an upper class.

VI

ETHICS—LEGISLATIVE, JUDICIAL, ADMINISTRATIVE

One basic principle is dominant in legislative, judicial, and administrative ethics in a representative, responsible government. It is the principle that issues should be decided on their merits. The principle has been recognized longest in the courts, where it has been accepted from the beginning of history. The American Bar Association formulated its "Canons of Professional Ethics" in 1908 and its "Canons of Judicial Ethics" in 1924,[1] but the spirit of the Canons is indicated in a few lines from Deuteronomy which preface the 1924 code. These instructions of Moses to the first judicial hierarchy of Israel go back some 2600 years.[2] "I charged your judges . . . Hear the causes between your brethren, and judge righteously between every man and his brother, and the stranger that is with him. Ye shall not respect persons in judgment; but ye shall hear the small as well as the great; ye shall not be afraid of the face of man; for the judgment is God's." These same principles of even-handed justice were reported by Moses as part of the divine mandate[3]

"Judges and officers shalt thou make thee in all thy gates . . . and they shall judge the people with just judgment. Thou shalt not wrest judgment; thou shalt not respect persons, neither take a gift: for a gift doth blind the eyes of the wise, and pervert the words of the righteous."

The Ancient Standard of Justice

The ideal of justice, perhaps the oldest ideal in government, is essentially one of settling cases on their merits. Reason is at the very heart of ethics. It is natural that the obligation to act on the merits of the case should have been recognized first in the courts when public policy is most clearly set forth in known rules of law, and when most of the cases have involved private parties as adversaries, with the judge, as representative of the state, a disinterested third party. A judge must not only mean to be fair; he must be intelligent in weighing the evidence and applying the law. Morality and reason are linked in the ethics of government.

Of the thirty-five Canons of Judicial Ethics (plus a "Summary of Judicial Obligation"), seventeen bear directly on the judge's duty to act on the merits of the case and to avoid situations or actions that would tend to weaken his impartiality and objectivity; thirteen have to do with the efficient, courteous, rational conduct of judicial business; and five concern more general obligations of the judge to the public interest. These canons as an official statement of the Bar Association are new, but the underlying principles are old.

Legislative and Administrative Standards

The same underlying principle of deciding cases on their merits must govern the conduct of legislators and administrators. In fact, it is even more urgent that they stick to this principle. But it is also more difficult for them to do so. The urgency and the difficulty both derive from the discretion which legislators and administrators exercise. Since the prime function of legislators is to make public policy, if they do not decide questions on their merits, the law becomes perverted at its source. A bad tax law is far more immoral than bad administration of the law, although it is more difficult to agree upon what is "bad" in legislation than in administration. Defects in public policy which permit inflationary forces to go on unrestrained cost the public much more than carelessness or even corruption in placing defense contracts. But again, legislative defects, under our system, escape the scrutiny which administrative failures receive. It is not easy to determine the merits of legislative decisions, for the evidence at hand is seldom all that is desired to understand the problem. There are frequently imponderables involved, and the criterion of the public interest is only a general guide. Since there is necessarily so much discretion involved in a legislator's decisions, and since the standards he applies are the most general of all public officials, it is correspondingly important that he avoid all situations and all actions that would tend to make him biased. The greater the discretion the more urgent it is to be scrupulous in avoiding any motivation contrary to the public interest.

The legislator is in a very difficult position. The judge can isolate himself from the parties to the controversy and tradition supports him, but the legislator cannot. As a representative of the public he must keep his touch with the public. He must be accessible, and the parties who seek him are the most avid and highly organized interests. Furthermore, the personal power which present legislative organization and present legislative practices put in his hands make the legislator peculiarly vulnerable to the pressure of special interests. To be truly objective and sharply rational in his judgments (in the public interest) an American legislator today needs to be both a moral giant and an intellectual power.

Administrators, by and large, have not so much discretion as legislators, but many important officials have broader discretion than do judges. They must, therefore, be scrupulous in making decisions on the merits of the case, and must take precautions to be sure that their judgment is not improperly influenced. It is not enough to avoid error; they must also avoid both temptation and appearance of favoritism. When much depends upon human judgment, it is only prudent to safeguard intellectual integrity.

The judge's moral problem is simplified by the fact that he does not have to take the initiative. Others act to bring controversies to him. One private party brings another into court. The state acts to prosecute an individual who violates the law. Or an individual takes some action under the law against the state. The responsibility is upon others to act, to prepare the case, to submit the evidence, and to clarify the issues. The judge's task involves a minimum of positive responsibility.

Passive Immorality

The duties of legislators and administrators differ from judicial duties. Legislators and administrators are essentially active, not passive. If they do not act, or act too slowly, the public may be injured more than if they err in acting. This is a serious problem, in part because a legislator or administrator can betray his trust by seeming to be judicial, that is, by becoming passive and leaving the initiative to others. Failure to provide for an adequate national defense can clearly cause fatal damage to the public. Failure to control extravagance or obsolescence in defense measures can also damage the public. The failure to support a League of Nations had something to do with the unresolved frustrations of the nineteen-thirties and the advent of World War II. The delay in controlling child labor was at the expense of many generations of children (and of handicapped adults). Legislative inaction in dealing with hazardous industries, e.g., mining, permits mine disasters to continue, and breeds bitterness which also costs the public dearly. Who can estimate the cost to the public of failure to act promptly, vigorously, and incisively in dealing with unemployment or inflation? It escapes moral censure because it is so vast as to escape measurement. The measurable dollar costs are less significant than the disorganizing and depressing effect upon society.

Although the obligation of administrators to act is usually legal as well as moral, much is necessarily left to their discretion, and the opposition which is provoked by any change in the *status quo* tempts administrators to go slow. In a period of rising costs the public-utility corporations will ask the regulatory commission for rate increases. But in a period of falling costs, or in a situation where costs could be reduced with good management, if the officials who have the duty to regulate do not act, the public has to pay more than it should for services furnished by a licensed private monopoly, or has to forgo the better services which it could have.

The tendency to be passive when the public interest requires positive action is so prevalent among regulatory agencies that it now has a name, "administrativitis," according to Senator

Douglas, and "quasi-judicialitis," in the lexicon of Louis Brown-low. The phenomenon is well-nigh universal. In the states pub-lic-utilities commissions created for administrative regulation, i.e., to give active supervision and direction to public-utility corpo-rations in the public interest, have tended to fall back into the more passive role of the courts, for which they were intended to be a remedy. In the federal government the Federal Trade Commission has abandoned its early role of dynamic defender of the competitive vitality of the business system for a less am-bitious policing job. The commissions which have regula-tory responsibility for a single industry or single segment of the economy (such as the Interstate Commerce Commission or the Federal Communications Commission) invariably tend in time to become the captives of that industry, concerned with its welfare as much as with the public welfare, painfully conscious of the desires of the industry's leaders, and much less sure of the public purpose in establishing the regulatory program. Reg-ulatory commissions, newly established after a period of in-tensive study of a recognized problem, retain their original fer-vor for a time. But sooner or later quasi-judicialitis, to use the Brownlovian term, overtakes them and they settle into the groove of passive conservatism.

The tendency of regulatory officials to reach a *modus vivendi* with the regulated interests is general. In part it accounts for the prosperity of organized crime despite the duties of state and local police authorities to enforce the criminal code. It was a contributing factor to the decline of state governments in economic regulation, e.g., banking, corporation charters, corpo-rate finance, and public utilities, although interstate competi-tion and the weaknesses of state legislatures were probably more influential. The tendency is more pronounced, however, among the so-called "independent commissions" than in the executive hierarchy of the state or federal government. The responsibility of the chief executive to the public tends to keep subordinate officials more alert to the public interest and also affords some protection from aggressive attacks by pressure groups. Once quasi-judicialitis grips an independent commission, it is difficult to arrest the course of the disease, which is progressive and leads to chronic invalidism.

The causes are not too obscure. An organized group that believes itself to be adversely affected by a new regulatory program does not give up when the new law has been enacted. It attempts immediately and persistently to get "sound" men appointed to the independent commission. The distinguished members of the bar who represent it can be most gracious, not to say ingratiating, to members of the commission who seem to deserve the industry's confidence. Some commissioners so win the confidence of industry that industry weans them away from the public service into its own employ. Commissioners who prove "difficult" are subject to constant attack in the public press, in trade publications, before committees of Congress and on the floor of Congress itself; and their reappointment is bitterly opposed. In these maneuvers the pressure group also works through party organizations and legislators. The defeat of Leland Olds, renominated by President Truman after ten years of distinguished service in the Federal Power Commission, is an example of what happens.[4] The attack was personal; his record as a responsible administrator was unchallenged. The success of such an attack has its inevitable effect upon other commissioners. In addition to attacks on personnel, the legislation is challenged in the courts, frequently with at least partial success; remedial legislation is offered, also usually with some success; and economy is urged in appropriating funds for enforcement of the law. "Independent commissions" are peculiarly vulnerable to such attacks. They are not independent of politics, of pressures, or of legislative committee controls; but they are not administratively responsible to the Chief Executive and he is not obligated to defend them.

Regulation is by nature a political process until the regulatory policy comes to be accepted and observed voluntarily by all concerned. Until that time comes the regulatory program is at the center of political storms. It needs the support of a responsible chief executive to carry it through the crucial years. Although the President of the United States is more or less held responsible by the public for the success of the total operation of the government, his responsibility for the independent commissions is marginal and at best very general. He appoints and reappoints members, but he can remove them only on formal charges, and it is doubtful that the courts would hold "dignified lethargy" to be a proper cause for removal.

One remedy for quasi-judicialitis is preventive. It is to recognize that new regulation is inherently a political process and so to organize the administrative work that it is in a department under the general direction of the Chief Executive. The danger of deciding questions on other grounds than their merits in the public interest is decreased, not increased, by this step. This pattern is sometimes followed in the national government and it does not lead to personal interference by the President or to arbitrary decisions by the department head. For example, the Secretary of the Interior and the Secretary of Agriculture have important regulatory powers, which are exercised with professional competence and reasonable objectivity. The administration of regulatory measures affecting industry, however, is normally entrusted to "independent commissions." Perhaps, as Louis Brownlow has suggested, this reflects chiefly the traditional attitude of the Committees on Interstate and

Foreign Commerce, which derives from a historical accident, the antipathy of Senator Reagan for President Benjamin Harrison.[5] "The first regulatory commission was the Interstate Commerce Commission. It was first set up in the Department of the Interior. Then there was a Presidential election and Mr. Reagan of Texas, the author of the interstate commerce bill, said that since a railroad lawyer named Ben Harrison had been elected President, he did not trust the President any more with this matter, so he invented the . . . independent commission. Thereafter, any bill or a regulatory matter that came to the Interstate and Foreign Commerce Committee resulted in the appointment of a commission."

Political Ethics and the Highest Courts

Although most judges in most of their cases have less difficulty in concentrating on the merits of the case, the highest courts which pass on questions of constitutionality of acts of Congress and the state legislatures do have so much discretion that they are in effect exercising a policy-making function of the legislative type. In defining the meaning of the term interstate commerce as employed in the Constitution of the United States the Supreme Court has in effect delimited the power of Congress to regulate industry. In defining the meaning of "due process of law" the Supreme Court has from time to time set limits on the power of legislative bodies to alter or regulate property rights. In elaborating the concept of the "police power" the Supreme Court has at other times excepted certain situations from the limitations on legislative power. Even in deciding so apparently simple a question as to whether an income tax is "direct" or "indirect," the Supreme Court has made public policy. During the nineteenth century and a large part of the first half of the twentieth, the Supreme Court was an influential factor in shaping the economic policy of the nation. When, in considering the economic legislation of the New Deal, the Supreme Court eventually determined that Congress had power to deal effectively with national economic issues, it seemed that the Court's withdrawal from political questions was imminent.

That expectation, in retrospect, seems to have been a phase of past naïve preoccupation with economic matters. The Supreme Court is again back in politics. That is, it is confronted with broad questions of public policy. It is involved in matters of civil rights, in questions of freedom of speech and freedom of belief, racial segregation, and relations of church and state. Apparently it will continue to be occupied with such questions for some time.

These broad matters of public policy confront justices of the Supreme Court with some of the same ethical problems that legislators face. In so far as the language of the Constitution gives them discretion, they have to determine what the public interest requires. Since they are in no sense representatives and are traditionally isolated from overt political pressure, they are thrown back upon the fundamental values of our culture for their standards. Their responsibility emphasizes again the interdependence of reason and morality. Absolute dedication to the public interest is essential but not enough. They also need prophetic insight into the moral and political nature of society and the vision to lay down a public policy that is in the public interest as the years will reveal it.

An old rule of liberal justices was to uphold the acts of responsible legislative bodies and of responsible administrators if compatible with constitutional language as a reasonable man might reasonably construe it. Is this still the liberal rule when personal rights, not property rights are at issue, and when the popular impulse of the moment is to curtail, not expand, freedom? Over the years the conclusions emerged that there are no absolutes among the property rights of a changing economy. Does this principle hold also for personal rights, or is man himself so unchanging that there are values, and rights, which inhere in his very nature and the nature of the universe? If moral law is not valid to defend man's property, is it valid to defend man himself? The role of the prophets has not been easy, and a thoughtful person does not now envy the justices of the supreme bench.

Judicial Appointments

The inescapable policy-determining function of the Supreme Court throws a great responsibility upon the President and Senate who nominate and confirm judges for positions on the federal bench. The justices of the Supreme Court obviously must be men of great learning (for it is from our culture that they draw basic public values) and of great integrity (for in their decisions of a policy-making type, they are responsible only to their consciences). To be true to their responsibility the President and the Senate dare not put untried men on the supreme bench. They must appoint men whose values and dedication to the public interest have been as fully proved as their professional competence. Since there is no place these qualities can be so well tested as in the lower courts, the same standards must be applied in appointments to district and circuit courts, if promotion is to be possible, and in the selection of state judges. Unfortunately there is no well-established policy of promotion. Only two justices of the Supreme Court now serving were promoted from lower federal

courts, and none from the highest state courts which have produced such outstanding justices as Holmes and Cardozo.

Why is there no tradition of promotion? One explanation is
that carelessness and the pressure for patronage have weakened the federal bench. The rule of Senatorial courtesy is enforced rigorously with regard to judicial appointments and not
always for the purpose of raising standards. Using judicial appointments to reward party service or to strengthen a local political machine cannot be justified in the public interest. As
President Theodore Roosevelt said, "Nothing has been so
strongly borne in on me concerning lawyers on the bench as
that the *nominal* politics of the man has nothing to do with
his actions on the bench. His real politics are all important." [6]
By real politics, T. R. meant the man's views on public policy.
Party patronage is bad enough, but personal favoritism is even
less justifiable. Senator Douglas of Illinois, by invoking the rule
of Senatorial courtesy in 1951, blocked the confirmation of an
organization candidate said to be the nephew of the chairman
of the House Rules Committee, but the rule usually works the
other way. It is not too difficult today to identify federal
judges who are better known for their relatives or political connections than for their opinions.

Drew Pearson may have been putting it strongly when he told
a Senate committee,[7] "This practice in my opinion has made
the Justice Department a dumping ground for political hacks,
and is responsible for a system where justice is administered
not for the benefit of the American public but for the political
benefit—or sometimes the law practice—of some Democratic
Senators—who now to some extent virtually appoint the judges
and district attorneys." The columnist, when challenged by
Senator Douglas on his certainty that giving up Senatorial courtesy would improve judicial appointments, quickly ad-

mitted that he could not be certain, but bubbled over with horrible examples of narrowly partisan appointments.[8] Perhaps the quality of judicial appointments is like the middle-aged cynic's view of the times. "They aren't what they used to be; and what's more, they never were."

If the lower courts are not being used today as a testing ground in which to discover judicial statesmen, where can men be tested for their basic values and integrity? Members of the present Supreme Court largely won their spurs in other fields —one in academic halls; one in administration; one in the House of Representatives, the lower courts and administration; one in the Senate and the lower courts; two in the Senate; and three in the Department of Justice. Despite the fact that it has often been done, the promotion of the Attorney General to the Supreme Court is risky business. A short period in the Attorney General's office gives little opportunity for either the President or the public to judge the man's inner qualities which become so important on the supreme bench. Historically there have been some notable surprises. Long service in the House or Senate is more revealing.

Secondary Vices

Although the primary ethical obligation of all public officials, legislative, judicial, and administrative, is to decide questions of public policy on their merits in the public interest, there are also secondary moral obligations related to this basic standard. One is the obligation to avoid the appearance of evil as well as evil itself. That is, an official must act on the merits, and he must avoid conduct or situations that would create a presumption that he is not acting on the merits. The importance of this meticulous conduct is not so much to preserve his own reputation as it is to protect the government itself from undue pressures. The appearance of favoritism can create almost as much pressure for favors as actual favoritism. The greater such pressures become, the greater is the probability that they will somewhere find a weak point and produce real favoritism. Then the problem snowballs. Corruption breeds corruption, and more and more men try to twist the government to their own ends, using the rationalization that it is necessary in self-defense.

Venality is a kind of stealing that can tempt men in any walk of life. It is not a peculiarly public vice, but it can compound almost any of the moral deviations to which men in public office may be tempted, or it can lead into them. In a pecuniary economy, with rising standards of living, and a wickedly unstable price level, it is not too difficult to go from innocent means of supplementing one's official income to things which are wrong without being clearly conscious of the transition. Venality cannot be tolerated, however, and the chief reason is not that it is stealing from the government (it may not be), or that it is taking unfair advantage of the public (e.g., getting an advantage in speculation from inside information). The reason why venality cannot be tolerated is that it is progressive and quickly destroys the ability of the public official to concentrate on his job and make decisions on their merits.

The Pyramid Upside Down

The effect of combining industrialization and modern technology with the ideals of responsible, representative government has been to turn the ethical pyramid upside down. The ancient ideal of justice stressed the need of a just judge but tolerated arbitrary legislative and administrative power. In the delicately adjusted life of present-day America, where political decisions shape the economy and the culture at pivotal points, the just judge is still essential, but it is even more important to have legislators who decide basic questions of policy on their merits in the public interest, and to have administrators who are completely dedicated to the public's service. The discretion placed in the hands of legislators and administrators by a people who idealize government-according-to-law is in one sense a measure of the necessary role of reason in governing. We have recognized the role of reason in science but have not realized that it is the intelligence of political, social, and economic policies which has created conditions in which men with free minds could discover science. Survival of an advanced culture such as that in America and Western Europe depends upon capacity to be intelligent in making and administering basic decisions of public policy. But reason is worse than useless unless it is dedicated to the public interest. Reason and morality depend on each other for fulfillment and must be combined in American politics of the twentieth century.

Varieties of Moral Hazards

The various threats to the integrity of a public official are alike in attacking his ability to act on the merits of the matter before him. They come from many directions but all approach this critical point of decision-on-the-merits. The instances of impropriety, corruption, illegal action which have been brought to light by the investigations of the Dawson, Buchanan, Fulbright, Hardy, Hoey, Kefauver, King and Chelf Committees, by the revelations of Senator Williams, by the disciplinary actions of Secretary Pace, and by the crusading journalism of the *Post-Dispatch* can all be fitted into a rough classification used by the Douglas Subcommittee of the Senate. The subcommittee found that threats to the integrity of public officials fall into five broad classes:

1. Influences carrying over from prior employment.
2. Influences of possible, probable or certain future employment.
3. Undue personal, social, or economic involvement.
4. Political involvement.
5. Simple venality.

If it is any comfort to him, the worried citizen (who in picking up his daily newspapers is almost certain that he will be faced with a new scandal or a fresh episode in an old one) can reassure himself that there is no need to extend the decalogue. It covers the situation very well. In fact, the ingenious devices of the crooked, the corrupt, and the shady men, both in and out of government, who try to get something they are not entitled to on the merits, all rely on a relatively small number of appeals to the frailties of human nature.

Influences Carried Over from Prior Employment

Acute problems of prior employment are largely a phenomenon of periods of war or industrial mobilization when it is necessary for the government to employ large numbers of men in key positions who have spent their lives in a particular business or industry. They are naturally steeped in the values and point of view of their industry. Their closest friends are in the industry and they have a stake in it. Business is a way of life, not just a means of making a living. It is not easy for successful executives in middle life to reorient their values and change their perspectives when they suddenly become public officials.

"Can they be perfectly fair if cases come before them which

directly or indirectly involve the company from which they came? Can they be completely objective in decisions which affect their industry, for example, where the industry favors a policy divergent from public policy or from proposed public policy? Can these men be completely detached in determining what the public interest requires?" [9] These questions of the Douglas Committee are questions which are asked quite generally. There is also agreement on the real moral hazards involved. The experience of the government in three industrial mobilizations since 1917 would seem to show that the hazards can be minimized but not avoided. Gross abuse of discretion can be prevented in particular matters, but the public must reconcile itself to some twisting of public policy.

In defense crises the government needs industrial talent. Since it is not feasible to maintain in normal times a civil service adequate for all the tasks of war, it must expand and contract, drawing men from industry and sending them back again. The moral hazard is accentuated (but not created) by the difference in the executive pay scales of business and government. In World War I and II and in the present crisis (1950-52), the policy has been to employ considerable numbers of businessmen without compensation ("W.O.C.") and to allow them to continue on the payrolls of private corporations. They are public officials, but privately paid.

In World War II there were, in early 1942, nearly 1300 dollar-a-year men and W.O.C. employees in the War Production Board alone. About half of this number was shifted to the War Manpower Commission when the Training-Within-Industry program was transferred. But the number of dollar-a-year men and W.O.C. employees again rose to nearly a thousand in WPB and continued at a high level throughout most of the war.[10] Other war agencies, such as the Petroleum Administration, also had large numbers of businessmen. The dollar-a-year arrangement has since been abandoned for the W.O.C. status, which is a more regular civil-service procedure.

Almost everyone agrees that the W.O.C. status is undesirable for full-time public officials vested with public authority. It is in fact generally illegal for public officials to be paid privately for work done for the government, and it is also illegal for them to work for the government free of charge. It takes special authorizing legislation to permit the dollar-a-year or W.O.C. employment of full-time officials. Despite the known difficulties such legislation has been enacted in each period of industrial mobilization as an emergency measure.

During World War II Senator Truman and his Senate Committee Investigating the National Defense Program gave a good bit of attention to the problem of the dollar-a-year men. They investigated several times; they had Donald Nelson, chairman of WPB, on the carpet repeatedly to defend the policy; and they exerted consistent pressure for safeguards and administrative vigilance. Various critics of the dollar-a-year men charged that (1) they held to a business-as-usual policy too long, held up the conversion program, and delayed in expanding productive capacity; (2) they favored big business in preference to small business; (3) they favored their own companies or industries in such matters as allocating materials, fixing prices, and awarding contracts; and that (4) they held back reconversion of industry after the defense-production peak had passed—until the big concerns could start even with the others. There was some truth in all of these criticisms, although most of the charges were not well proved. Instances of deliberate and direct favoritism were not numerous.

More difficult to control was the general distortion of policy because of deep-seated attitudes or convictions which were business-oriented rather than government-oriented.

World War II policy to reduce the hazards of this type of employment in the War Production Board included a number of steps. (1) President Roosevelt, who began the recruitment of businessmen for the National Defense Advisory Commission in 1940, insisted on careful selection to get men of integrity as well as industrial know-how, and began the practice of having the FBI check each man. This practice continued. The policy was also established of not appointing any men who were involved in anti-trust suits. (2) John Lord O'Brian, General Counsel of WPB, made it a rigid rule to employ attorneys only on a regular government salary. Legal positions were not filled with dollar-a-year men. Attorneys were required to sever their connections with private firms. He established his point that there must be no conflicts of interest influencing decisions on legal matters. (3) The appointment of trade-association officials to positions in the government was discontinued. Despite the value of their broad knowledge of their industry, early experiments with trade-association officials raised many questions, and it was concluded that they could serve their country better outside the government than as public administrators. This prohibition was also extended to private consultants. (4) The general policy was established in 1942 of not assigning a dollar-a-year man to a key executive position at the head of a branch or section which represented his industry. The purpose was to avoid direct conflicts of interest. Exceptions were always permitted in special circumstances, however, and in 1944 the rule was relaxed so that it barred employment of a dollar-a-year man only where he "could be required by his position in the War Production Board to make decisions directly affecting his own company or its competitors." [11] The exceptions under this rule were approximately one in eleven to the positions covered. This prohibition did not extend, however, to men on leave without pay from industry who were on the WPB payroll as experts and specialists. The shaping of policy was thus in the hands of industry men. (5) Finally dollar-a-year men were required to certify, upon taking office in WPB, "that in accepting this appointment as a government official, and in the course of my official duties, I will not represent my employer or any industry and that all my actions will be taken in the public interest." [12]

As chairman of the Senate Investigating Committee, Mr. Truman was perhaps the most vigilant watchdog to prevent abuse of discretion by men from industry working in the government in the years 1941-1944, and the situation always troubled the Truman Committee. In 1950, when a new industrial mobilization was called for, Mr. Truman as President found himself in the position of his predecessors, searching industry for men of talent and integrity and bringing them to Washington to work for the government without compensation. The 1949 legislation establishing three new higher grades in the hierarchy of civil-service positions with salaries ranging from $11,200 to $14,000, and raising the salaries of political officials heading departments and agencies so that they ranged from $15,000 to $22,500, actually put the government in a more advantageous position than it was in 1941 to employ men on a regular government salary.

The Defense Production Act of 1950 authorized the President to fix the salaries of the heads and assistant heads of the emergency defense agencies at levels comparable to those of other department heads, and their assistants,[13] and also to make use of the new higher grades of the civil service.[14] In addition, however, the Act also authorized the employment of persons without compensation in several categories, and authorized the President to exempt them from the conflict-of-interest statutes.[15] Under this legislation President Truman authorized the heads of the emergency defense agencies "to employ persons of outstanding experience and ability without compensation."[16] Except for the substitution of the W.O.C. arrangement for the dollar-a-year status and the somewhat higher regular government salaries, the situation in 1951 was much like that ten years earlier. In the spring of 1951 a newspaper estimate put the number of businessmen serving the government without compensation as high as six to eight hundred.[17] A subsequent check of eight defense agencies by the House Committee on the Judiciary,[18] however, turned up only 274 W.O.C. employees plus eighty paid part-time consultants.[19]

In proceeding under the Defense Act of 1950 President Truman attempted to utilize the experience of World War II as to safeguards. Persons employed without compensation are not exempt from the conflict-of-interest statutes in taking official actions and making recommendations with reference to contracts and other *direct* applications of their private employers, or any other private enterprise in which they have an interest. This rule tends to keep W.O.C. employees out of specific government business in which they might have a conflict of interest. Regulations also require the appointing officer to certify that he has not been able to fill the position with a man of the required competence and experience on a full-time salaried basis.[20] The appointments are recorded with the *Federal Register*, and the chairman of the Civil Service Commission is directed to make a quarterly survey of them and report any recommendations to the President.

No one argues that the employment of men who inevitably tend to represent a particular industry in key government positions is an ideal arrangement or that it should be continued for any length of time. It is an emergency policy made necessary by the present state of our politics and the present development of the civil service. It should be noted that criticism has always been directed more at the system than at the men. Blanket criticism of dollar-a-year and W.O.C. men from the business world would be quite unfair. Despite unfortunate individual failures, most of these men have conducted themselves surprisingly well, considering the anomalous situation in which they must operate. Very probably American businessmen as a whole have shown greater capacity to acquire a public point of view and to adopt the criterion of the public interest than have their counterparts among the more class-ridden societies of Western Europe.

Even if it be true, that fact does not make the situation acceptable, and the only escape from it is to avoid it by preventive measures. That calls for a much broader base of recruitment and a much larger number of men in the group whom we call politicians. The country needs men of business experience and competence, who have already proved by service in responsible public offices that they are faithful and competent public servants. When a national emergency comes such men cannot be improvised. The nation needs businessmen who are willing to serve the state as well as the corporation and who make it a point to do so in normal times. By and large their training and testing must take place in local governments and state governments. The federal government is too small and too central to train men in politics. There are only 533 elective offices in all and only one elective executive office. Not many of the political offices in the executive branch of the federal govern-

ment can be used for training or testing purposes. The Chief of
Naval Operations does not put an officer fresh out of Annapolis
to command a battleship. Neither can the President commit executive departments to the charge of neophytes. Wendell Willkie's
failure to win the Presidency in 1940 is an example of the difficulty of a businessman's beginning his political career at the top.
There is no similar difficulty at the bottom. Businessmen have
always been welcomed in local government, and those who have
won their spurs there as public servants have been able to go
ahead. More are needed. Many elective local offices also have the
great advantage of being part-time jobs which permit men to
continue in their business calling. Positions in state legislatures
have the same advantage as training schools. Until the ranks of
"politicians" are enriched with a wider variety of men from business and professional life, the national government will be hard
put to find tested men for responsible posts in every emergency
involving the economy.

The second preventive step is to develop the civil service at
the highest level, along the lines earlier suggested. The existence of trained men of high competence in career positions at
the departmental level will make it possible to assume additional
responsibilities with less stress in emergencies and to fit in men
drafted from business at lower echelons as reserve officers are
absorbed into the wartime army.

Until these steps are taken it must be expected that in
emergencies public policy will be skewed this way or that. The
most that can be expected of procedural safeguards is to keep
within moderate limits the individual abuses of discretion
which will inevitably occur.

Influences of Future Employment

"Coming events cast their shadow before, and if the possibility of lucrative employment with a private concern should be raised in any way, directly or indirectly, while the public servant is negotiating or doing business with that concern, it also casts doubts on the merits of the pending business." [21] This warning of the Douglas Subcommittee points up the problem. Toward the end of World War II it was foreseen that there would be serious difficulties in terminating war contracts. In the interest of quick reconversion to civilian production, in order to avert feared post-war unemployment, it was decided to negotiate settlement quickly. This was a firm recommendation of the famous Baruch-Hancock Report of 1944, which was largely adopted as the policy of the government.[22] The discretion given to government officials in making firm settlements made the moral hazards inevitable. The Comptroller General estimates that mistakes, of stupidity or cupidity, by federal employees cost the government between a half-billion and a billion dollars in a total of $65 billions in terminated contracts, a percentage charge to human frailty in the neighborhood of 1 per cent.[23] This seems to be a good record, or a bad one, depending upon the standards employed.

This sort of thing is an old problem. It gave rise to the Act of 1872 which forbade previous employees of the government to serve as attorney or agent in prosecuting any claim, or to aid in the prosecution of any claim, that was pending in the department in which he was employed while he was there. The prohibition extends for a two-year period. The act continued in force during the Spanish-American and First World Wars. But in the intensive total mobilization of World War II competitive procedures were impossible. Contracts were negotiated, re-negotiated, and later terminated by negotiation of the war agencies in an effort to convert all industry to war production quickly and then to reconvert with still greater speed. It was agreed that speed was more important than care; that moral hazards would have to be risked; and that costs of delay would be greater than some abuse of discretion. It was further generally argued that the government could not get and hold the experienced (in business) employees that it needed if men were in any way barred from subsequent re-employment in industry. Most of the emergency war agencies, where officials had been given great discretion, were therefore exempted from the Act of 1872. This policy may have been a mistake, and there was some anxiety at the time among career administrators over the absence of safeguards; but in authoritative circles there were no strong objections expressed when the decision was made to act quickly rather than carefully.

The Comptroller General, whose lack of speed in settling contracts was a principal reason for by-passing the General Accounting Office, has been the most consistent critic of discretionary contracting and of the lack of safeguards. In hearings before the Ethics Subcommittee in 1951 Senator Douglas asked:[24]

Did you find many cases, Mr. Warren, where men did resign from the war agencies and from the military service and then represent private parties in the prosecution of claims against the agencies with which they had formerly been connected?

Mr. Warren. Senator, we found former employees of the contractor assigned to the termination and settlement of that particular contractor's claim. We found them going back on the contractor's payroll, in one case the day after they got out of the Government. . . .

Senator Aiken. You found cases where an accounting office would be preparing claims for private industry against the Government that was also passing on those claims for the Government?

Mr. Warren. That is correct.

Senator Aiken. I refer particularly to the cases where there was a transportation subsidy on gasoline, and I recall very well the same accounting firm was preparing claims for many of the big oil companies that was also passing on those claims for the Government, although they employed different men to prepare the claims and pass on them.

Senator Douglas. Did you find many cases of high-ranking Army and naval officers retiring from the service and then accepting positions in concerns which had furnished supplies to the Government, and with whom they had dealt when they were Army or Navy officers?

Mr. Warren. I think I can recall several; yes, sir.

Senator Douglas. Who continue to draw retirement pay from the Government since they have gone into private employment?

Mr. Warren. Yes.

More recently the Fulbright Committee's investigation of the RFC brought to light instances of employees leaving the government under questionable circumstances when there were no extenuating conditions of wartime pressures or hurried industrial mobilization.[25] James C. Windham, an aide to (then) director George Allen, left the RFC and became treasurer and director of the J. L. Jacobs Co. shortly after the RFC made a $300,000 loan to the company. In 1949 the RFC made two loans to the Central Iron and Steel Co. totaling $6,300,000. "The loans were granted [by the Board] over the objection of all examiners and reviewers with the single objection of the substitute examiner, Hubert B. Steele," who had been assigned to the case by Director William E. Willett.

"One month after the second loan was authorized, Steele left the RFC and obtained employment at $15,000 a year with Goodwin, Rosenbaum, Meacham and Bailen and Joseph E. Casey, jointly. He received a payment of $5,000 on the day he reported for duty. Rosenbaum explains that the $5,000 payment was for four months' salary in advance.

"Casey was the principal advocate of the Central Iron and Steel Co. loan. He worked with his brother-in-law, Robert W.

Dudley, a member of the firm. Both made their principal contacts in the RFC with Willett." [26]

In commenting on post-government employment of this sort the Douglas Subcommittee said,[27] "These circumstances are in fact inherently so suspicious that a public employee who values his reputation for integrity should feel himself disqualified for employment with a firm to which he has made valuable awards until a considerable period (e.g. two years) has elapsed after that business has been completed. Governmental employers should discourage such transfers by all possible means." RFC's last board of directors apparently did not share this view.

The Ex-Government Lawyer

The vocational group which transfers most freely from the public service to the business world is the lawyers. The best place to learn tax law is in the Treasury Department. In the Department of Justice a young attorney can quickly become an expert in any one of a number of fields in which business corporations have continuing legal problems. In the regulatory agencies of the government a lawyer learns more about that special field of administered law, with more valuable complementary insights into economics and public policy, than he can learn in any other place. This is a well-understood fact. The demand for competent lawyers in these complex fields is strong and continuing. An able young attorney going into the government knows that after a few years, if he should choose to leave the public service, he may do so at a very considerable increase in salary either as a member of a law firm, usually with an "administrative practice" or on the legal staff of a corporation. This does not imply or require any impropriety on his part. In the course of doing an honest job his competence will win recognition from his legal antagonists and from persons with whom the government has litigation, as well as from his administrative superiors.

In a sense this situation has advantages for everyone. The government attracts a better legal staff than it has to pay for, or than it could secure even by paying more. It keeps a young and vigorous staff and avoids the costs of stagnation. Although it loses legal talent in its prime, there is no serious damage as long as a few of the able mature men stay on and as long as replacements keep coming. The situation benefits the employee; for he is sure of increasing responsibility, growing professional competence, and advancement in the government or of a better-paid job in private life. Business benefits by having a certain source of trained legal talent. The public benefits by having in the corporation influential men who have been exposed to the public point of view in matters of business policy and who can see things from more than one angle. The lawyer who leaves the government for private practice can and usually does render a valuable professional service which is socially useful.

Five-Percenters, Fixers, and Frauds

But the situation is not all sweetness and light. Even a casual reader of the daily press who has paid even slight notice to the findings of the Hoey and Fulbright committees knows that the activities of men trained in the law shade off from strictly legal work into several other kinds of activity. In addition to the (1) attorneys, strictly speaking, there are also (2) the "influence peddlers" or "five-percenters" (to use Hoey's phrase), (3) the fixers, and (4) the frauds.

The attorney is concerned with representing his clients, e.g., taxpayers, regulated corporations, or contractors in handling business with the government in which there are legal questions involved. If the attorney served the government for some time and in a position of important responsibility he will for several years have a good many friends in the government in high places. This makes it easier and more pleasant to handle business with the government even though he and the public officials are both scrupulously correct in all their dealings. This is natural, normal, and inescapable. Most of the more respectable attorneys with a government practice, it may reasonably be assumed, are correct in their dealing with the government—and equally correct are the great majority of public officials. The reputable attorneys practicing in Washington will say, if pressed, that they do not use influence. But they prefer not to have to say so publicly. The idea that these men may have influence keeps clients coming. The weakness of their moral position is that they are exploiting the presumption that they use influence and that in so doing they help to bring about conditions that create the influence peddler.

The influence peddler, who is frequently an attorney (but need not be in some lines, e.g., representing clients who want to get contracts), goes one step further. Instead of avoiding the impression that he does not use influence, he tries to create the impression that he has great influence and uses it successfully. He has signed photographs of influential officials on his office walls, testimonial letters where they can be seen, and is apparently on a first-name basis with the politically great. Some public officials play into the hands of these influence peddlers inadvertently, and a few have done so deliberately. One conclusion which has come out of the investigations of recent years, however, is the certainty that the influence of the influence peddler is greatly exaggerated. It is also clear that the number of attorneys who do more than use their good will to help them make an honest case for their client is small. But behind the smoke of exaggerated claims by the influence peddlers there is, unfortunately, the fire of some reality. Even though relatively small, it is dangerous to the security of the state.

Beyond the influence peddler is the Fixer, who is not content with getting a quick or favorable decision within the ultimate limits of official discretion, but tries for the decision he wants whether or not it is legal. To be successful he needs more than the weak official who is guilty of favoritism. He can be successful only if there is deliberate corruption. The Fixer does not flourish generally at the federal level, despite the publicity a few fixers have attracted. The temporary success of John F. Maragon, who exploited his contacts with General Harry H. Vaughan, was something of a shock to even the cynical, although no more so than the General's peculiar insensitivity to the requirements of his high position.[28] But it does not establish the fix as a feature of federal administration. The Fixer tends to be more present in local governments, where the pecuniary strength of commercialized crime and vice create irresistible hazards for commercialized political machines. This the Kefauver Committee well documented.

The Fraud is simply another variety of confidence man who pretends to have influence, either within the law or beyond it, which he does not in fact possess. He preys upon the ignorant, the greedy, and the unsophisticated.

The fantastic frauds of Samuel D. Mussman, alias Sam D. Mason, who relieved a variety of credulous victims of a quarter of a million dollars would be laughable (except for the plight of the victims) were it not for the belief in the corruptibility of the government which they attest.[29] Persons who advance funds to an agent for "sewer money" should be sufficiently suspicious to question the agent's integrity as well as the government's. The fact that so obvious a faker could operate in the middle of the twentieth century is embarrassing to everyone with any national pride.

The categories of Five-percenter, Fixer, and Fraud are not necessarily exclusive. One activity leads rather easily into another, and the same man may operate in several roles at different times, handling some legal business, using his personal influence for other clients, and attempting a fix when the conditions seem right. The Fixer and the confidence man, however, are likely to find their operations interrupted by periods of difficulty in keeping out of jail. Witness: Maragon and Mason.

Men of Influence?
Despite the exaggerations which becloud the influence racket, some undoubted and prime examples have come to light. The Fulbright Committee in 1950-51 exhibited Mr. Joseph E. Rosenbaum, of the Washington law firm of Goodwin, Rosenbaum, Meacham and Bailen, who claimed that he had two RFC directors, Willett and Dunham, "in his pocket," [30] and whose fees for handling loan applications ran well above the market rate. Mr. Rosenbaum was involved in a number of loan applications which to the Committee seemed very questionable on their merits. Former Congressman Joseph E. Casey was also associated with this firm (although not a member or employee) and was in fact the firm's "key representative in RFC matters," [31] for example, the Central Iron and Steel Co. loan mentioned above. Mr. Casey shared to the extent of 20 per cent in the firm's fees on clients' business with RFC. But these professional fees were not so remunerative as his leadership

and participation in an entirely different group which did business in the purchase, chartering, and sale of ships, especially "surplus" tankers, bought from the government. This group of unquestionably distinguished men made profits of $3,250,000 on an investment of $101,000 through transactions which were apparently legal. Depending upon one's point of view, the profits can be attributed to entrepreneurial genius, luck, peculiar post-war conditions, influence and inside information, lax administration, and/or defective legislation.[32]

The Casey ship deals, which an investigating Senator conservatively called "a little complicated," involved successive sales of the ships, or owning corporations, or the stocks of the latter so that the "surplus" ships sold immediately to American buyers wound up ultimately in the control of foreign nationals.[33] American ownership was clearly legal; but the legality of resale to bring about foreign control has been challenged. There were a number of interesting aspects of the ship transactions. (1) The Maritime Commission made something of a record for speed in approving a proposal to sell three tankers two hours before the final application was filed and a day before the buying corporation was incorporated. (2) The law firms acting as attorneys made very substantial fees. Mr. Casey's fees totaled $104,000 from the Rosenbaum firm with which he was affiliated. Mr. Newbold Morris' law firm received fees of $120,000 to $160,000.

(3) The participants in the ultimately very profitable transactions, as time and events have disclosed them, were a varied and interesting group. In addition to Mr. Casey they included Secretary of State Stettinius, Admiral Halsey, Julius S. Holmes, the University of Chicago ($15,000 invested brought, two and a half years later, $420,000), the China International Foundation, Inc., a philanthropic organization of which Mr. New-

bold Morris was President and Trustee. Benefiting in one way or another from the ship transactions were a former member of Congress, an influential Washington lawyer since indicted for perjury, a Secretary of State, a diplomat, a former Admiral, professional ship brokers, Chinese emigrés, an illustrious university, and a foundation giving relief to stranded Chinese students (headed by the man whom President Truman chose to investigate corruption in the national administration). The ship deals are hardly typical, but in the wide range of people involved they are perhaps symbolic of the problem of ethics in public affairs. As of March 19, 1952, no illegal action on anybody's part had been proved, yet the transactions as a whole, as more and more of the details come to light, can only be embarrassing to men and women who take pride in the nation's character and integrity.

A man of influence who got his first Washington experience not in practicing law, but as a dairy-business employee, was the now famous E. Merl Young.[34] His first government employment was with the General Accounting Office. After wartime service in the Marines, he became an RFC examiner. When he left the RFC to take simultaneous employment with two RFC borrowers, his salary jumped from $7,193 to a total of $28,000 from the two debtor corporations. In 1950 he went into the insurance business financed exclusively by the firm of Goodwin, Rosenbaum, Meacham & Bailen. Mr. Young's tax declaration for 1950 indicated that he had an expected income of $60,000. Despite this striking success story, Mr. Young was somewhat overshadowed in the press by his wife, the White House stenographer of mink-coat fame who had gone to work in Senator Truman's office in 1940.[35] The Fulbright Committee came to the conclusion that there "were close personal relationships . . . between Dawson [a former RFC official then an administrative assistant to President Truman], Merl Young, Rex Jacobs [an RFC borrower], James Windham and RFC directors Dunham and Willett. These friends, with others, constitute a group [the committee said] who appear to have exercised influence over RFC." [36]

The exact nature of the relationships of the influence-group may never be clear, even with the aid of continuing investigations and prosecution for violation of the law. But the composition of this group is of some significance. The attorneys-at-law provided the center for operations; to them were added a former Congressman, also an attorney, former RFC examiners who took employment with RFC's clients and with the law firm's clients, a former RFC employee who was promoted to the President's staff, an RFC director promoted from the RFC staff, an RFC director appointed through the influence of the national party committeeman from his state, and an RFC borrower who doubled as an RFC agent. This combination suggests the variety of people and experience that may contribute to "influence."

Undue Involvement: Personal, Social, and Economic

This example of an influence-group exhibited by the Fulbright Committee serves to emphasize the fact that "a recognized problem of long standing is that of public officials becoming unduly involved with persons, concerns, or industries which are affected by their decisions." [37] This conclusion of the Douglas Committee does not overstate the facts. "There is a strong presumption that a substantial economic involvement will create either a bias or an emotional problem through fear of bias. It is generally agreed, therefore, that any such involvement should be avoided. This is the purpose of the conflict-of-interest statutes, and of the law of incompatible offices.

"Involvements which it is generally agreed must be avoided include salaries, fees, and other compensation from business concerns, direct or indirect ownership of concerns doing business with the Government, speculation in securities or commodities in a field touching that in which the public servant has official functions. Somewhat less clear but also coming under the taboo for administrators is substantial investment in an industry affected by his official functions. How much is 'substantial'? That probably depends in part on its ratio to the individual's total investments. On these points there is not much disagreement. There is some feeling that public officials should be permitted to own businesses which do not concern their official function in any way and which they can operate through an agent or employee. But this, too, is frequently forbidden by law, perhaps to make sure that his official duties will have a public servant's full attention." [38]

What happens when these safeguarding principles are ignored may be illustrated by the case of Mr. James V. Hunt, who, while employed as a War Assets Administration consultant at $50 a day, also represented clients, for a fee, in buying property from the War Assets Administration. The Hoey Committee found that this conduct, although not illegal, was "wholly indefensible." [39] One thing leads to another. In time Mr. Hunt's "contacts" became so close with General Alden H. Waitt, Chief of the Chemical Warfare Service, that: "Hunt succeeded in influencing General Waitt to give special and unusual consideration to his client, because he felt that Hunt could help him in the furtherance of his military career." [40] When favoritism was brought to light, General Waitt was first suspended by the Secretary of War and then retired.

Hunt used his service in the Quartermaster Corps also to establish a friendship with General Herman Feldman, Chief of the

Corps. Despite the fact that the character of Hunt's activities as an influence peddler after he left the government was not concealed, the general "in his official position on several occasions displayed favoritism toward Hunt." [41] For this he was suspended and reprimanded, but was reinstated, because of his forty-two years of otherwise honorable and efficient service.

How do such obvious mistakes occur? How can public officials and employees be drawn into such situations which are so embarrassing, and which in retrospect look so indefensible? One way obviously is through friendships formed in government employment which are continued when one man leaves the government and goes into business with the government. The Douglas Committee observed that: [42] "Ethical difficulties are inevitably created when cases come before public officials in which they are personally involved. It is obvious that if a man representing the Government deals with personal friends or relatives on the other side of the table, he tends to be less objective than he should be in coming to terms. The remedy is for the official to disqualify himself and turn the matter over to some one else. This is the rule which prevails in the courts and by which judges are presumed to act.

"Wherever a public official has discretionary power to make decisions the terms of which are of great concern to individual businesses or to groups of businesses, he must be on his guard against being unduly influenced."

Personal involvement of public officials with men doing business with the government may also arise out of the business transactions themselves, if the public employee and the businessman are thrown together frequently. These are not necessarily improper, of course; in fact they are quite desirable unless and until one party to the friendship tries to make something out of it that he is not entitled to on the merits. In the

Hunt-Waitt case, Hunt deliberately sought special favors, and Waitt was beguiled by the idea that Hunt's imagined political influence would further his military career. When one party to the friendship begins to have ulterior motives he usually attempts to build up the friendship, and if he is outside the government he may do so rather naturally. "For example, a contracting officer and his family may be drawn into a social program of dinners, parties, golf, and other social engagements by a contractor or his agents. If this continues, it makes the contracting officer and the contractor members of the same social circle. Even if the engagements are purely social, the official may find it hard to be completely detached when it comes to handling official business with his new friend. If business matters are discussed during social engagements, complete objectivity becomes more difficult still." [43]

At some point in the process of involvement, purely personal or social relationships tend to be supplemented by economic advantages. Then the public official is securely caught in the gossamer web. But even this involvement is not so easy to avoid as one might think.

"The line between the proper and improper begins to be less certain when one looks for a consensus of opinion as to favors, gifts, gratuities, and services. The exchanging of gifts and favors is reported to be rather general in the business community. What is it proper to offer public officials, and what is it proper for them to receive? A cigar, a box of candy, a modest lunch (usually to continue discussing unfinished business)? Is any one of these improper? It is difficult to believe so. They are usually a courteous gesture, an expression of good will, or a simple convenience, symbolic rather than intrinsically significant. Normally they are not taken seriously by the giver nor do they mean very much to the receiver. At the point at which they do begin to mean something, however, do they not become improper? Even small gratuities can be significant if they are repeated and come to be expected. But here, too, convention must be considered: gifts to school teachers are now generally forbidden by law, but a Christmastime present for the postman, usually on engraved green paper, is almost as well established as holly.

"Expensive gifts, lavish or frequent entertainment, paying hotel or travel costs, valuable services, inside advice as to investments, discounts and allowances in purchasing are in an entirely different category. They are clearly improper. On this, there is substantial agreement in the governmental community, and any one who thinks them proper must have already lost his perspective. The difficulty comes in drawing the line between the innocent or proper and that which is designing or improper. At the moment a doubt arises as to propriety, the line should be drawn. Innocence is perhaps lost when one is conscious that it exists." [44]

Public officials may become involved because they are venal. But these are few. Of the vast majority who mean to do right, some become unduly involved because they are not alert to the ulterior motives of others and to their own vulnerability, and because they are not scrupulous from the beginning in attempting to keep personal feelings and attitudes out of public decisions. One of the disadvantages of our civil service which draws men in from other walks of life at high as well as low levels is that these men will bring the ethics of their particular business or calling with them, and the service will not be as consistently indoctrinated with the ethics of the public service as in a closed civil service.

The Hoey Committee noted that,[45] "Standards of conduct for the public official are of necessity different and more stringent than those commonly accepted in private business. For instance in the field of sales promotion and public relations, gratuities and other favors are extended or exchanged as a common practice. However, this practice cannot be condoned if engaged in by a public official. Most departments and agencies of government prohibit the acceptance of gratuities by their employees. The Administrator of GSA [General Service Administration], for example, states: 'No employee shall accept any gratuity or favor of any nature whatsoever, directly or indirectly, from any person, firm, corporation, or other entity which has done or is doing business or proposes to do business, with this Administration.'

"The reason for such a rule is obvious. A public official must conduct himself so he can give equal consideration and service to all persons doing business with him. If he becomes obligated in any measure to any particular person then he can no longer serve the public impartially."

The little foxes spoil the vines. Carelessness creates suspicion. Favoritism sets off a chain reaction that creates constantly increasing pressures. In an explosive situation of this sort the only safe policy is to respect the "no smoking" signs.

Political Involvement

"Politics itself can give rise to embarrassing conflicts of interest," said the Douglas Committee.[46] "When men are appointed to important administrative positions, often with the clearance and approval of county and State political organizations, or national committees, or Members of the Senate and House of Representatives, should they feel especially obligated to their political sponsors? If so, to what extent? Is there any obligation touching specific administrative decisions? If there is no obligation to the sponsor which can affect handling of administrative issues strictly on their merits, how can political sponsors be induced to accept this role of impartiality? Often political sponsors take a proprietary interest in departments or agencies in which they have helped to place men in key positions, and if their interest is pushed aggressively, it creates serious ethical problems for the administrator."

This problem is one which should be and could be minimized by proper institutional arrangements. If it is common sense so to design a bridge that it will carry the anticipated load with an ample safety margin, it is equally elementary to plan an organization and to staff it with people so selected and so protected by their status, duties, powers, relationships, standards, and public standing that there is maximum certainty that the organization will carry the administrative load.

The failures in the federal service in recent years were in a sense predictable in that they occurred chiefly where the design was known to be faulty. The three departments in which the nineteenth-century practice survived of making extensive partisan appointments to positions which are not properly posts of broad political responsibility were Treasury, Justice, and Post Office. The patronage practices affecting these departments were designed to accommodate the local political organizations, and the appetite for patronage of the members of Congress, rather than to meet the administrative needs of the departments.

One should be very clear that political appointments have their proper place in our administrative system. Positions of broad political authority and responsibility must be filled by able politicians who have capacity for leadership. This is an essential element in the scheme of responsible government. Such officers as heads of departments are clearly in this class unless the department, despite its size, does not involve broad questions of policy. Most of the Assistant Secretaries as well as the Secretaries should also be politicians. There is just as much need for good politicians as for good career administrators.

When the patronage policy dips down to the bureau level within the department, however, it is quite questionable. The trend is away from this plan. Most bureau chiefs are now career men, and experience increasingly indicates that they need to be. If the Secretary of the Treasury is politically responsible for his department there is no reason why the Commissioner of Internal Revenue needs to be, or logically, that he should be. Public political responsibility is by nature more or less exclusive. It cannot be shared. A political bureau chief is *ipso facto* that much of a challenge to the authority and political responsibility of the Secretary of the department. A political appointment at the bureau level tends to challenge the unity and discipline of the department without any compensating increase in public control of the bureau. A Presidential appointment decreases not increases the Chief Executive's control of the bureau, for the President cannot now keep track of department and agency heads, let alone bureau chiefs, and the fact that a bureau head is a Presidential appointee makes him more difficult for the Secretary to control. The only controls which are increased are those of the pressure group that is interested in the bureau and of particular politicians whose nominee the President accepts. A patronage appointment at the bureau level, furthermore, weakens management at a point where it needs to be professionally strong, with adverse effects upon administration throughout the bureau. The wise policy and the trend of practice, fortunately, is to pick men for professional competence to head the bureaus.

When patronage appointments are made within the bureau itself to head divisions or to head field offices, the administrative integrity is so weakened that a tight, well-managed, efficient organization is almost impossible. The costs shape up in both poor administration and moral failures. A strong organization is impossible with weakness in key positions. The Chief Executive and his party are overtaxed to find able men to fill positions at the departmental level. Nothing is clearer in American politics than the failure of the patronage system to produce good administrators on any continuing dependable basis for the lesser administrative posts; and patronage appointments in field offices have always been unsatisfactory. Loose organization, lax management, low morale and the patronage system go hand in hand.

The Treasury, the Department of Justice, and the Post Office Department have all suffered from this handicap. Until the Bureau of Internal Revenue was drastically changed by the President's Reorganization Plan, effective March 15, 1952, the Commissioner, his four top assistants, and the sixty-four regional Collectors have all been political appointees. The old organization was not able to carry the increased load of work or stand the greater moral strain.[47] Since 1940, federal taxpayers have increased fourfold to 82 millions, and the collections have increased tenfold to more than $50 billions—perhaps $61 billions in 1952.[48]

The Bureau of Customs has had the same type of political organization. The Commissioner, Assistant Commissioner, and fifty-one regional Collectors of Customs have always been political appointees. In addition to the political ties of the Collectors, many have been accustomed to engage in private business or professional activities. Conflicts of interest, political and economic, have thus been invited rather than avoided in the key executive positions which so largely determine the tone of the service.

In the Department of Justice, where the need for strict impartiality is not challenged by anyone, key offices in the administration of justice always have been in the hands of political appointees. That is, the ninety-four United States Attorneys and Marshals in effect have been chosen by the Senators or the local political organization of the President's party. They operate with a high degree of autonomy and rather meager supervision from the Attorney General and his Washington staff. As political appointees, the men who decide what to prosecute, whom to prosecute, and when to proceed are tied more tightly to a local party organization than to the Department of Justice or the Attorney General or the President.

The Post Office Department, one of the biggest public-utility enterprises in the world, has operated with an organization in which 22,000 key executives were "Presidential Postmasters" in first-, second-, and third-class post offices. The turnover was checked somewhat when the four-year term of office was replaced by continuous tenure in 1938 and the Hatch Act kept these men out of active political campaigning, but the support of political organizations continued to be an important factor in their selection. The key executive positions in the postal service were still not integrated in the career service, and had political obligations to fulfill in some way.

Executive Reorganization Plans No. 2, 3, and 4, submitted to Congress by President Truman April 10, 1952, abolished the political positions (that is, the Presidential appointment with Senate confirmation) in the Bureau of Customs, the first, second and third class postmasterships, and the U. S. Marshals (not attorneys); and transferred their functions to positions in the classified civil service. These long-overdue reforms, if they become fully effective, will greatly strengthen the Treasury and the Post Office Department. The Department of Justice will also benefit; but the key legal positions of U. S. Attorney in the local administration of justice are still patronage for the Senators and the local party machines.

The views and desires of members of political organizations, local, state, or national, can be quite properly considered when matters of broad policy are at issue. But when the political organization puts pressure on an administrator to decide a particular case, or to act in a specific situation, it is no more and no less than any other pressure group. The administrator's obligation is to act on the merits of the case without favoritism or consideration of extraneous matters.

The Venal Administrator

Wherever there is power it may be exploited for sordid personal advantage. In a pecuniary society the temptation to commercialize an administrative position is frequently present. Some men will yield to it, particularly if they do not have good leadership and supervision and are not part of a well-managed organization. The Douglas Subcommittee noted that,[49] "Differences of degree, usually accompanied by differences in motivation, change the character of improprieties. Gifts and favors which may begin as entirely innocent practices become improper when they begin to affect the public servant's ability to act for the public as agent or representative, fairly and objectively. They are improper as subtle influences upon his point of view.

"If carried further, they become ends in themselves, a way of increasing the public servant's income. At some point, the receiver becomes venal. He is, in effect, taking bribes and graft to enrich himself. This has been recognized to be wrong as long as Western civilization has existed. One can find it vividly depicted and scornfully denounced in the pages of the Old Testament. It is always a problem, but it is a less important problem today in its effect upon the conduct of public affairs than subtle economic involvement."

It is nevertheless a constant hazard and a problem to be dealt with. Where there is power someone will be tempted to use it to his own ends, to make something out of it, and temptation comes from within as well as from without. First Deputy Fire Commissioner Moran, in New York City, was properly impartial in issuing permits to install oil burners. But he had to be paid (as well as the city) to issue the permit. This is graft in perhaps its purest form—proper decisions, properly made, but for a price (which grossed the Deputy Commissioner and his associates $500,000 a year). No form of corruption is so old as to be obsolete, and no moral failure in politics so simple as to be outgrown. Any of the situations in which moral problems arise, past employment, future employment, or personal, social, economic, and political involvement may be exploited by the venal man.

The Idealist Administrator

Above and beyond the moral problems of public administration of which the public is aware, administrators have ethical problems of a professional character which are so subtle or so embedded in a technical context that the public overlooks them. The ultimate ethical criterion is still one of loyalty to the public interest, but usually that is only a way of stating the problem, not of finding the answer. An alert administrator may frequently find himself torn by conflicting but indirect loyalties to the same public. This confusion is in part a by-product of both the complex social structure of American life and the somewhat confused organization of most American governments.

Consider the position of a bureau chief in the national administration, for example. He is at the head of a bureau responsible for certain activities or functions based upon statutory authority and financed with appropriated funds. He is responsible to the Secretary of his Department and to the Chief Executive for the performance of his duties. He also has many direct contacts with the legislative committees and the appropriations committees of Congress, all of which have definite ideas about what he and his bureau should do. Some of these ideas get into the Acts of Congress, some get into letters addressed to him, and many are given to him orally, frequently in formal "understandings." The clientele of his bureau looks to him to carry out a program for their benefit. They take a great interest in the program and may be organized to make their wants known. The clientele, moreover, may not be unified, but may contain several different groups.

On any specific issue it may be difficult to tell what the public interest requires. This would be true even if there were only the bureau and one department in the entire federal government. But there are scores of departments and agencies and hundreds of bureaus in the national administration. In pressing his own program, how much is a bureau chief obligated to consider the interests of the other programs of the government? This is no academic question, for these programs have an impact upon each other. They are not isolated.

For example, how vigorously and by what methods should the Commissioner of Reclamation press forward with a river-development program of dams, irrigation projects, and hydroelectric facilities? The Director of the Fish and Wildlife Service is also responsible for conservation policies which may be adversely affected by the dams, and the Director of the National Park Service may find that present parks or potential park sites are inundated by new reservoirs. The Power Administrations, which market at wholesale the current from major hydroelectric projects, are concerned about technical aspects of construction. Indian Reservations may be flooded, and the Commissioner of Indian Affairs may wish to have Indian families relocated on newly reclaimed lands. What are the obligations of the Commissioner of Reclamation to his fellow bureau chiefs in the Department of the Interior?

The Reclamation program impinges also upon programs outside of Interior. The Department of Agriculture is concerned with effects upon tillable land resources, and the Rural Electrification Administration has found multi-purpose projects a vital source of power for the local farm co-ops. Furthermore, the Army's Corps of Civil Engineers has an extensive dam-building program for flood control in some of the river basins that Reclamation is reclaiming. The interpenetration of these many separately conceived federal programs creates ethical problems for each of the bureau chiefs. When federal activities were fewer and simpler these ethical obligations were seen only dimly; but now they cannot be ignored. How aggressively should the bureau chief push ahead with his own program regardless of its impact on other programs? At what stage should he consider other programs which he affects, and how far should he go in attempting to reconcile his own objectives with the objectives of other bureaus?

These are ethical problems of the greatest practical significance that occur on many levels, perhaps all levels, in public administration. If, for example, the Secretary of Defense pushes aggressively for national security with great single-mindedness and without much broadmindedness, he may so affect the foreign policy of the government as to make national insecurity inevitable. Similarly, fixing doggedly on the goal of military security may destroy the economic vitality of the country on which military strength depends. Yet if the Secretary of Defense is not vigorous and determined in attempting to promote the national defense, policies of other department heads also may endanger the nation. A department head's moral obligations to the country as a whole are such that he must consider other objectives and policies than his own, and he must find ways of accommodating other programs in carrying out his own.

It is no solution of their moral dilemma to push ahead aggressively, relying on the next higher official in the hierarchy to settle disputes. This policy quickly swamps the responsible superior; and matters which come to him as fully matured interdepartmental disputes can seldom be settled except by unsatisfactory compromises. A rationally integrated program for the government at large has to be built from the bottom up with co-operation at all levels if it is really to serve the public interest. In other words, judged by the standard of service to the public, an administrator cannot be measured by *his* program alone. It is his impact on the total program, including his own particular program, that counts.

In the abstract the administrator's duty is clear. But in his day-to-day operations things are more confused. The clientele of his bureau or department judge him by specific results within his own program. They define the public interest in terms of things they want—a dam, a battleship, a contract, a ceiling price, a rate decision, a franchise or permit. They try very hard to get the things they want without regard for things that other people want. The overt influence and pressures of the legislature are also particular, not general. In Congress, for example, as has been noted, the scores of committees and sub-committees, dominated by specialist chairmen, without a nationally oriented or representative leadership of a responsible character, tend to be so many pressure groups, needling the administrator to make particular decisions, and further twisting public policies and their administration to particular ends. The easiest thing for the federal administrator to do is to go with the tide and assume that the voice of the committee is the voice of the people. But his knowledge of the substantive problems frequently tells him this is not so, and usually he finds several voices shouting different instructions.

When the bureau chief looks to the Secretary, so that he can be guided by departmental policy he may find it far from clear, or that the department has not yet achieved a coherent policy. When the Secretary looks to the President or his Executive Office for the guidance of national policy, he may find it inchoate, confused, or non-existent. The tasks of government have in thirty years changed so much in nature and scope that its habits, its organization, and its personnel have not yet caught up with the over-all problem of consistent and coherent policy. The national administration is an adolescent giant, better muscled than co-ordinated.

This situation puts enormous moral strain on the administrator. It is easier to be the agent of special interests than the executive representative of the total public. If he is embarrassed by too many back-seat drivers he can at least listen to the one with the biggest voice or the most muscle. If he tries to determine the public interest honestly and realistically and to be guided by it in his administration, he still gets much less guidance, and support, than he needs from his superiors in the administrative structure. The myriad agencies of the national administration are in process of becoming one government, but progress is slow, halting, and not unopposed.

Legislative Morals

"The problem of . . . involvement is probably more difficult for Members of the Congress than for administrators. There are fewer traditional safeguards, temptation is more subtle, there is no higher authority, and discipline is rare even for illegalities. Men tinged with sovereignty can easily feel that the King can do no wrong, and in American politics as it now is, it is easy to feel that many things are justified which one heartily wishes were not necessary. The ancient Greeks with great insight pictured their gods as wise and usually benevolent, but also busy rationalizing their little peccadillos and not infrequently venting their wrath to satisfy somewhat personal ends. Capitol Hill, to its occupants, seems somewhat closer to earth than Olympus, and mortality is painfully evident except for those fortunates from one-party districts or States. The pressures are great, perhaps too great for mere mortals, and those who have not experienced the pressures and the dilemmas of the Olympian heights should perhaps first try to understand the situation before passing judgment." [50]

These words of a thoughtful and conscientious group of Senators are, if anything, an understatement. To understand the legislator's moral dilemmas, however, one must view them in the context of party and pressure politics, the subject of the next chapter. Moral problems of the legislator will be considered there.

Some Things to Be Done: The Criminal Code.

There are a number of things that can be done to tighten up the moral standards of public officials in conducting public business. Some are direct in their nature, others are indirect.

The first and most obvious thing is to extend and stiffen the criminal code on bribery and conflicts of interest. Present federal laws are incomplete and inconsistent. Some recognized problems are dealt with; others are not. What is a crime in one agency is sometimes permitted in another. To strengthen the law on bribery, for example, the Douglas Subcommittee on Ethics in Government proposed: (1) prohibiting bribes in other media than money (e.g., jobs, promotions), (2) prohibiting the use of third parties to receive bribes, (3) prohibiting payments that are in the nature of bribes, without the necessity of proving intent to influence or be influenced, (4) prohibiting payment of public officials to influence other officials, (5) prohibiting bribes in connection with a wide variety of administrative decisions in addition to contract matters, (6) stiffening penalties, and (7) punishing the briber as well as the bribed.[51]

To reduce the number of conflicts of interest affecting federal officials a number of steps have been suggested.[52] For example, (1) it is proposed to curtail the exemptions of salaried employees from general conflict-of-interest legislation (W.O.C. personnel would not be affected). (2) The prohibition of government contracts with members of Congress could well be extended to corporations (owned or controlled by members of Congress), and (3) in the same fashion government contracts with federal officials should be proscribed. (4) The policy of no contracts with members of Congress does not now apply to RFC loan contracts, contracts with government corporations, or any of the agricultural benefits or farm-credit agencies. The

Douglas Committee suggested that RFC loans to Congressmen should be barred. (5) The ban on officials doing business with the government (in their private capacity) should certainly cover the independent agencies as well as the executive departments (to which it is now limited). (6) The prohibition of speculation, by public officials, and the use of confidential information for that purpose should be extended to securities. It now covers only agricultural commodities. (7) Restrictions upon ex-government employees' doing business with the government could be extended and enforced with criminal penalties. To be effective in this field a policy of general prohibition must be both precise and realistic. The Douglas Committee urged that the problem be studied further and that action be taken.

Professional Codes

A step that could obviously affect the conduct of public affairs is the preparation and adoption of professional ethical codes by discrete groups that participate in public affairs. Many if not most of the professions have done this, with an effect that is on the whole beneficial. "One of the oldest and best known of professional codes goes back to the Hippocratic oath of the fifth century before Christ. It was a pledge to mutual assistance within the medical profession and to further extension of the healing arts; it bound the physician to put his professional duty to his patients first, and to resist temptation to exploit his unique position for personal ends. It protected the patient, the physician, and the profession." [53]

The American Bar Association drew up a code in 1908 which has been amended occasionally since then. Justice Robert Jackson believes the Bar Association's code has been moderately useful "particularly because the code is the basis of disciplinary proceedings, and is the basis of educational programs in the schools and colleges where young men are studying for the bar." [54]

Most of the codes of the recognized professions, however, are oriented toward problems of relations of the professional man and his private patient or client. They do not face up to the problems of the professional man and the government. The Bar Association's forty-seven canons of professional ethics, for example, do not even mention "administrative" practice, the representation of clients before executive departments and agencies, and administrative tribunals. If Washington attorneys had to make a living on the kinds of business that are covered by the canons, most of them would starve.

Various groups of public officials have adopted codes. Two of the best known are those of the International City Managers Association and the National Educational Association code for public-school teachers. They face the moral problems of their respective groups rather frankly. To the extent that such codes of public officials are kept up to date, kept in mind, and made the basis of disciplinary action, they can be a powerful force in maintaining high standards in the conduct of public affairs. This calls for leadership and some sense of public function within the professional group itself. Every group tends to have standards of some sort, and it has it within its power to set high standards.

"When a specific group with a socially useful function begins to wield great power, it stands at a moral crossroads. It must recognize its social or public function and accept its obligation to protect that function against the exploitive tendencies which power brings, or else its exploitive tendencies will tend to become predominant. There are many forms of exploitation, but in a commercial order, commercial forms of exploitation are naturally predominant. Probably the severest pressure on any professional group today is a temptation to commercialize its power. A code is essentially a measure to safeguard the integrity of the professional function." [55]

This is a challenge to all professional groups that have anything to do with public affairs. "The broad moral code, to which members of society owe allegiance, is not enough. Its principles must also be applied to the professional activities in anticipation of the issues and dilemmas which arise, so that professional obligations can be seen clearly and understood, free from the tensions and temptations which beset a busy professional life. Professional codes are a recognition that professional status brings with it the power to exploit its position—to use it for personal rather than professional ends." [56]

A Code of Official Conduct

Reform through voluntary codes, however, is a slow process. The Douglas Committee came to the conclusion that something more is needed right away in the national government. It said: [57]

> The Administrative Procedure Act should be amended to provide that the following practices shall be improper for federal officials and employees and shall be grounds for summary dismissal from the federal service:
>
> (a) Engaging in any personal business transaction or private arrangement for personal profit which accrues from or is based upon the official position, authority, or confidential information of the official or employee.
>
> (b) Accepting any valuable gift, favor, or service directly or indirectly from any person or organization with which the official or employee transacts business for the Government.
>
> (c) Discussing future employment outside the Government with a person or organization with which there is pending official business.
>
> (d) Divulging valuable commercial or economic information of a

confidential character to unauthorized persons or releasing such information in advance of its authorized release date.

(e) Becoming unduly involved, for example, through frequent luncheons, dinners, parties, or other expensive social engagements with persons outside the Government with whom they do official business.

The Administrative Procedure Act should be amended to prohibit federal officials who participate in the making of loans, granting of subsidies, negotiation of contracts, fixing of rates, or the issuance of valuable permits or certificates from acting in any official transaction or decision which chiefly concerns a person or organization by which they have been employed previously in the preceding two years or with which they have a valuable economic interest. Any violation of this prohibition should be grounds for summary dismissal.

The Administrative Procedure Act should be further amended:

(a) To provide that former federal officials and employees shall not appear before agencies in which they were formerly employed in cases which they previously handled or of which they had some direct knowledge as federal officials or employees and that they shall not participate in the preparation of such cases.

(b) To provide that for a period of two years following their termination, federal officials and employees of the ranks GS-15 and above who leave the Government shall not appear before the federal agencies in which they were formerly employed as the representative of a person or organization doing business with the Government.

The penalties of disbarment from practice before a federal agency and of cancellation of contract in appropriate cases should be authorized to discourage those who would corrupt as well as those who allow themselves to be corrupted. Publicity for findings of improper practices would serve as a further deterrent.

Counteracting the Influence Peddler

A number of steps have been suggested to deal with the problem of influence peddling. The Hoey Committee in 1950 recommended strengthening of official information services to get information to the businessman before he falls into the hands of the influence peddler, and commended steps being taken to do so through the Federal Supply Inquiry Office of the General

Services Administration, the Defense Department's Military Procurement Information Center, and the Commerce Department's procurement service in its field offices.[58] A spot check of the latter indicated that the service was good. The Committee also suggested a gray-listing of contractors known to have violated procurement laws or regulations (instead of blacklisting to bar them from doing business) to alert procurement officers to the hazards involved in dealing with these men. The Hoey Committee also counseled strengthening of investigating staffs and commended the revision of procurement regulations and contract clauses to require the full disclosure of all agents employed by the contractor. Finally, Senator Hoey and his associates challenged the necessity for so heavy reliance upon negotiated contracts (in preference to open competitive procedures) in a period of only partial mobilization.

Antibiotic Therapy

Like the antibiotic drugs that have checked some of the most troublesome infections and painful maladies in the human organism, there is available a remedy for some of the moral maladies in the body politic that would be like the antibiotics in its positive impact. This remedy is disclosure. All that is lacking is the courage to apply it. The Douglas Committee in reviewing the testimony taken reported that:[59]

> There was perhaps more general agreement upon this principle of disclosing full information to the public and upon its general effectiveness than upon any other proposal. It is hardly a sanction and certainly not a penalty. It avoids difficult decisions as to what may be right or wrong. In that sense it is not even diagnostic; yet there is confidence that it will be helpful in dealing with many questionable or improper practices. It would sharpen men's own judgments of right and wrong since they would be less likely to do wrong things if they knew these acts would be challenged.

The disclosure of income, assets, and transactions in the securities and commodity markets was proposed for all Members of the Congress and for higher administrative officials of the Government. . . . It was proposed that all Senators and Representatives in Congress, all administrative officials receiving a salary of $9,000 or $10,000 a year, and all federal judges should make such disclosures. To cover officials serving in important positions without compensation or with nominal compensation, the requirement of reporting might well extend to all officials in positions classified at GS-15 or equivalent ranks, regardless of salary actually received.

More recently it has been proposed by the President that disclosure also be required of high political-party officials. In view of the close contact of the parties with the Government and their influence upon its operations, this recognition of the public responsibility of such party officials seems wise, and the subcommittee had previously come to the same conclusion about the desirability of such a requirement.

Disclosure of this type would be helpful in dealing with conflict-of-interest problems. A Member of the Congress, for example, would not have to divest himself of any of his assets, but if they were of such a character as to influence his attitude toward particular industries or particular companies, the absence of concealment would free him from any charge of trying to put something over on the public, and would permit congressional colleagues and the public to judge better the weight of his arguments. Similarly a legislator could continue to receive any type of income he was willing to justify. If he doubted that he could justify it to the public, the requirement of disclosure would deter him.

For public administrators who, at certain levels, are more or less anonymous, the disclosure provision could help materially to guarantee their impartiality. Superior officers would be responsible for seeing that administrators were not economically involved in such a way as to jeopardize their impartiality. It has also been suggested that administrators of junior rank should be required to make similar disclosure to their superiors, so that conflicts of interest can be avoided. Disclosure is proposed also in some form for committee staff members and for witnesses testifying before committees. . . .

More complete disclosure is similarly proposed for registered lobbyists, legal representatives and other persons employed to influence administrative as well as legislative decisions. It is suggested that if the funds backing these activities are traced to their source, and if all payments by and to lobbyists are known, the public as well as responsible legislators and administrators will be able to make decisions with a better understanding of the situation. This plan would require administrative departments to maintain a register of lobbyists and of lobby finances for all lobbyists appearing before them.

There is some feeling that contingent fees for influencing legislation, particularly public bills, ought to be prohibited. But those who oppose the prohibition argue that contingent-fee arrangements should be disclosed—and in administrative matters as well.

It is also proposed to apply the disclosure principle to the problem of influence and pressure exerted upon administrative agencies for possible decisions. It is suggested that administrators be required to keep a docket for each case showing all contacts with all persons who sought to influence the decision, whether the contact occurred in regular channels or at a social gathering.

The Committee was not prepared to endorse all of the proposed uses of the disclosure principle without further study, but it did strongly recommend "that legislation should be enacted requiring all Members of Congress, all federal officials receiving a salary of $10,000 or more or who are in positions of grade GS-15 and above, or of equivalent rank, and the principal officials of national political parties to disclose their incomes, assets, and all dealings in securities and commodities." [60]

The Committee said,[61] "It is difficult to think of any good reason for not taking this action. It will help to protect the public interest, and will do so without moralizing. It may be an inconvenience, but it can do no real injury to public servants or political leaders, and it will protect from innuendo at the same time that it encourages self-examination of the propriety of one's income and assets. In our opinion this is a reasonable and moderate measure on which Congress should not hesitate to act at once."

Basic Hygiene

Public-health authorities have long taught that one of the best ways of avoiding sickness is to build up a strong constitution that will have the vitality to resist and throw off disease. This method of preventing moral failure is also fundamental in public administration. In the vernacular of public administration it goes by the name of "better management."

How can the federal government get better management? There is no mystery about it, and most of the basic steps are well known, but really good management cannot be improvised. It has to be developed over a period of time through a realistically rational organization of the government's work, through "a corps of administrators of the highest level of ability with an interest in the program of the Government as a whole,"[62] through a continuous revision of procedures, and through the growth of standards and professional ideals that put the public interest first in the thinking and the values of all officialdom. The Brownlow Committee pointed the way to better management in 1937, and that was also the Hoover Commission's theme in 1949. Governments either go forward or backward, and public administration has been moving toward better management. Public administration in local governments has been revolutionized in the past fifty years.[63] The State governments have also made notable progress in public administration, despite the stagnation in legislative institutions. There has also been great progress in the national administration since the middle twenties. But the progress has not been fast enough to keep pace with the pressures and the goal is not yet in sight.

The Hoover Commission said of the national government,[64] "The executive branch is not organized into a workable number of major departments and agencies which the President can effectively direct, but is cut up into a large number of agencies, which divide responsibility and which are too great in number for effective direction from the top. . . .

"The line of command and supervision from the President down through his department heads to every employee, and the line of responsibility from each employee of the executive branch up to the President, has been weakened, or actually broken, in many places and in many ways. . . .

"The President and the heads of departments lack the tools to frame programs and policies and to supervise their execution. . . .

"The federal government has not taken aggressive steps to build a corps of administrators of the highest level of ability with an interest in the program of the Government as a whole."

The Commission went on to point out general weakness in over-elaborate and over-rigid procedures, budgetary methods, and accounting; and it also recommended a number of specific and carefully considered improvements in the organization of the executive branch. President Truman got behind these proposals looking toward better management and supported them wholeheartedly, although his action did not in all cases agree exactly with that proposed by the Commission. Under the Reorganization Act of 1949 he has sent to Congress forty "reorganization plans." Twenty-nine have gone into effect, as provided by law with the concurrence of both House and Senate.[65] Either house by the adverse vote of a majority of its entire membership may block these reorganization plans. Eight plans have been so blocked, of which two were revisions of plans blocked earlier.

An important action in 1952 was the reorganization of the Bureau of Internal Revenue which became effective March 15th. The new plan abolishes the political positions of the sixty-four collectors and sets up a more rational field organization in twenty-five district offices, entirely under professional career administrators. Only the Commissioner of Internal Revenue will be a political appointee. In the successful Senate fight to approve this reorganization plan, led by Senators Hubert Humphrey, Mike Monroney, and Blair Moody, supporters of the reorganization brought out the fact that none of the seventeen collectors promoted from the career service had been found at fault, while eight of the remaining forty-seven had failed. Of the 57,000 civil-service employees, only 166 had recently been removed for moral failures.

A number of improvements have also been effected by statute in recent years. The 81st Congress and the first session of the 82nd Congress enacted forty-six laws more or less carrying out Hoover Commission recommendations. These included an act changing the National Military Establishment into the Department of Defense and strengthening the position of the Secretary of Defense, reorganization of the Department of State, and creation of a General Services Administration (consolidating many of the "housekeeping" activities of the government). The Citizens' Committee for the Hoover Report estimates that more than half of the Commission's objectives have been achieved. This is a notable and commendable record which will bear good fruit in time.

But realism compels the student of administration to note four facts.

First, the Hoover Commission did not cut deeply into the extravagantly dispersed organization of the executive branch. It merely recommended pruning conservatively here and there. If and when everything is done that the Commission proposed, the benefits will be notable; but it will still be impossible for the President to be in full control of the government as Chief Executive. The demands of subordinates upon him will still exceed his span of attention by 200 or 300 per cent. Much more forthright action is needed to solve this problem of high-level management. Reorganization is not enough; some fresh thinking on organizational problems is needed.

The second fact is that good management is not something that can be attained once and for all by even the most heroic effort. It is essentially a continuous as well as progressive process. Constant awareness of problems, an alert critical faculty, and consistent effort are needed to have good management in the "big democracy" of today.

A third fact must be accepted also. "Management" in public administration is not a matter of very general public interest. It seems too technical and too mundane to get very general attention. It is hard to develop popular interest in good management, even though it does largely determine what standards of morality as well as standards of efficiency will operate in the public service.

A fourth fact is that responsibility for better management falls most directly on political leaders. In the national administration it falls upon the President and his principal appointees and upon members of Congress; for Congressional support is needed to solidify "good management" in the law and practice of government. The bill to take 22,000 postmasters entirely out of politics and rationalize the operation of the postal system was left in committee, but the President moved vigorously to curtail patronage in Reorganization Plan No. 2 of April 10, 1952. Action to put the appointment of district attorneys and their staffs on a professional basis is quite remote. The quality of administration, at least the possibility of attaining a high level of administrative competence and integrity, depends most directly upon the political leaders of the country.

Honor and Prestige

Do political leaders and do members of the public want public administrators of high competence and integrity? If they do, why do they not honor administrators who distinguish themselves for these qualities? We do not pay the judge as well as the leading members of the bar are paid, but we honor him, and so does the bar. This is essential if the competence and integrity of the judiciary are to be maintained; and the necessity is so well accepted that we honor the judiciary as a whole despite the presence of some undistinguished members.

We do not pay public administrators as well as responsible executives in the business world. Nor can we, although too great a differential must be avoided. But unless the public and its political leaders honor public administrators—individuals for distinguished service, and the service as a whole for its essential role in modern life—it is ridiculous to expect that men of high competence and integrity will dedicate their lives to the public service. The public must choose. If it wants a reasonable proportion of its best men in public administration, it must be honest enough to recognize the public service as a high calling.

It is obvious that better management, administrative reform, and high standards of morality in public administration are not isolated phenomena. They are related to the politics of representation, and to the politics of parties and pressure groups which are discussed in the following chapter.

VII

PUBLIC, PARTY, AND PRESSURE POLITICS

Our consideration of questions of morality in American politics has run through problems of the several members of the cast of characters: the traditional big three, the legislative, executive, and judicial branches; the new members, administrators, the political parties, and the pressure groups. To do justice to the moral problems of party and pressure politics, however, we must come back to ourselves, the men and women who together constitute what Walter Lippmann long ago called the "phantom public." Each of us should start with himself in attempting to understand American politics of today.

If I am an average American man, four key words explain a great deal about the way I live. The words are specialization, organization, loyalty, and pressure.

Specialization

In making a living, the average man may say, I am a hard-working specialist. I know my own line and I know it well. Although I am a specialist, my specialization has a relatively broad foundation. If I am a professional man, my professional training was preceded by a liberal education. If a businessman, I probably completed college before going into business, and probably had a varied business experience before settling into my present groove. If I am a skilled laborer, I may have completed high school before going to work, and I have not been tied to one job, one company, or one city. If a farmer, I have almost certainly a secondary-school education and may have gone to the state college of agriculture. Yet although a specialist with a broad training I am by necessity a specialist, taking my job seriously, working very hard at it, and having very little time or energy left over for other things. My job is more than bread and butter. It is a competitive game, a way of living, and the pace is swift. Due allowances must be made of course for age (younger men have had greater educational opportunities than older men), and for difference between callings. But in general, it is true that American men of all classes are specialists concentrating heavily on their job.

Organization

Organization is the second key word in my life as a normal American man. I work not as an individual alone, but as a member of an organization—a law firm, a university, a business corporation, a labor union. Even as an avowed individualist in the American Medical Association (which is engaged in a very collective campaign to oppose "socialized medicine"), I make every effort to be on at least one hospital staff, a very complex organization, and I may be a member of at least an informal medical group. Even as a farmer, the traditional epitome of individualism, I am now a participant in organized agriculture, receiving conservation payments, covered by crop insurance, getting a government-guaranteed price for certain crops, being a member of Farm Bureau, Grange, or Farmers Union, and perhaps buying or selling through a co-op.

The American economy is dominated by organizations; I am almost certain to be a member of one and perhaps several. The organization in which I am directly a member is also a member of other and larger organizations. My local is a member of a union which probably belongs to A.F. of L. or C.I.O. My corporation probably belongs to a trade association, or several of them. Although the economic organizations are perhaps dominant, other aspects of my life are also highly organized; I participate in organized religious, social, political, and recreational activities. Part of my Americanism is my ability to fit into a team or group which has an end in view.

Loyalty

Loyalty is the third key word in American living. As a normal American I expect to give a very high order of loyalty to the organization to which I am most strongly committed—which is in most instances my vocational organization. If I am a union man, I stick to my union, come what may. If I am part of the "management" of a corporation, I give it a loyalty far beyond the call of duty. The giant corporate empires of America are as much the product of the devotion of dedicated men as of technology and finance capitalism. The middle-aged businessmen who end their earthly careers with heart attacks are not men who hold something back. They give everything they have to their job (and their organization). If the business seers of *Fortune* are to be credited, businessmen are also willing to pick their wives and make over their family life to please the corporation.[1] This is loyalty to the corporation for sure. What happens to the family is another question. *Fortune's* generalization, whether true or apocryphal, suggests the intense loyalty of men today to their organizations, primarily their economic or vocational organizations.

Pressure

The fourth key word in American life is pressure. This is a natural product of specialization, organization and intense loyalty. By concentrating their thinking and their energies on the activities of the organizations in which they work, by pushing aside competing interests and competing loyalties, Americans have created a society which, although it is known the world over for its productivity, might better be known for the pressures it generates. The pressures are enormous, and the breakage is high. Men work under pressure day after day and year after year. Ultimately the pressures are personal. They place enormous strain on physique, emotional stability, and character. Some men are destroyed by the pressures and all suffer some stress. The pressures also put a heavy load on institutions, particularly political institutions. Some, which have not been designed to carry such heavy loads in high voltage, have short-circuited. The consequent overload on other parts of the system puts them in danger also. Obviously the factors of load, design, and human capacity must be brought into line.

"Not a Politician"

As a normal American, one may say, there is another aspect of my attitudes and way of living which is not so easily expressed by a single word. It takes a sentence, and the sentence is "I am not a politician." How many times have you heard it? How many times have you said it? The idea is fixed in the minds of most of us, and it pops out frequently.

What does it mean? First of all, it means that we do not hold public office or become candidates for public office. Nor do we take an active part in persuading other men to be candidates and in helping them to get elected. Probably we do not even vote in the primaries, at least not very regularly, and we may be far from faithful in voting in even the most important general elections.[2] America leads the democracies of the world in non-voting. The sentence, "I am not a politician," also means that we have no considered political philosophy expressed in a coherent set of ideas or a positive program for the problems of the day. Finally, we do not have a positive responsible attitude toward public affairs at all. We have a sure and certain position on matters that affect our specialization, but beyond that segment, our political horizon is void. Positive responsibility for politics, for government, for public affairs generally we leave to the "ambiguous they"—the they of "They ought to pass a law," the they of "They ought not to allow it," the they of "They ought to know better," and the they of "They are all a bunch of politicians." As normal Americans, we protest, "I am not a politician!"

Are Leaders Different?

If specialization, loyalty, pressure, and an aversion for politics dominate the lives of average Americans, how about the men who are above average in qualities of leadership? How different are they? The answer is inescapable that they are not much different. The men who are leaders in their field and in their particular organizations also live lives dominated by specialization, organization, organizational loyalties, pressures, and aversion for politics. If there is any difference from the average man it is that these factors are more pronounced in their lives. They are the leaders in their special fields. They give life and vigor to their organizations. Their loyalties are more intense. And they are more emphatic in proclaiming that they are not politicians. The fact is that these men, the natural leaders, the established leaders, of American life generally do not become political leaders. Normally they do not stand for public office, and they do not help to choose and elect other men. There are of course exceptional men, and a few exceptions in the lives of otherwise normal men. The exceptions may even be increasing, but they are still deviations from the norm; they are not the norm.

For at least seventy-five years, the natural leaders of American life have usually been too busy with their business or professional duties to be publicly active in politics. They have not been willing to accept public, political responsibility for leadership in public affairs.

The leaders of American life are not uninterested in politics, but their interest is specialized. They look out for their special interests but avoid public responsibility for the interests of others. They keep out of party politics except when it is a phase of pressure politics. The latter is the natural outlet and, in a sense, the inevitable product of the specialized, organized, high-pressure life of present-day America. If the natural leaders of the country will not go into politics, but are zealous in attempting to protect or promote their particular interests, especially economic interests, through governmental action, some form of pressure politics is inevitable.

The shift from party politics to pressure politics is one phase of a general tendency to narrow or limit responsibilities and concentrate efforts. The corporation itself has served that purpose, limiting the risks and the personal incidence of losses. The universal use of contracts in business transactions similarly pins down the obligations to the narrowest possible point. Land, jobs, capital, raw materials, and salary are all covered by contracts in a legalistic maze that obviously would not work at all if it were not for the dedication of management to the corporate enterprise which breathes life into it. The device of narrowing responsibility is applied to government itself.

Suburbanism is an example. It is easier to build a Winnetka than to clean up Chicago and make it livable. It is simpler to move to Westchester than to make over New York. More generally it has been easier to set up an "independent" school board than to perfect local governments. The independent boards and commissions which still dot the governmental landscape are the ideal devices for pressure groups which are interested in their function. The leaders of American life have preferred the easier way, the simpler way, of pursuing limited, selected political objectives unencumbered by broad political responsibility.

This strong preference for the specialized approach and for strictly limited responsibility has been dominant but not complete. The exceptions are significant. Americans can always be drafted for public service in emergencies when the need of the community, the state, or the nation is so obvious that it cannot be ignored. The emergency of war is the clearest example, for then loyalty to the nation takes precedence over other loyalties. No other needs are quite so clear. Men of leadership can also be called upon for civic services. They will organize the community-chest campaigns, put over the philanthropic appeals, support the opera, and manage the museum. This willingness to be called for duty in civic enterprises seems to be increasing and suggests that the aversion for public affairs may not be unassailable or unchangeable. This is confirmed also by the occasional participation of leaders from the normal groups in reform campaigns to push over a corrupt local machine and to clean up after it.

Party Politics

Party politics in many places, particularly the cities, has been left in the hands of atypical men. If the normal leaders of American life will not accept broad political responsibility, it must obviously fall upon someone else. This is what has happened. For many years urban party organizations have been run by the least typical Americans of their generation. Immigration solved the problem for a time. First- and second-generation Americans manned the political machines of American cities, and judged by the standard of maintaining the machines' vitality, they ran them rather well. This source of political talent is approaching extinction, and the thin trickle of D.P.'s will not be sufficient to restore it.

If the new representative Americans do not staff political organizations, who will carry on? It could be men who are below standard in education, income, and business success. Or it could be men of such independence of mind and personality that they ignore the normal patterns of behavior and go into politics because of its intrinsic importance. Men of such independence, however, are not numerous, nor are they often good organizers who take naturally to group life. The chances are that until the stereotyped aversion for politics changes, responsibility for organization politics will usually go by default to men from whom one could least expect distinguished leadership in the public interest.

Political Organizations

The stable political organizations of American politics are the local organizations, the city and county "machines." State political organizations are usually weak. The dominant leadership of some city or county boss may at times give stability and apparent strength to the state organization, but this is never permanent, and usually the state organization is no more than a loose federation of county organizations. National party organization is weakest of all. The national-party committees are in effect no more than interim agencies to give the appearance of continuity to the organizations which are established quadrennially to run the Presidential campaigns.

Local political organizations are essentially commercial in motivation. They tend to be manned by people who make a living or a partial living out of politics. Characteristically they are not voluntary organizations of dedicated men and women who want to do something for the public interest. The men who run the local political organizations, however, do have a point of view which is public in character, as compared with that of a pressure group or special interest. They have some sense of responsibility for the whole public, perhaps as much as they can reconcile with the commercial success of their organization. Commercial necessity forces some "loading" for overhead to be added to the direct cost of government. This seems to be inevitable as long as volunteers are not available for the day-to-day work of political organizations.

The indirect costs of commercialization are probably much greater than the overhead loading. It can be more expensive to put important business in the hands of an appointee who is only partially competent, or faithful, or honest, than to put such matters in the hands of a fully qualified person and to subsidize political organizations directly. Incompetence can lead to such catastrophes as the failure of a bridge, the spreading of epidemic or endemic disease, the growth of narcotics addiction, playground accidents and fatalities, and the "blighting" of urban areas.

More important than the administrative cost of incompetence, commercialization of politics tends to create a very insecure base for defending the public interest. Local political organizations which cannot count on volunteer workers are inherently vulnerable to groups which have something to offer in exchange for something they want.

Gambling is a good example. To a conscientious political broker who has some respect for the public interest, it must seem relatively harmless to the public to take protection money from professional gamblers who give the public what a substantial portion of it wants. Since the money comes out of the pockets of those who want to throw it away, anyhow, what is the harm? Being paid not to enforce laws which a large number of people do not want enforced and about which the rest are apathetic must seem to the professional machine politician an innocent graft. Once the commercial principle is introduced in politics, however, it is difficult to stop. A mind which cannot see the cost to the public of commercialized gambling usually fails to see the harm in selling public-utility franchises, health standards, safety standards, educational standards, tariff duties, tax concessions, loans, and the public domain. If they are sold one at a time and in small quantities, there are ways of rationalizing the process so that it does not seem too bad. It is hard to keep "honest graft" within bounds.

How Strong Are the Machines?

If the local machines, which tend to be expensive at best and grossly venal at their worst, are not so constituted as to be reliable defenders of the public interest, how strong are they and what can be done about them? The answer is the same when derived logically and historically. They rule by default of leaders from the main stream of American life. They have never been able to stand up very long against a sustained attack from well-led amateur politicians. The ability of reform movements to overthrow city "bosses" is well established. Most of the famous machines have been upset at least once and some of them many times. Tammany, the most famous of all, has gone down to defeat repeatedly. The winning power of amateur politicians is not in doubt—just their staying power. The lack of staying power brings us back again to the aversion for political responsibility of the normal leaders of American life; for an amateur who is willing to stay in organization politics becomes a professional, a new kind of professional, but, nevertheless, a professional.

Both technology and changes in public policy have weakened the position of the old-fashioned local machine. An army of doorbell ringers and ward workers is not so indispensable when the candidate himself comes into everyone's home via the radio or television. At least the organization need not be so large. With adequate publicity a strong candidate can make an effective appeal to the public through the daily press, periodicals, the radio, television, and by direct mail.

The issues of politics also have more appeal to a much larger number of people than they once did. National-defense measures and foreign policies are obviously important in a period when it is no longer possible to rely for protection on any kind of isolation—geographic, economic, or cultural. The problems of unemployment and inflation, as is now accepted, are entangled in many aspects of public policy. The Christmas basket of groceries and load of coal from the ward boss had their place, but they cannot compete with an orderly public-assistance program, social-security benefits for particularly needy groups, such as dependent children, and social insurance. The farmer who regularly cashes soil-conservation checks and gets a loan on his crop at 90 per cent of the "parity" price does not have to be told that he should take an interest in politics. Few in the ranks of organized labor are so unthinking as to be unaware of the change that has taken place in the union movement under the aegis of federal legislation. As long as wage disputes in railway, coal mining, and steel industries go to the White House for settlement, the interest of both management and labor in national politics is not an abstraction.

Party organizations are still important, and will always be important in politics. But the trend of events is against the old-fashioned type of local machine. Permanent organizations can be smaller than they once were, and it is easier for the part-time volunteer to play an effective role. The potential strength of the rational appeal is greater, and can be exploited in press, radio, and television discussions.

Pressure Politics

In the political processes of agitation, discussion, and persuasion, pressure groups, not party organizations, dominate the scene. This has become a truism of American political life. At election time particular groups put pressure on the parties; and the campaign manager and platform draftsmen in turn cultivate special-interest groups. The groups may be dilatory in supporting candidates, but they are certain to be vigorous

n opposing candidates who have affronted them. Between elec-
ions the activity and influence of pressure groups are still
greater. When, for example, a new Congress convenes, or a
new President takes office, the campaign organizations melt
away, and the residual party committees and bosses take their
place in the array of organized groups that look over the shoulder
and try to guide the hand of the man in the office. Although perhaps a little broader in outlook than the special interests, the
ocal party machines are in many ways like them.

To the man charged with authority, legislative or admin-
strative, the political world is a sea of special interests: individuals and corporations who want something for themselves;
organized industries such as steel, textiles, petroleum, electric
utilities, processed foods, brewers and distillers, dairy products,
etc., which are powerful and strongly organized segments of
the economy; economic associations which include more than
a single industry, for example the National Association of Manufacturers and the Chamber of Commerce; labor unions, indi-
vidually and in federated form; professional associations, for
example, the American Medical Association, the American Bar
Association, the National Education Association; veterans' organizations; and "masked" organizations such as the Committee for Constitutional Government, the National Economic
Council, and the Foundation for Economic Education, which
have fancy titles, frequently patriotic in tone, but which usually have some very particular axe to grind. Most of these organizations are concerned with public policy or specific governmental decisions in economic matters. But there are at least
a few which are not, for example, the Anti-Vivisection Society,
the National Catholic Welfare Conference, the National Committee for Mental Hygiene, the National Congress of Parents
and Teachers, the National Council of Jewish Women, the

YWCA, and the League of Women Voters. But the proposals of even the non-economic groups very often have economic consequences for the government.

There are literally hundreds, perhaps thousands, of organizations active in American politics. The (Buchanan) House Select Committee on Lobbying Activities in 1950 listed almost a thousand organizations that had registered or filed financial reports under the Federal Lobbying Act in the period January 1, 1950, through October 20, 1950, and its list cannot be presumed to be complete. In the years 1946-1950, more than 2000 individuals also registered as lobbyists, but these were only the front men. Many of them had strong organizations and staffs behind them. These lists suggest the volume of pressure-group activity to influence federal legislation, but they do not cover administrative lobbying or lobbying of either variety in state capitols and city halls.

The expenditures regularly reported by registered lobbies to influence federal legislation are only a fraction of the total financial outlay for pressure politics. In 1949 and 1950 they were at the rate of more than $10,000,000 a year. The Buchanan Committee came to the conclusion, however, that lobbying "in all its ramifications" is a billion-dollar business. The multi-purpose organizations which have lobbying as only one of their functions secure funds by dues and assessments upon their members. The "masked" organizations which operate as "foundations" or "educational" committees rely chiefly on contributions and get most of their money from relatively small numbers of generous donors. The largest sums come directly or indirectly from the business world and are credited as a business expense (before taxes) or as tax deductions.[3]

Although lobbying gets its name from the time-honored practice of buttonholing legislators in the lobbies of legislative halls this is now only one phase of lobbying. Although it is still an important activity, the means of contact have been greatly enlarged. Letters, telephone calls and telegrams supplement the professional lobbyist's work, and the pressure group may bring in large delegations to see the public official or rely upon selected third parties who are in a position to have particular influence with a member of Congress. The National Association of Real Estate Boards, for example, has selected "contacts," totaling more than six hundred, among whom appropriate persons can be found to put pressure upon any influential member of Congress. "The expectation is . . . that the 'contact's' political, business, or personal acquaintance with the Member of Congress . . . will enable him to make a decisive impression on the member's thinking." [4]

Pressure groups offer legislators an array of services: collecting data and research of a sort, drafting bills, writing speeches, "arranging remunerative speaking or writing engagements," even helping new Congressmen to find a place to live in Washington.[5] The social lobby is also still very much alive. Parties and dinners have a place in pressure politics.

"Lobbying at the grass roots" is an equally important phase of pressure politics. This is the systematic and concerted effort to mold public opinion in such a way that it will be generally favorable, or unfavorable, to a broad program, a general policy, or an entire category of political actions. This may be done through widespread distribution of books and pamphlets, getting prepared stories or editorials into the press through particular papers or news services, inducing colleges to offer certain courses of study, and regular distribution of printed materials.[6] An organization such as the National Association of Real Estate Boards, which can rely on co-operation of local real-estate boards, is particularly effective in work at the grass roots.

The volume of activity is impressive. One organization alone, for example, the Committee for Constitutional Government, between 1937 and 1944, sent out "eighty-two million pieces of literature" including 760,000 books, "more than 10,000 transcriptions carrying fifteen-minute radio talks . . . three hundred and fifty thousand telegrams . . . many thousands of releases to daily and weekly newspapers" and "full-page advertisements." [7] "Institutional advertising" which blossomed during World War II has continued to be a phase of present-day pressure politics. Magazine readers are now accustomed to full-page ads with impressive art work editorializing as to the merits of free enterprise, and paid for with the corporate funds of perhaps a licensed industrial monopoly—funds which otherwise could be distributed to stockholders, passed on to the consumer in reduced rates, or collected in taxes by the government. There are no reliable figures as to the total cost of this part of pressure politics. But the expenditures for this purpose which may be observed in periodicals issued during a single week are not small.

The world of pressure groups has taken on some of the complexities of corporate business. Organizations have subsidiaries and affiliates. There are combinations, interlocking directorates, and joint programs. In some areas also there is concentration of control in the hands of a few large donors. At one extreme are financially strong organizations like the American Medical Association, which spent more than $1,500,000 in a single year.[8] At the other are men with a letterhead and a paper organization. In all pressure groups the organization's officers, secretariat or bureaucracy have a great influence, and it has frequently been demonstrated that they do not accurately reflect the views of all their members. The defects in representativeness and responsibility which beset government itself are in fact much more acute within the world of pressure groups.

In the flood of pressures which swirl about public officials a number of characteristics of pressure groups are apparent, but one is paramount. Pressure groups are diligent in watching the course of legislation and administrative decisions; they are versatile, persistent, and skillful in influencing both legislators and administrators; but most of all they are zealously single-minded in almost exclusive concentration upon their own special interests. By and large they are not concerned with anything else and accept no responsibility for adjusting their own driving purposes to the purposes of others or for fitting them into the overriding general welfare.

This narrowness and intensity of purpose is to be expected. As has been noted in Chapter 2, Americans subconsciously cling to the notion that the economy in the abstract is an automatic system which manages itself regardless of what individual men may do. They also have confidence, despite their traditional anti-government grousing, that the system of representative government has inherent, automatic qualities of mechanical stability, no matter what individual citizens may do to influence governmental decisions. These illusions are still sufficiently strong in an America of big business, big labor, and big agriculture that the generality of leaders in nearly all walks of life can and do dedicate themselves unrestrainedly to the pursuit of their own particular interests, without taking much thought of what the effect will be for the public as a whole.

Public Officials on the Spot

According to the doctrines by which we live, the unvoiced assumptions, and the prevailing attitudes, the only men in all American life who are supposed to have any moral obligation to consider the public interest are public officials, elected or appointed, and elected representatives. Elected executives and legislators are directly or indirectly responsible for the appointed officials, and such independence as they all may have to act in the public interest and to make decisions on the merits of the case is directly related to the system by which men are nominated and elected to office. The source of moral security or insecurity is in electoral politics. Some examination of the electoral processes is necessary to an understanding of the moral problems of the elected representative and the elected public official.

Campaign Obligations

By an evolutionary process a system of nominations and elections has been developed in most states which keeps the door of opportunity open. Experience with the caucus, the legislative caucus, the mixed caucus, and conventions led to the deliberate creation of the primary-election system which now prevails for nominating candidates to local and state offices in all but four states.[9] (Connecticut and Rhode Island still use the convention system generally, and New York and Indiana use it for state officers.)

The evolutionary process in nominating candidates for President is not so far along. The national nominating convention is an extra-legal institution, admittedly not satisfactory, yet neither perfected nor replaced. In its present form it has continued without much change for thirty years. Delegates are chosen in a variety of ways—by primary election (fifteen states), by state or district conventions (twenty-nine states), and by party committees (four states).[10] The choice may or may not be regulated by state law. It is not regulated by act of Congress. Roughly 40 per cent of convention delegates are chosen in primary elections. They must be pledged in four states, may be pledged in five states, cannot be pledged in three states, and are bound by the presidential preference primary in two states. Six other states also have a presidential preference primary which is advisory to the delegates; and one of these, Maryland, is a state which chooses its delegates by convention. The situation is confusing to the public in general and to some delegates in particular. It is possible to have a delegate pledged to one candidate and advised by the preferential vote to support another. Some further evolution in the process of nominating presidential candidates is to be expected, but perhaps not until one or more of the national conventions affronts the public with its choice.

The great virtue of the direct-primary system is that it keeps the door open to competition. It is an achievement of the progressive movement in the years prior to the First World War, and was a deliberate and successful effort to break the monopoly grip of party bosses and organizations on the nominating process. It was a reaction to the abuse of power in specific situations where men with wide public support were in one way or another denied the party nomination. There were enough instances of corrupt conventions, and more than enough of perfunctory machine-run conventions to arouse popular indignation, which progressive political leaders were able to capitalize in reform legislation—the direct primary system. In the reaction of the nineteen-twenties direct primaries were attacked, but unsuccessfully, except in New York and Indiana.

It is relatively simple to run for office. A candidate gets his name on the ballot by petition or by merely filing and paying a fee or deposit. If you as a reader of these lines are not familiar with requirements as to registration, filing dates, and other details, it is because you have never considered running for office and have never seriously considered putting up someone else as a candidate. There is no mystery about it.

For a person who is well known, well liked, and respected in his community, the direct primary system is ideal. If he obeys the Scriptural injunction to seek the lower honors before the higher, he is certain to make a respectable showing, and perhaps to win the nomination on his first try. If he wins the nomination, he will have the more or less active support of his party organization in the ensuing campaign. Being the official candidate of his party brings with it a certain amount of publicity, and it is entirely possible for him to make an effective appeal to the public for support in the election. If he wins the election, his public position will keep him before the public, and he will have many means of keeping in touch with the public. His actions are news; he is in demand as a speaker, and both individuals and organized groups seek him out to ask assistance or favors. A first candidacy, particularly if it is successful, makes a second one easier. Success in representing a small constituency also is the best preparation for representing a larger one. It is not difficult for the person who is well known, well liked, and respected in his community to go into politics and make good.

The joker is that by and large the men who have these natural qualifications for representing their fellows do not go into politics. They leave it to someone else. Although the most careful students of the party system agree that it is now possible to challenge the machine in running for office, they also agree that the machine is not often challenged. Many of the complaints about the difficulties of running for office come from nobodies who lack the natural qualifications, or from men who try to start too high on the scale of political responsibility. Of course they have difficulty. Of course they need strong organization support to get anywhere. Of course they need money for extensive publicity. A candidate with no previous experience as a public servant or with no natural appeal to the public will have to be carried by the organization, and his public personality will have to be created by publicity.

The man with natural qualifications for leadership has none of these handicaps. If he is a leader in his business, profession or vocation he is used to responsibility, and he is familiar with the process of getting his ideas over to a group and of winning their support. If he has participated in civic affairs, he has broadened his horizon of responsibility and has widened his circle of friends. If this sort of person is interested in having good men in public office, he can usually persuade them to run and help them get the nomination. He can also get others to help, and can organize their efforts in the pre-primary and primary campaign. If he himself is willing to run, others will be willing to help him. He will not have great difficulty in getting volunteer workers and in building up a campaign organization. It is relatively easy if men start soon enough and at a modest point in the hierarchy of offices. The Henry Fords and Wendell Willkies who start and end their political careers in our desperate campaign for the United States Senate or the Presidency merely emphasize the fact that one does not begin any career at the top, even a career in public life.

The door is open for men with qualities of leadership to go into politics. But success is not automatic. There are difficulties, and they must be faced. Almost nothing can be done alone in this world. A candidate must have some help, organized help; and he will need money for campaign expenses. Where can he get personal and financial assistance? Clearly, the stronger the candidate, the easier it is for him to get volunteer help. He can build his own organization. A strong candidate is also more likely to attract financial support than a weak one. But if he is a strong candidate because he is already a public figure with a known position on issues, he may also encounter strong opposition. Then a good organization and adequate financial support are necessary. This will be particularly true if he is a progressive in politics, who favors changes in the *status quo*, particularly changes affecting the business world. Most independent candidates, who are not merely the obedient pawns of a local party machine, feel very acutely the problem of organizing and financing their electoral campaigns.

Since many of the men who could run for office most easily refuse to do so, it follows that the less well qualified (in experience, reputation, and recognition) who do run will find the difficulties still greater. How can the ordinary candidate meet them? How can he meet them and still keep sufficient independence of thought and decision to be able to decide issues that come to him in his official life on their merits?

Consider the problem of the average candidate. Shall he go to the party organization and ask for their support? If he does, it is with the understanding that he will be faithful—a voice that speaks, not the brain that decides. Should he seek support of business groups, or farm groups, or organized labor? Will not each group expect something in return—something that will limit his freedom of action? Should he accept support generously proffered him by men who represent organized gambling and vice? Some say this group attaches fewer strings than do others. There is no special-interest group that he can go to, not even the party organization, that will not demand something in exchange for its support. Can he afford to accept this support? And can he get nominated or elected if he doesn't? That is the dilemma.

The only alternative is to appeal to his friends and to the general public. Perhaps candidates are too reluctant to do this. Possibly the public is ready to respond to direct appeals for personal and financial assistance. There is some indication that this is true, and that more ordinary people would pitch in and help to nominate and elect a good candidate if he would ask them. But the tradition is against it, and will not be quickly changed. The law is also against it; campaign contributions are not tax deductible. In making out his income-tax return one can deduct contributions to the church, the Red Cross, the Tuberculosis Society, the March of Dimes, the Heart Fund, and the Cancer Fund, and to "masked" lobbies, but not a nickel to nominate and elect a good man to office. The law does not permit a citizen to be philanthropic in his approach to politics even if he wants to be. He must make an investment; he can't make a donation—and get credit for it.

Campaign costs are increasing. Radio and television time is expensive, and the rates are raised at election time! Other forms of advertising or of appealing to the public are also expensive. In the nineteen-twenties the higher campaign expenditures were attributed to the direct primary by its critics. But campaign costs have gone up since then, as the electorate has grown and as the commercial radio and television industries have established themselves. Some recently successful candidates think that costs have increased four or five times since the twenties.[11] But the official records of campaign finances are notoriously incomplete, and all estimates are highly speculative. Men who have been long in politics and who have won a place as public figures can get public support without elaborate and expensive campaigns. This is in part because they sometimes run almost unopposed. When strong opposition develops they also have to fight, and to spend money to do it effectively.

After considering a candidate's difficulties in financing his campaign, the Douglas Committee observed that it was "No wonder [that] the old system of finding a financial 'angel' and then of sending him on a flight to the embassy in Graustark has its attractions, even from an ethical point of view." In a day when the conduct of foreign relations seemed unimportant, this logic was compelling, although it sounds dated in 1952.

Campaign Ethics

The ethical problems of a candidate are not over when he gets the nomination. A number of questions confront him. Consider, for example, the situation of a candidate for Congress. On what basis shall he appeal for support? There is no recognized party program which has been threshed out in the halls of Congress that he can advocate and explain to the voter. The platforms improvised at party conventions are so obviously intended to please everybody without offending anybody that they are very little help even if interpreted literally; and they have been so consistently ignored that it is difficult to take them seriously. The candidate thus lacks a body of principles or a set of coherent proposals with which he could make a positive and rational appeal to the voter on important issues of policy. If he wants to discuss issues on their merits, he will find that he has to make bricks without straw. A genius can do it, but it is difficult for an ordinary candidate.

It is much easier to wage a negative campaign by picking out the mistakes of the administration if one's own party is out of power, and arousing fears about the malevolent and incompetent opposition if it is in. Republican candidates can exploit failures of the Democratic administration, and it is always possible to argue that achievements should have been much greater, even when they have been very substantial. Democratic candidates can warn that a Republican victory would end business prosperity and bring dire consequences to farmers and to labor. This is a telling argument; the Republicans also used it for years; but it backfired most unpleasantly in Mr. Hoover's administration. He who claims credit for prosperity must also accept responsibility for depression.

When campaign tactics are negative it is easy to get into personalities. This is the tendency—deplored but prevalent. No man is perfect and few are so discreet as to keep their sins entirely to themselves. When skillfully brought to public attention in a variety of ways—rumors, a whispering campaign, suggestive comments or bold allegation—they get some attention. Even a paragon of virtue can be lampooned, insulted, and vilified. The charges themselves are interesting even if unsupported, and the election will be over before they can be answered effectively. At election time the ordinary restraints which men exercise to avoid slander and libel are thrown to the winds. The tradition is that men do not sue to recover damages for campaign insults; they merely reply in kind. It is difficult not to. If his opponent shouts enough insults, it is hard for even the most conscientious candidate to preserve his restraint.

"Mudslinging" was the old-fashioned term for tossing insults. But techniques have advanced and now we have the improved "smear," a more deadly device. Of all the smears, the quickest and most effective in 1952 is to call a man a "communist." It carries the taint of traitor without the necessity of proving treason, espionage, or sedition. The fact that there are communists in the United States and that the Soviet government uses them for espionage lends just enough color to the danger of espionage to make the charge of "communism" a potent one in this period of much publicized international tension. To the extent that the public accepts guilt by association it is possible to smear a great many people. To the extent that men are considered communists who have not disagreed with or opposed everything the communists have proposed, the circle of potential victims grows still wider.

The present furore over loyalty, "disloyalty," and "communism" in American life is essentially a domestic political phenomenon. It is the mid-twentieth century variant of old-fashioned mudslinging, and it should be so recognized. There is a problem of espionage, but it is a separate matter with which public "disloyalty" charges have little connection. Espionage is a problem for the FBI and the counter-espionage forces of the government. Public charges and committee publicity of the Dies Committee type add nothing to what these responsible agencies know about communist infiltration. It is clear that Soviet efforts to place men in the government, in labor unions, and in many other walks of life have not been entirely unsuccessful. But there is no evidence at all that the smear by individuals or committees has helped to prevent espionage. If the testimony of distinguished counter-espionage agents is to be accepted, the activities of political red hunters may have actually hampered the counter-espionage program.[12] Wholesale charges of communism or disloyalty by individuals or committees are not an effort to catch traitors. They are an attempt to make political capital by slandering an opponent, an opposing party-faction, or an opposing party.

If a useful function of the Committee on Un-American activities has been to alert the public to the problem of espionage, the question at once arises: Why did the Committee at so many periods in its history use smear tactics? Would not careful, painstaking investigation followed by well-considered and precise reports have been more convincing to the public? It is difficult to answer this question. Due care and objectivity in investigating and reporting would avoid creating doubts as to the Committee's reliability, and would avoid injuring innocent men and women. In the long run, such work would be more enlightening and persuasive to thoughtful people. But perhaps the taste of a large segment of the public is such that it enjoys what traditional standards permit—mudslinging and the smear. Mudslinging is a reflection upon both the slinger and the public, and its prevalence reminds us that even in a well-educated and humane people there are counter-currents of irrational feeling.

Under these circumstances, what are the moral obligations of a man in public life? Is he justified in using the smear because he is sure of a considerable audience? Is it right to get publicity for himself by vilifying others? It is possible to appeal to man's worst nature as well as his best.

The danger of dissipating the strength of the rational and humane tradition in democratic politics is so clear that it is not unreasonable to expect a well-qualified candidate for public office to be faithful to the truth in all public discussions, including his own campaign for election. Men who have really distinguished themselves as public servants have usually done so. Political foes as well as friends respect the Norrises, the La Follettes, the Aikens, and the Douglases even though they are at times misguided or misinformed. The best men in public life are expected to adhere to a high standard of veracity and they do so.

But what about the ordinary men who lack distinction of any

kind, the men who lack the qualities to be real leaders, the mediocrities? What basis have they for appealing to the public? As we have noted, they have no firm party platform on which to stand. Their own record is no asset to them. All they have is ambition. Will they not almost certainly turn to mudslinging and vilification? This is their only hope, and all except the morally strong will resort to it if the public permits them to do so. There is no escape from the conclusion of the Douglas Committee that "People have an obligation not to be 'suckers.' " [13] The public must discriminate; it must be skeptical; it must insist on evidence; it must by its own rationality force all candidates for public office to discuss issues on their merits.

Persistent mudslinging by a candidate is at least *prima facie* evidence that he thinks he has nothing positive to offer the public in his own life and record. He resorts to the smear presumably because he has no better course open. In a period in which a new word has been coined, "McCarthyism," one may speculate on the place of Senator McCarthy in history. Will he be remembered as a citizen and taxpayer? Probably not, although his fiscal obligations to his state have received some attention. Will he be remembered as a pamphleteer? That seems unlikely, although that capacity has also received publicity. Will he be remembered as a military figure? Apparently not. Will he be remembered for distinguished professional service at the bar of justice? On the basis of the official and public records to date, that, too, seems improbable. The probability is that he will be remembered as the outstanding mudslinger of the mid-twentieth century, a man who shrewdly exploited the much publicized international tension to advance his political fortunes by smearing other men in public life—men both great and small, ranging from a fine military leader of unquestioned integrity and selfless devotion, to obscure civil servants whom the public never heard of before.

Who is most responsible for McCarthyism—the junior Senator from Wisconsin or a gullible public? "The person who swallows a plausible falsehood without at least pondering over it is almost as much at fault as the person who perpetrates the falsehood." [14]

The low plane of campaign ethics is in part responsible for the low prestige of politics as a profession. It is thus a deterrent to entering politics, and in turn feeds back to lower political ethics still farther. Campaign mendacity, if unchecked, sets in motion a downward spiral.

The renowned authority on public opinion, George Gallup, argues that the effectiveness of mudslinging and vilification as a campaign strategy is greatly exaggerated, and that candidates commonly underestimate the horse sense of the public. He says, "I do not claim that acting as a gentleman will elect a candidate, but I do firmly believe that such behavior will not lose him any votes and almost always will win him votes." [15] True or not, the public has no chance to prove it unless at least one of the candidates in a campaign puts it to the test. An often overlooked requisite for democratic self-government is faith in people and their rational capacity by candidates for public office. Democracy cannot be made to function by leaders who have no confidence in the public.

The Senate Subcommittee on Ethical Standards in Government faced this problem squarely and came to the conclusion that, "The present period is, in one sense, a test of faith in the capacity of mankind for self-government. Distress over intemperate, reckless, and irresponsible statements or over emotionalism and appeals to prejudice should not become an anxiety complex. The tendency to exploit fear and prejudice is not new in politics. The corrective for an emotional appeal to the worst in men is both an appeal to deeper emotional values, and a skillful and persistent challenge to man's highest powers of reason and judgment. . . . Public discussion is in itself both a crucial test and an evidence of that faith. This is a time for men who believe in the power of truth and reason to stand to their guns and keep firing." [16]

Day-to-Day Dilemmas

Winning an election brings with it a new set of moral hazards. At first, with a mandate from the people, the newly elected representative seems to be the master of his soul and captain of his fate, that is, if he has been able to avoid too many commitments during the primary and election campaigns. But as time passes, the day-to-day challenges to his integrity make themselves felt. Basically his obligation is to decide all issues on their merit in the public interest; and his problem is to retain his public values and his public point of view in a legislative world where the general public is inarticulate and where all the organized special publics speak emphatically.

Again the absence of a legislative program developed by representative and responsible leadership in the legislative body is a great handicap to him in safeguarding his faithfulness to the public interest. Neither the majority nor the minority prepares such a program in any publicly responsible, rational way. In the states the Governor's program, and in Congress the President's program, is the legislator's only point of departure in attempting to define a public position for himself on legislation. Since the bills which the administration sponsors are quickly scattered among the many legislative committees, the individual state legislator or member of Congress has no contact with any of them except those which are assigned to his own committee or committees, unless and until they are reported back to the legislative chamber.

In the meantime as has been noted in Chapters 2 and 3, the legislator devotes himself to running errands for his constituents. That is, he finds himself increasingly active as an administrative lobbyist, and discovers that he is only a part-time legislator.

Members of Congress have an added difficulty in maintaining their integrity and independence of judgment, growing out of the onerous nature of their task and the financial burdens that are involved. Membership in a city council is a part-time job and need not take a member away from his occupation or his home. State legislatures also meet for relatively short periods, or for a few days at a time over a longer period. Half of the state constitutions limit the length of session (the limits vary from thirty-six to ninety days) and all but six of the state legislatures meet only every other year, unless called in special session. Being a state legislator is everywhere a part-time job that does not involve serious personal or financial sacrifice. Members of Congress always found their duties much more burdensome, but in the old days (before 1933) Congress had one long session and one short session. It convened in December and adjourned in June for the long session, and then it expired after the December-March short session. The regular sessions required attendance in Washington for only nine or ten months in a two-year period. Those days are past. Congress now convenes on the first week in January each year and continues in session through the summer and well into the fall months.[17] In times of war or other crisis, Congress is in almost continuous session. A member must be in Washington at least seven-eighths of the time during his term. This takes him out of his normal business or professional life and either separates him from his family or requires him to establish a second residence in Washington. For all members, except those who are independently wealthy, service in Congress brings with it financial problems which create moral hazards.

The salary and expense allowance, totaling $15,000, and the funds for office expenses and travel do not cover expenses. The few members who live on their official incomes tend to be older men, whose families are grown, and who come from safe districts. The expenses of other members run beyond their official income, typically by more than $3,000; and about a third of the Representatives and a number of Senators are in debt.[18] Members with heavy personal expenses for education or family medical bills, Senators from populous states who have a very heavy correspondence, and members who face a stiff primary or election fight find their expenses running still further ahead of their official income.

Members obviously have to balance their budgets in some way. Where does the money come from? Private wealth is one source, and the number of rich men in Congress is reported to be increasing. This has its disadvantages. The public can hardly afford to depend upon rich men exclusively to represent it, and the millionaire may find it difficult to keep his mind on the public interest rather than on his investments when he is making decisions on public policy. If there is a drift back to making the Senate a "rich man's club" it should give alarm to all, including the rich. On this point no one has reliable information. Incomes are not disclosed and tax returns are confidential. Members of Congress have shown no enthusiasm at all for any abandonment of their financial privacy.

A second source, and the most general one, is a business or profession in which the member of Congress continues to take a more or less active part. Since two-thirds of the Senate and one-half of the House are lawyers, it is natural for them to have a law practice. They may even find that it flourishes mightily after the election results are announced. The new business and the lawyer's new status as a representative of the public, however, raise some ethical problems for him. If he is in fact fully occupied in Washington, how much can he draw from his law firm for leaving his name on the door? Which clients come to the firm for legal services and which because a member of the firm is in Congress? If the firm becomes heavily involved in work for particular business concerns or particular industries, can the member retain his objectivity in deciding legislative questions which affect them? And can he avoid becoming an indirectly paid administrative lobbyist for that business or industry? The latter goes beyond impropriety and verges on illegality. It is against the law for a member of Congress to take a fee for representing a client before a federal agency. Is it any better for a firm in which he has an interest to do so? This sort of practice by law firms which have members in Congress is quite general.[19]

Businessmen, farmers, and journalists find it more difficult to keep their business going while serving in Congress. An insurance agency is perhaps an exception. It does not require the owner's constant personal attention; public office has an advertising value; and business may actually pick up while the agency head is away. A conscientious member of Congress, however, must make sure that he is not being paid for his influence when his agency begins to write new and large policies; and like every other member who is a businessman, he must also make sure that his objectivity is not impeached by his particular business involvement.

Doctors, journalists, teachers and other professional men find that service in Congress cuts them off from their calling. How are they to balance the family budget? There are various sources, although none is so easily lucrative as a law practice. Fees for writing articles, lecturing, and public speeches are old standbys. Nowadays a well-known member may also get fees for radio and television appearances. These fees for *bona-fide* services performed involve no particular moral hazard unless the fees are out of proportion to the service and unless they come from one or a few sources which have an interest in legislative or administrative decisions. When an active lobby begins in one way or another to contribute substantially to the support of a Congressman, he need not be surprised if others question the independence of his judgment. The Buchanan Committee found in 1950, for example, that the Committee on Constitutional Government, a registered lobby, was contributing as much as $500 a month for "research expenses" to Representative Ralph W. Gwinn who wrote a "column" for the lobby.[20] If such arrangements with pressure groups should become general, how well could the Congress represent the public?

The public's elected representatives are its chief agents in promoting and defending the general public interest. On them rests the responsibility of government—the responsibility to make public policy serve the general public rather than any special group or particular interest. If they are not clear-sighted and faithful, the entire structure of representative government totters. Yet it is not easy to be clear-sighted and faithful. Many factors conspire to make it difficult for a legislator, as we have noted: the lack of general public interest and support in nominations and elections, the difficulty of financing a campaign without making embarrassing commitments, the financial pressures, and legislative organization and procedure which tend to drive the representative into the arms of special interests.

To the extent that legislators become the agents of special interests rather than the trustees of the public, the moral position of appointed administrators also becomes more difficult. They are then beset by pressures from all sides, from within the government as well as without. In considering the party and pressure politics of today it is difficult to escape the conclusion that an undue share of the responsibility for defending the public interest is thrown upon administrators and civil servants.

Perhaps American politics compensates for its faulty safeguards elsewhere by extraordinary precautions to strengthen the administrator and the civil servant. Great honor accorded faithful and competent administrators, for example, would have that effect. Is this the American tradition? Everyone knows it is not. Administrators and civil servants are "bureaucrats" by definition, referred to disparagingly as a matter of course in too many political speeches, and sometimes subject directly to violent and reckless attacks. It is almost redundant in American usage to say "lazy public official." The tendency to make light of the public services is well-nigh universal. One can find slighting references or deliberately insulting statements in campaign speeches, in debates reported in the *Congressional Record*, in the literature of taxpayers' organizations, chambers of commerce, and business groups, in full-page "institutional advertising" of public-utility companies, and in dinner-table conversations. This tendency is so prevalent that it is hard to escape the conclusion that something more than inertia is keeping it alive. The remarks of a former president of the United States Chamber of Commerce quoted by the Commission of Inquiry on Public Service Personnel now seem slightly out of date: "The best public servant is the worst one

. . . A thoroughly first-rate man in the public service is corrosive. He eats holes in our liberties. The better he is and the longer he stays, the greater is the danger." [21] This is not the position of the Chamber in the nineteen-fifties, but the anti-government philosophy is still current and one of its forms of expression is systematic disparagement of the public service. The Government of the United States is probably the single most important organization in the world today, yet it is still the fashion to ridicule its employees. That is hardly the way to treat men upon whom falls much of the responsibility for protecting the public interest in the conduct of public affairs.

It is just as important to recognize good work and to avoid unfair disparagement, as it is to be accurately critical of specific misconduct. To the extent that recent disclosures of official misconduct in the public service lead to loose condemnation of the public service as a whole, the effect will be to lower, not raise, standards, to discourage able people from staying in the public service, and to deter promising young people from entering. In a democracy the public is indirectly the employer of the civil service. It follows that the public and its agents, its elected representatives, must be scrupulously fair in their appraisal of the public service and in their expressed attitude. The consequences of loose talk are too costly.

The federal "loyalty program" has a subtle bearing on the integrity of the federal civil service, and, strange as it may seem, the total impact is negative. Viewed in perspective, the Truman administration's loyalty program was set up as a political counter-measure to a persistent political attack on the New Deal and the Fair Deal by men hostile to it in the Congress. Although chronologically speaking most of the pressure over a period of years came from the President's own party, Republican victories in the 1946 elections and the possibility of hostile legislation in the 80th Congress apparently prompted the President's action. By executive order he set up elaborately systematic machinery for investigating and determining the loyalty of *all* federal employees, and "stole the Republican thunder." [22] But seemingly unaware of the consequences of this maneuver, the President by implication made concessions which were damaging and which perpetuated a political issue that he wished to dispose of definitively.

The federal loyalty program is widely criticized on many grounds, for example: it inflicts a severe penalty, the stigma of "disloyalty," without observing the standards of judicial procedure; similarly, it falls short of the standards of administrative procedure which are established by law for comparable governmental decisions affecting persons outside the government; it is an extravagance as an elaborately expensive procedure which has no bearing on the real problem of espionage; some critics find the program unsatisfactory because it has not disclosed appreciable disloyalty within the civil service; and, last but not least, the more philosophically mature critics point out the fact that in attempting to measure "loyalty" and "disloyalty," which are subjective states of mind that cannot be measured unless expressed in overt action, fallible man is attempting the impossible.

In appraising the effect of the loyalty program on the quality of the civil service, however, these criticisms are less significant than two other features which are easily overlooked. First, the President as Chief Executive took what was basically a weak and evasive position with regard to the integrity of the civil service. The administration had made two complete and apparently thorough investigations of employees accused of disloyalty and had dismissed or disciplined all persons of doubtful loyalty—forty-six persons out of 3,500 complained of in

1942, and twenty-nine persons out of 700 complained of in the 1943-1946 period. The President could have said with complete reasonableness, "The Federal Service is loyal; it has been carefully checked; I and my subordinates vouch for it; and we welcome and will continue to act on all evidence of misconduct that comes to us from any source." That would have meant taking full and complete responsibility for the patriotic integrity of the service. His position would have been no less strong in fighting the Rees Bill, which passed the House but not the Senate; for the President's Executive Order was cited in the House debate on the bill as evidence of the reality of the problem and of the need for legislation. Even if the Rees Bill had passed both Houses, and if Congress had overridden a veto, the administration would have been in no weaker position, for in forestalling the proposed legislation, the system set up in the Executive Order accepted many of the basic features of the Rees Bill (to establish a "loyalty program" by statute).

The second weakness was that that action tended to keep the political issue of civil-service loyalty alive instead of settling it definitively. This indeterminateness flows from both the machinery itself and from the administration's acceptance of the principle that a chain of associations proves a disloyal state of mind. Any accusation, no matter how irresponsible or unsupported, can set the entire machinery in motion once more, and an employee can be accused over and over again. Instead of settling a political issue, the Executive Order of 1947 has preserved it.

Looking at the situation for a moment from the civil servant's point of view, one can see something of the emotional consequences. In attempting to explain his feeling to his political superiors a civil servant might say something like this. "If you do not have full confidence in me, say so and I will get out, or fire me; but as long as I work for you, I expect to be defended against outside attack." And is it not reasonable for him to make one point further, "You may fire me for any good reason or for no reason at all. But if in doing so you attach a severe penalty (the stigma of 'disloyalty' which will go with me through life), you have a moral obligation to safeguard the validity of your judgment by following judicial standards." In some ways, it would have been less damaging to the civil service to have dismissed men arbitrarily, merely on the grounds that they had been criticized and were therefore embarrassing the administration.

The loyalty program does not protect civil servants as a whole against unfair attack; it does not protect an accused civil servant against either bad judgment or administrative timidity; and it does not protect the government against espionage. It was harder to see this in 1947 than it is now, when it is difficult to escape the conclusion that the program has instilled fear and weakened the public official in his function of upholding the public interest in the face of pressure or attacks from greedy or aggrieved interests. A maneuver that was smart legislative tactics has had unfortunate administrative consequences.

Steps to Be Taken

The present pattern of American politics gives very little protection to men who seek or accept political responsibility and to the administrators for whom they are directly or indirectly responsible. Institutions mold men, but men also shape institutions. In a democratic society which attempts self-government, it is only a matter of common sense to set up incentives for faithfulness to the public interest and safeguards against unfaithfulness. There is no panacea, but there are a number of useful steps.

Some have been mentioned earlier, for example: making the internal organization of Congress representative and responsible, and thus avoiding the deadly and irresponsible particularism which has gripped Congress for so long; making Congress a real forum for debating basic issues, and so giving a boost to positive party politics; fair representation in state legislatures; better organization and management in the executive branch; clarified codes of official conduct; and required disclosure by legislators and executives of income, assets, and speculative transactions as recommended by the Ethics Subcommittee of the Senate.

The therapeutic effects of the disclosure principle cannot be doubted. But it is medicine which Congress itself is not yet prepared to take. In every session of Congress since 1947 Senator Wayne Morse has introduced a disclosure bill, a simple, perfectly feasible piece of legislation; but, for some reason or other, all of these bills have died in committee. Why do members of Congress object to making public their income and its sources? Are they ashamed to be poor, ashamed to be rich, ashamed to be getting poorer, or richer, or ashamed of the ways in which they are becoming poorer or richer? Do they place great value on privacy for its own sake? One doubts that they would be in public life if they had not at least a trace of the extrovert in their make-up; and they are ready enough to invade the privacy of other citizens when the public interest seems to be served by it. The principle of disclosure has many applications in addition to Congress: party officials, administrators, contingent-fee arrangements of lobbyists, the financial backers of witnesses and lobbies, and a public docket showing the intervention of Congressmen and other lobbyists in administrative decisions. But Congress can hardly apply the principle to others until it is ready itself to accept it. President Truman strongly recommended legislation making disclosure mandatory in the fall of 1951; but his enthusiasm for the principle apparently evaporated when his corruption investigator, Newbold Morris, proposed to use it seriously in the spring of 1952.[23] The reluctance of Congress and the Administration to apply the disclosure principle is not a little disquieting.

Certain additional specific steps could also be helpful. Codes of legislative conduct, perhaps along the lines suggested by Senators William Benton and Paul Douglas and Representative Charles E. Bennett, could be very helpful, particularly if they were used as a basis for disciplinary action by legislative bodies. The general public would also welcome in these codes reasonable standards of restraint as to nepotism and personal patronage, as an evidence that the public interest comes before personal or family interests.

Higher compensation has been proposed to reduce financial pressures upon members of Congress. It might take several forms; rent allowances to help meet the double-residence problem; enlarged travel allowances to cover several trips home; substantial pensions or even terminal compensation to encourage ex-Congressmen to go home instead of hanging around Washington as lobbyists; and higher basic salaries. Increases up to $10,000 have been suggested. The best figures available indicate that at least $3,000 is needed to balance the Congressman's personal budget in 1952. But Congress as a whole seems quite relaxed about the problem of inflation, and continued inflation will gobble up any small increase. Perhaps there is a certain amount of logic in a relatively stable Congressional compensation, if the public is ever to expect price stability.

Revision of the Corrupt Practices Acts governing campaign

contributions and expenditures is much needed and long over-due. The consensus is that there should be full disclosure of all sources of funds and of all expenditures, but that the limits should be more realistic than the statutory maxima, which are generally evaded today.

A most challenging proposal is that the public should assume directly at least part of the costs of political campaigns for *bona-fide* candidates. This is an old idea going back to Theodore Roosevelt, and is essentially conservative; for it would be cheaper in the long run than forcing candidates to shop around among the special interests and pressure groups for funds. There would be a good many difficulties to be worked out in carrying out a policy of public support, but none would be insuperable. Should the public meet the expenses of candidates or of parties? President Theodore Roosevelt proposed an appropriation for each of the great national parties.[24] How "great" should a party be to qualify? The door ought not to be closed to third parties. The direct-primary election is in itself an aid to candidates; but should the government meet primary-campaign expenses? Unless it did so in one-party states, where the election is determined in the primaries, public assistance would not serve its purpose. What type of campaign expenses should be met? And should public assist-ance be supplementary or exclusive?

Although such questions are admittedly difficult, they can be answered, and certain states and cities already have pro-vided assistance to candidates, usually in the form of printed pamphlets distributed to voters. Oregon has had such a vot-ers' pamphlet since 1908. If one accepts the principle that the public interest is to get the facts before the public regarding candidates and issues, and that there should be widespread discussion of these facts, he has a basis for justifying a policy of public support and also for avoiding endless expense. If facts are made generally available, and if they are brought to public attention in at least one comprehensive or dramatic presentation, the basis for a rational election decision is laid. The public policy might well be to try to guarantee this foundation. There would of course be additional campaign efforts privately financed; and discussion, it might be hoped, would continue in widening circles until the last ballot is cast.

A political scientist, Professor Jasper Shannon, has suggested a way to circumvent some of the difficulties that might otherwise arise in providing public assistance for campaigns. He has proposed a public or quasi-public corporation to be responsible for giving adequate publicity to issues, and presumably also to candidates.[25] By focusing on issues it could serve all parties and all significant candidates. It could use established media—press, radio, television—and also issue its own publications if necessary. It could use appropriated funds and also accept private contributions. Independent voters would be more inclined to contribute to a corporation of this sort than to a political party, or a particular candidate.

There are also indirect ways in which public policy could contribute to campaign financing. One is to require radio and television stations, as a condition of their licensed operation, to provide specified amounts of free time for political discussion. Broadcasting companies may not care for this idea, and they will also call attention to their free coverage of national conventions, but it is not an unreasonable plan if required of all, and it makes more sense than the practice of raising rates for political speeches. The present anomaly of public policy which does not make campaign contributions tax-deductible or permit personal campaign expenditures to be charged as a professional expense should certainly be corrected. Abuses can be avoided if the credits permitted are not too large. The objective should be to encourage the general public, rather than special interests, to contribute to campaigns.

Proved Measures

Formal governmental institutions have a bearing on the public's participation in politics. This has long been recognized and is sometimes forgotten. The long ballot with many minor offices to be filled by election handicaps the public while appearing to increase its power. The short-ballot idea, which is being applied increasingly, is to concentrate the public's decision on a few important and responsible offices. The council-manager form of city government is a successful application of this principle to local government. It is in accord with the facts of life today in that it does not overtax the public and provides essential professional specialization. It centers authority and responsibility in a relatively small governing council elected by the public and provides for professional leadership in administration through the appointed city manager. It works. Almost eleven hundred cities have adopted the plan—despite the persistent opposition of local political organizations—and the number has doubled since 1945.[26] It provides optimum conditions for general public participation in local self-government, without putting unnecessary burdens upon the public.

The public's effectiveness in elections has also been increased by the trend toward small city councils and away from ward representatives. In the forty-eight states there are also changes taking place which help public control. Constitutional revision is a slow process, but the number of administrative officials chosen by elections is declining, and the trend is toward concentrating the public's decision upon the office of governor and upon the state legislature. One state, Nebraska, has created a unicameral legislature, something which all but a few cities came to long ago.

These are encouraging trends; but there is one area in which progress has been quite disappointing. That is the metropolis. Metropolitan growth continues, with expanding suburban satellites. Central cities have lost many of their leading men (voters, leaders of opinion, potential office holders) to the suburbs. Efforts to check the political disorganization of metropolitan areas have been largely unsuccessful. Metropolitan areas, which are the key centers in American life, have governmental institutions which are least well designed for both their political and administrative needs. Political disorganization is such that it is almost impossible for the people of the metropolis to grapple with their problems, and the rurally dominated state legislatures, which have power to act in matters of local-government organization, do nothing.

Rational Limits of Specialization

The shape of institutions can help or hinder men in self-government. But the complex of constitutional documents, laws, formal organizations, offices, traditions, parties, and pressure groups are not government. In the last analysis men govern. Governments do have momentum and inertia, but they are not machines. Men must govern themselves in a complex society as well as a simple one.

In appraising the state of American politics, the average American must come back to himself and face up to some questions which have to do with his role in modern life. The basic question he must ask himself is: How much of a specialist do I have a right to be? That is, how much is it right and reasonable for me to concentrate on my business, professional or other vocational interests to the exclusion of other responsibilities, particularly political responsibilities? If every one else concentrated as strongly as I do, what would happen to representative government? Obviously the average man must give most of his time to earning a living, but there are limits to concentration on his job and his career if the health and vitality of the family, the state, and of religious and cultural institutions are to be preserved. It is unreasonable, of course, to expect the average man to spend all of his time on politics. This is a world of specialists, specialists in government as well as specialists in business; and the average man will have to rely upon specialists to administer public affairs. But it is his moral obligation to himself and to his fellows to give enough attention to the issues and processes of politics to make an intelligent choice of specialists. He must give enough attention also to the machinery of government to be sure that it is not too cumbersome or archaic to be workable. And he must at times consider specific issues of public policy with enough detachment to come to a decision as to what the public interest (not just his own special interest) requires.

In order to meet these obligations, the average man may have to set limits to his specialization. He may have to give up something in his career in order to fulfill his obligation to his country, his family, and their future. He recognizes this obligation in wartime, and it is equally valid, although less dramatic, in peacetime. The average man's real interest is in a peaceful and prosperous America in which men are united by bonds of understanding and good will, and in which institutional adjustments, economic and cultural, are made reasonably. No fame and no future can compare with this estate, either for the average man or for his children. It is equally true for the man who is a leader among his fellows. What are riches in an unstable economy? What is security in a society torn by fear, hatred, or violence? What is fame if civilization crumbles?

A second fundamental question an American must ask himself is: How aggressive have I a right to be in pressure politics? If I and my special-interest group are unrestrained in playing pressure politics to get what we want, and if all other special-interest groups are equally aggressive to get what they want, what will be the effect upon public policy, public welfare, and the stability of the state? If he is realistic he will be forced to conclude that although counter-forces sometimes contain each other, many times they do not; aggressive forces frequently combine; aggressiveness breeds aggressiveness; and in a politics of unrestrained special interests, it is unlikely that public officials who are the formal defenders of the public interest will long be effective. If democratic self-government is to be a reality, is it not essential for the men who are leaders in special-interest groups to have some active sense of their group's responsibility to society as a whole? The power which inheres in great pressure groups can be tolerated only when there is also some restraint, some sense of responsibility in its use.

How can the American, who is typically a specialist and a member of a specialized organization, keep sufficient length of perspective and breadth of values to make sure that through his zeal and drive he will not in his specialized success destroy the nation and the culture in which he lives—and with them himself? Some way he must preserve or re-create the whole man if representative self-government is to continue.

VIII

INTEGRITY—MAN AND THE STATE

It is the many ramifications of the problem of morality in American politics which lead to confusion in thinking about it. Taken one at a time, each phase of the problem is understandable. But each is involved with others, and it is almost impossible to settle any one of the numerous constituent problems unless related questions are answered simultaneously. It was this quality of baffling complexity in the moral problem that led the Senate Subcommittee on Ethics in Government to conclude that a thorough study by an authoritative commission is needed to make clear the nature and dimensions of the problem.[1]

At the risk of oversimplification one is tempted to search for a central difficulty or a nuclear problem that could provide the key to solution, or at least to substantial progress. Running back quickly over the major pieces in the puzzle, the searcher notes: a certain complaisance over early and substantial American success in securing human rights and promoting individual welfare; subconscious confidence in the automatic qualities of the economic and political order; legalism; and philosophical naïveté. He notes also that the pattern of American life is dominated by specialization, organization, loyalties, and pressures. He is further impressed by the fact that the typical American with qualities of leadership has a pronounced aversion for "politics" in the broad sense, but is head over heels in the narrower variety of pressure politics.

Both individual and public moral standards seem to have been slowly rising in all particulars that can be measured, yet the making of public policy and the conduct of public affairs are embarrassingly below the standards which one can accept as satisfactory today.

One of the major difficulties is obviously the delay in making institutional adjustments in the political world. Obsolescence places more strain on human flesh than it can stand. Intelligent design can and does relieve these stresses. On this point there is convincing evidence, for example: steady progress in rationalizing city government; less but still substantial change in state administration; commendable improvement of administrative institutions in the national government; and a primary election system by which it is possible to keep the door of opportunity open to all in politics. This evidence is encouraging.

The lag in modernizing political institutions, however, is discouraging. Progress has been slow at best and in some areas there has been almost none. Very little has been done to correct the disorganization of metropolitan areas. The system of nominations and elections was left half-modernized forty years ago, and almost nothing has been done since. Institutional failure is perhaps most acute among legislative bodies which, although intended to be the generic center of American politics, have become unrepresentative and irresponsible. This weakness has crippling effects throughout all politics. To the extent that the central problem of morality in politics is institutional in character, it is here at the heart of representative government, in the legislative assemblies.

But at this point in the search for the key to moral difficulties, one begins to doubt that the basic problem is exclusively institutional. No one of the institutional maladjustments is mysterious, nor is a remedy lacking. But there has been so little action. Why? As Americans we are normally challenged by difficulties. Why have we not been challenged by representative government? We fought for it. We won it. But do we have it? Perhaps "the fault . . . is not in our stars but in ourselves."

If the moral problem of American politics has a single center, a point that is more causative than any other, that point seems to center in the peculiar pattern of loyalties which Americans have to the organizations that they have created and of which they are a part.

In contrast to the monolithic state, the strength of American political, economic, and social organization is its laminated structure. American life is a maze of interlocking organizations which exist because of the loyalties of their members. In the conflict of organizations and organizational loyalties, many moral dilemmas of politics have their origin.

In this laminated society of pluralistic loyalties, it is obvious that the country is able to preserve its strength and unity, literally its integrity, so long as each of the constituent organizations makes only such demands upon its members as can rationally be reconciled with their obligations to other organizations. If one organization does not claim all of a member's energy and devotion, there can be many of them. Organizational pluralism is dependent upon organizational moderation in both the extensiveness of their activities and the intensiveness of their demands. As long as this principle is respected the adjustment between the demands of organizations can be made by their members, in a process of free choice without undue emotional stress.

A legalistic balancing of obligations would obviously not be workable. A pluralistic society thrives because there is leeway in it, and because some members of every group go far beyond the call of duty in their loyalty to it and their work for it. A family is the most obvious example. It thrives because some members, usually both parents, contribute to it whatever it needs. They do not begrudge the time, energy, or devotion that may be required. The family survives also because most of the time it does not demand too much. It leaves its members some freedom for other loyalties and other groups. If the family should become so greedy in its demands upon its members that it began to monopolize the life of its members it would to that extent challenge the pluralistic organization of society. One interpretation of traditional Chinese culture is that the family did so dominate life as to weaken political and economic institutions. Conceivably the church could also so extend its demands and jurisdiction as to challenge other groups. Similarly, if the state should be so extensive in its demands as to preclude loyalty to the family and economic or social groups, the monolithic state would replace the laminated structure with which we are familiar.

In America there is as yet no challenge to pluralistic organization from these sources. The state's demands upon its citizens are paramount if it chooses to make them so. But actually the demands are few, except in times of national danger, when it expects men to defend the state with their lives. As long as pluralism continues in the organization of American religious life there can be no challenge to the laminated structure of society from that direction. The American family is certainly in no mood of aggrandizement, but, rather, is fighting to hold its own integrity.

If there is a challenge to the pluralistic freedom of American life, it comes not from political, religious, or social organizations, but from economic groups which, although economic in origin, have become active politically and socially, and which demand of their members unlimited loyalty. This presents a dilemma. None of these organizations could exist if their relations with all members were mechanically contractual. Some dedicated men are necessary to keep them going through hard times, to carry them over obstacles, and to overcome opposition. Great industrial organizations and labor unions alike require leadership and devotion that are beyond what can be purchased on a contractual basis. Yet if great organizations both widen the range of their activities and insist on preclusive loyalty from their members, they are more than a threat to the state; they challenge the basic organization of society itself. The reportedly growing policy of business management to draw wives and children into the "corporate family," to consider wives "members of the team," and to look over the wives of executives in hiring or promoting men is therefore a little frightening in its suggestion of a trend toward corporate omniprevalence. Labor-union expansion into the social life of its members would be similarly disturbing as a move toward a rigid class organization which America has so far escaped.

If the characteristic pluralistic organization of American life, which is one measure of present-day freedom, is to be preserved, it behooves each organization to avoid jurisdictional expansion and constantly to strive for moderation in its demands upon its members and upon society. Organizations, of course, are more or less fictions. They live only in their members. Organizations do not think or act; men make the decisions and do the work.

This brings us back to the individual American, the average man, and the leaders who direct the organized activities of their associates. The battle for the integrity of American life is fought in the minds of men. The potentially explosive forces which are inherent in the specialization, extensive organization, and high pressures of American life can be kept in control only so long as the key men throughout all of organized society keep their loyalties in balance and their special zeal in check.

The business executive who thinks only in terms of his corporation, the labor leader who thinks only in terms of his union, and the leader of organized agriculture who thinks only in terms of his farm organization are all a menace to the basic integrity of the nation. The leaders of men and also the average men must have the long perspective and the broad values of statesmen if the integrity of American life is to be preserved. Every great organization, in proportion to its economic and political power, has become vested with a public interest, and its leaders must recognize a public responsibility. If the entire responsibility of looking out for the public welfare is left to men who are formally in government office, they will either fail or, in succeeding, they will be forced to substitute a monolithic state for the freedom and strength of our laminated society. There is no escape from this dilemma. In a free society the responsibilities of the statesman fall on everyone, and upon each person in accordance with his power and ability.

The moral problem of American politics is ultimately personal. How can I as an average American keep a public perspective as to the things which I do that affect public policy and the general welfare? How can I make sure that my values are consistent with the welfare of society? How can I avoid the crippling bias of intensive and prolonged specialization? It is obvious that if I am going to have enough interest and understanding and judgment honestly to consider the public interest in what I do, I dare not let myself be merely a businessman, or lawyer, or farmer, or artisan, or any other specialist. I must keep alive my interests in other phases of life than my job, and interest must be emotional as well as intellectual. I can do this only by participation. If I am active in cultural, religious, civic, and political affairs, I am more likely to have a balanced perspective and I am more likely to care about cultural, religious, civic and political values. But these activities also take time. The price of balance may be less concentration, slower advancement, smaller earnings, less distinction. To achieve a wholesome society man must first make sure that he is a whole man, for in his own life are the controls that determine society's integrity.

This may not be much of a sacrifice for the average person. But how about the leaders, the dynamic men and women who set the pace and who play key roles in their organizations? Will they also forgo the benefits of highly concentrated efforts in order to maintain wider contacts and a more socially reliable point of view? Before venturing a hasty no, one should be aware of compensations. A businessman may make less profit but have better health. A professional man may give his children less money but better guidance. A scholar may have less knowledge but greater insight. An executive may have less data but better judgment. Perhaps specialization is too often carried beyond the point of diminishing returns in American life, and possibly the time has come to be moderate even in things so important as one's calling. Division of labor and specialization have contributed greatly to progress, but these principles can be overworked. Why not look at them freshly?

The American concentration during past decades upon economic, engineering, and scientific tasks, and the preoccupation of political leaders in recent years with economic and military affairs have tended to obscure the reality of moral ideas and moral forces. Americans tend to assume that only economic interests and motives are compelling, although many of their actions challenge this idea. Contributors to voluntary religious, civic, and charitable organizations are spending more than $2 billions a year from other than economic motives, and for other than economic purposes.[2] Religious bodies in the United States are spending $1.3 billions of this sum and also maintain a force of tens of thousands of missionaries in foreign lands.[3] The growth of public education, the most elaborate and costly system of education in the world, came about not because Americans saw it would be a great economic asset, but because it seemed like a "good thing to do." It is a product of American idealism, not of economic foresight. In addition to the system of public education there are in the United States more than 1200 privately supported colleges and institutions of higher education.[4]

Probably the greatest number of men and women are not moved primarily by economic motives. Other motivation plays a larger part in their lives. The most obvious group of this sort are women who are wives and mothers of families. Despite the glamorous advertisements, and the well-advertised labor-saving appliances, they lead a strenuous life which stresses the welfare of others, not self.

Is not the dominance of economic motives in American life greatly exaggerated? American materialism is the materialism of production, and is nourished by the fun of "doing things." There are few misers and few connoisseurs of wealth. American philanthropy is taken for granted. There is some general feeling that it is bad form to be too soft a touch, and perhaps there is a tendency to apply commerical standards at times where they are inappropriate, under the compulsion of a vague feeling that one ought to be able to show a profit on all transactions. But anyone who looks at American life freshly and intimately is bound to be impressed by the great strength of idealism.

Even such great public policies as lend-lease, the Marshall Plan, E.C.A., Point Four, and the mutual-security program tend to be distorted in discussion as if they were purely economic policies, or some form of imperialism. A discussion of Theodore M. Greene, a witness before the Committee on Ethical Standards, and Senator Humphrey on this point illuminates this tendency to distortion.[5]

> *Dr. Greene.* Is it not . . . true, Senator, that by and large we fail to give people in other nations a fair notion of our total national set-up? That is to say, we are interested in the dollar, we are interested in self-defense, we are interested in our own prosperity, but we also are fundamentally a humane people, we are fundamentally a just people, we do not like starvation, we do not like cruelty, we do not like exploitation. . . . As a people we are nowhere near as hardboiled as we try to make our spokesmen describe us.
> *Senator Humphrey.* I am not going to take too much time on this, but I had an experience two nights ago when two members of the German Parliament were guests of mine. They had been in the country two months as a part of the state program which brings in 2,500 people a year from Western Germany and other parts of Europe to visit the United States. These two young men both had doctor's degrees, both brilliant, both anti-Nazis, and now were leading political movements in Germany, I would say the middle center. One of them was in fact a Christian Socialist, and the other was what they call the Freedom Party or Free Party. I asked them what was their im-

pression of Americans, what was the impression of America in Germany and Europe.

They were very cosmopolitan men. They said the impression of the average European is that America is business. They are not saying that is bad. Business surely is good. But the fact is that when the Point 4 program was announced, he said that there was a seminar group or study group of younger men in the Parliament that got together for discussion and said, "What is in it for the United States?" That was the first thing. America could not be interested in this unless there was a pay-off. He said that opinion had been completely reversed after he had spent two months in this country, staying in the homes of American families. They were in Connecticut, Ohio, Wisconsin, also in Illinois, and all through the Eastern area. They were not visiting with Government people, but rather universities, and business and farm people. They said they came away from these visits with the feeling that the American people had sort of a mission. They never talked to anybody outside of the Government that ever said how much we were going to make out of it. They were primarily impressed by the fact that the average person they talked to about foreign affairs, the Marshall plan, or Point 4, thought these things were helping them and they got a sense of warmth and kindness out of knowing they were doing something for somebody else. Why is it we cannot project that? Why does somebody have to come over here and find it?

Perhaps the answer is that Americans are both slightly ashamed, and not fully aware, of their own idealism.

A sober look at the moral problem of American politics leads almost inevitably to the conclusion that the problem is colossal. If it is not enough to avoid corruption, if it is not enough to balance rights and duties in a legalistic way, if the Great Commandment is the standard to which men must now commit themselves, what chance is there of success? The complete answer to this question extends beyond the realm of politics, beyond the social sciences, beyond any one segment of life, even that of religion as it is conventionally defined. But an honest appraisal of moral resources, a look beneath the surface of American life leads to the conclusion also that there are no grounds for defeatism and despair. America is not doomed to failure. Although it is not the custom to appeal to idealism in politics, the record shows that when the appeal is genuine and straightforward, the response is unfailing.

NOTES

I. *American Politics—The Characters and Their Roles*

1. In most sections of the country a larger percentage of the electorate votes in presidential elections than in mid-term elections or in state and local contests. Even in this election, however, the participation seldom exceeds 60 per cent of the adult citizens, and sometimes falls below 50 per cent. In local elections participation of voters is frequently as low as 20-30 per cent. See V. O. Key, Jr., *Politics, Parties, and Pressure Groups*, Chapter 19. (Crowell, New York, 1948)

2. This tally is based on the Constitution as it appears in the *United States Government Organization Manual.*

3. Madison's famous essay No. 10, in *The Federalist* papers begins with this point.

4. *The Writings of George Washington*, Bicentennial Edition, John C. Fitzpatrick, ed., Vol. 35, p. 226.

5. *The Federalist*, No. 10.

6. U. S. Senate, Committee on Labor and Public Welfare, 82nd Congress, 1st Session. Report of a Subcommittee . . . *Ethical Standards in Government* (Committee Print), p. 14. This subcommittee is referred to hereafter as the Committee on Ethical Standards; and the report is cited as *Ethical Standards in Government.*

7. Employment figures are taken from the U. S. Civil Service Commission, *Monthly Report of Employment, Executive Branch of the Federal Government,* and from the Conference Board, *Business Record,* Vol. 6, July 1949, pp. 276-277.

8. The peak comes in summer.
9. Employment figures are taken from the *Annual Report of the U. S. Civil Service Commission*, its *Monthly Report of Employment*, and from the Tax Foundation's *Facts and Figures on Government Finance, 1950-1951*.
10. This was the situation before Korean fighting affected employment.
11. *Facts and Figures, 1950-1951*, p. 50. (The Tax Foundation, New York, 1950)
12. *Ethical Standards in Government*, p. 64.

II. *Morals and Politics*

1. For a brief discussion of the Declaration in its revolutionary setting see the Introductory Note, "Revolutionary Ideas in Ferment," in A. T. Mason, *Free Government in the Making*, pp. 81-87. (Oxford University Press, New York, 1949) The Declaration is printed in full in most source books on American government. See for example, J. M. Mathews and C. A. Berdahl, *Documents and Readings in American Government*, pp. 25-28. (Macmillan, New York, 1930) Generally regarded as the standard reference is Carl Becker, *The Declaration of Independence: A Study in the History of Political Ideas*. (Knopf, New York, 1942)
2. "But when a long train of abuses and usurpations, pursuing invariably the same Object, evinces a design to reduce them under Despotism, it is their right, it is their duty, to throw off such Government, and to provide new Guards for their future security."
3. *Ethical Standards in Government*, p. 11
4. U. S. Senate, Committee on Labor and Public Welfare, 82nd Congress, First Session, *Hearings . . . Establishment of a Commission on Ethics in Government*, June-July 1951, pp. 85-86. These hearings will be cited hereafter as *Hearings, Ethics in Government*.
5. *Hearings, Ethics in Government*, pp. 87-88.
6. *Ethical Standards in Government*, p. 10.
7. Comparing agriculture and manufacturing, the two largest elements in the economy, as to gainfully occupied and employed persons, we find that agriculture had 51.6 per cent of all gainfully occupied and employed persons in 1870 and manufacturing had only 16.4 per cent. In 1900 agriculture had 37.7 per cent and manufacturing 21.3 per cent. Agriculture did not drop behind manufacturing until the 1920's. In 1930 the percentages were agriculture 21.3 and manufacturing 22.3. Comparing aggregate payments on a percentage of the national in-

come, agriculture was overtaken earlier by manufacturing. In the decade 1869-79 agriculture's share was 20.5 per cent and the share of manufacturing 13.9 per cent. In the next decade they were approximately equal—agriculture 16.1 per cent, manufacturing 16.6 per cent. From 1889 to 1899 the percentages of the national income were agriculture 17.1, and manufacturing 18.2. The difference was not as much as 3 per cent of the national income until the period, 1909-1918; agriculture's share then was 17.7 per cent, and the share of manufacturing 20.8 per cent. Simon Kuznets, *National Income, A Summary of Findings*, 1946, pp. 40-41. (National Bureau of Economic Research, New York, 1946)

The distribution of population is also significant. In 1900 the population was still 60 per cent rural. In 1920 it was almost evenly divided, 49 per cent rural, 51 per cent urban. Preliminary figures released by the 1950 census show that the population was in 1950 59 per cent urban and 41 per cent rural, approximately the reverse of the distribution fifty years earlier. See *New York Times*, March 4, 1951.

8. Enacted almost casually and not regarded as of first importance in the legislative program of the day, the Sherman Anti-trust Act of July 2, 1890, 26 *Stat.* 209, had relatively little effect on the growth of monopoly in industry through "close consolidations," and was not vigorously applied for almost twenty years. Whether it has ever been applied with sufficient vigor and discrimination is still a matter of debate, with the doubters having most of the statistics of industrial concentration to support their doubts. The law is a landmark in the development of public policy, however, as the first important direct action by the federal government, aside from the tariff, to control industry generally. The Interstate Commerce Act of 1887, which preceded it, was a railroad measure.

The Sherman Act as interpreted by the courts had some effect upon the competitive methods of big business and was followed in 1914 by the Federal Trade Commission Act, 38 *Stat.* 717, and the Clayton Anti-trust Act, 38 *Stat.* 730, which stressed therapeutic measures to prevent growth of monopoly through unfair methods of competition.

A concise discussion of these measures and their administration is to be found in Merle Fainsod and Lincoln Gordon, *Government and the American Economy*, pp. 432-525. (Norton, New York, 1948)

9. Federal Reserve Act of December 23, 1913, 37 *Stat.* 251.

10. Measured in 1929 dollars, national income increased from $10.6 billions in 1875 to $32 billions in 1900, and to $69.5 billions in 1925. The income of gainfully occupied persons also increased during this half-

century; it was $701 per person in 1875, $1102 per person in 1900, and $1523 per person in 1925. Kuznets, *op. cit.*, p. 46.

11. The ranks of organized labor numbered less than 3,500,000 in 1929, and dropped still lower in the early 1930's. In 1949 reported union membership totaled 16,000,000. (Figures from the *World Almanac* for 1930 and 1950).

12. Agriculture has achieved political parity with other organized economic interests through the joint efforts of the farm bloc in Congress, the House Committee on Agriculture and the Senate Committee on Agriculture and Forestry, the U. S. Department of Agriculture, and the farmer organizations, American Farm Bureau, the Grange, and the National Farmers' Union. Ability to maintain a price-support program backed by subsidies in periods of food shortages, high food prices, and great farm prosperity is impressive evidence of political strength. An astute observer of American politics and administration, V. O. Key, says that American agriculture has become a "hard-boiled, crystallized pressure bloc constantly alert to its interests," and that its political activities "have the odor of the machinations of an old-style tariff lobby." *Politics, Parties, and Pressure Groups*, 2nd ed. 1948, pp. 30-31. On the political strength and organization of American Agriculture see Key's Chapter on Agrarianism, *op. cit.*, pp. 15-47; Wesley McCune, *The Farm Bloc* (Doubleday, New York, 1943); Donald C. Blaisdell, *Economic Power and Political Pressure*, TNEC Monograph No. 26, 1941, pp. 175-186; Stuart Chase, *Democracy Under Pressure*, pp. 90-104 (Twentieth-Century Fund, New York, 1945); Theodore Salontos, "The American Farm Bureau Federation and Farm Policy: 1933-1945," 27 *Southwestern Social Science Quarterly*, 313-333, March 1948.

13. Corporations have replaced directly owned private business; great business units much larger than it was once thought possible to operate have come to dominate many industries; "limited" competition has come to be as familiar as monopoly and competition; business generally and by industries is organized for effective political action; so also are labor and agriculture. Public enterprise, private monopoly, regulated industry, and unregulated industry are mingled in American economic life. Labor and agriculture are obviously "married" to government, and the mutual bonds of general business and government are only a little less obvious. An honest picture of the American political economy is to be found in Merle Fainsod and Lincoln Gordon, *Government and the American Economy*, 1948, especially pp. 3-45, 855-892.

14. *Hearings, Ethics in Government,* pp. 269-270.
15. *Ibid.,* p. 275.
16. *Ibid.,* p. 308.
17. *Ibid.,* p. 308.
18. *Ibid.,* p. 309.
19. U. S. Senate, Special Committee to Investigate Organized Crime in Interstate Commerce, 82nd Congress, First Session, Report No. 307, *Third Interim Report,* pp. 1-5.
20. *Ethical Standards in Government,* p. 7.
21. *Hearings, Ethics in Government,* p. 116.
22. *Ibid.,* p. 127.
23. *Hearings, Ethics in Government,* pp. 438-439.
24. *Ibid.,* pp. 263-264.
25. *Ethical Standards in Government,* pp. 10-11.
26. *Ibid.,* pp. 8-10.

III. *Morality and the Legislative System: Representation*

1. A person required to testify by Congress, however, may not be compelled to give evidence that might be used against him in a criminal prosecution. This constitutional right of the individual to avoid self-incrimination derives from the Fifth Amendment. *Cf.* Edward S. Corwin, *The Constitution and What It Means Today,* pp. 161-2. (Princeton University Press, 1946)
2. Madison or Hamilton in *The Federalist,* No. 51. (Everyman ed., p. 265)
3. *Ibid.,* p. 253.
4. The phrase is from Edward S. Corwin's, *A Constitution of Powers in a Secular State,* p. 2. (Michie, Charlottesville, 1951) Prof. Corwin has himself been a leading influence in adjusting and expanding ruling concepts of legislative power to the realities of the modern life.
5. George B. Galloway's count for 1950 was 131 standing subcommittees, the same number as in 1945. See his article on "The Operation of the Legislative Reorganization Act of 1946." 45 *American Political Science Review,* 43, March 1951.
6. The remarks of Representative George Meader reflect the views of many thoughtful members. "I have long felt that the one important improvement in Government needed today more than any other is the strengthening of the Congress. I think the constitutional responsibilities placed upon the Congress to determine policies are not being

discharged under modern times in the effective way that they ought to be. I have the general feeling that Congress has failed to keep step with the development of our national economy, which today is a far more complicated and intricate affair than it was fifty or seventy-five years ago." U. S. Senate, Committee on Expenditures in the Executive Departments, 82nd Cong., 1st Sess., *Organization and Operation of Congress, Hearings* . . . June 1951, p. 90. This document will be cited hereafter as *Hearings, Organization and Operation of Congress.*

7. Quoted by Comptroller Lindsay C. Warren, *Hearings, Ethics in Government,* p. 38.

8. *Hearings, Ethics in Government,* p. 158.

9. *Ibid.*

10. *Ibid.,* p. 96.

11. See the remarks of Senator William Benton, *Ibid.,* p. 39.

12. V. O. Key has called attention to the Congressional habit of passing bonus legislation over the President's veto in election years. *Politics, Parties and Pressure Groups,* p. 131.

13. "It ought to be on the record that the President did not take part in developing the National Labor Relations Act and, in fact, was hardly consulted about it. It was not a part of the President's program. It did not particularly appeal to him when it was described to him. All the credit for it belongs to Wagner." Frances Perkins, *The Roosevelt I Knew,* p. 239. Officials from the NRA and the Department of Labor, however, worked very closely with Senator Wagner in preparing his bill.

14. *Hearings, Ethics in Government,* p. 226.

15. *Ibid.,* p. 227.

16. Senator Estes Kefauver, "What's to Be Done about Congress?" *New York Times Magazine,* Sept. 11, 1949, p. 9.

17. Estes Kefauver and Jack Levin, *A 20th Century Congress,* p. 195. (Duell, Sloan and Pearce, New York, 1947)

18. U. S. Congress, 79th Congress, 1st Sess., Joint Committee on the Organization of Congress, *Hearings on the Organization of Congress,* March-June 1945, pp. 296-7. Mr. Ramspeck recalled this recommendation six years later. See the *Hearings, Ethics in Government,* pp. 448-9. See also a similar but allegedly facetious proposal of Representative Abraham J. Multer, *Hearings, Organization and Operation of Congress,* p. 512.

19. In a careful analysis of the work of committees handling Army appropriations for the period 1933-1950 Elias Huzar came to the conclusion that "the Committees on Appropriations should raise their

sights. In examining budget estimates for the Army, the subcommittees on military appropriations have been too much absorbed in costs and details. . . . Their concern with detail is understandable, but it has diverted the subcommittees from the more valuable work of scrutinizing military programs and policies. . . . The Appropriations Committees might exercise greater influence than they do if they concentrated on the larger issues of program and policy involved in military appropriations, such as the stockpiling of critical materials, the strength of the Air Force, and mechanization of the Army." *The Purse and the Sword*, pp. 398-9. (Cornell Univ. Press, Ithaca, 1950)

20. *Hearings, Ethics in Government*, p. 208.

21. *Ibid.*, pp. 206-7.

22. *Ibid.*, p. 414.

23. *Ibid.*

24. Article 1, Section 5.

25. In 163 years twenty-one members of the Senate have been expelled, two-thirds of them during the Civil War for treason or because of the secession of their states. *New York Times*, Sept. 30, 1951.

26. See Spencer Erwin, *Henry Ford vs. Truman H. Newberry*, especially Chs. 5-7 for a review of Senate action. (Richard R. Smith, New York, 1935)

27. See *Cannon's Precedents of the House of Representatives*, Vol. 6, Sec. 179, pp. 344-6. (Government Printing Office, 1935)

28. *Ibid.*, Sec. 180, pp. 346-351.

29. 71 *Cong. Record* 5131-2, Nov. 4, 1929, 71st Cong., 1st Sess.

30. *Literary Digest*, Nov. 16, 1929, p. 11.

31. No instance is reported in *Cannon's Precedents*, Ch. 42, "Punishment and Expulsion of Members."

32. H. H. Wilson, *Congress: Corruption and Compromise*, Ch. 3. (Rinehart, New York, 1951)

33. For discussion of the Cox episode see Wilson, *op. cit.*, Ch. 4.

34. *Ibid.*, Ch. 5.

35. The May case is discussed in Wilson, *op. cit.*, Ch. 6.

36. Quoted by Wilson, *op. cit.*, p. 108.

37. Recent news reports have alleged that Mr. Thomas was released from prison without paying his fine, contrary to the instructions of Judge Alexander Holtzoff, who imposed the sentence. *Compass*, January 8, 1952.

38. *New York Times*, Sept. 30, 1951.

39. See the review of the case in Wilson, *op. cit.*, Ch. 10.

40. *Ibid.*, Ch. 11.

41. Quoted by Wilson, *op. cit.*, p. 175.
42. U. S. Senate, Committee on Rules and Administration, 82nd Cong., 1st Sess., Report No. 647, *Maryland Senatorial Election of 1950*, Aug. 20, 1951.
43. *Ibid.*, p. 43.
44. 97 *Cong. Record*, August 6, 1951, p. 9711.
45. *New York Times*, January 9, 1952.
46. *Washington Post*, Jan. 24, 1952, p. 6.
47. *Hearings, Organization and Operation of Congress*, p. 327.
48. *Ibid.*
49. *Ibid.*, p. 328.
50. 95 *Cong. Record*, pp. 2665-7, March 17, 1949. In his remarks Senator Douglas also takes great pains to show that the liberal and progressive Senators representing a majority of the people of the country, and the people themselves, do not object to the heavy expenditure of federal funds for the benefit of minorities. In fact, they favor it. But, the Senator argued, minorities should not exploit their disproportionate power selfishly, especially to prevent majority rule by preventing the Senate from acting. Hence his opposition to a backward step on the cloture rule.
51. U. S. Conference of Mayors, *Government of the People, By the People, and For the People.* This pamphlet presents graphically a number of the examples of unequal representation which are discussed in these pages. The population figures antedate the 1950 census.
52. *Ibid.* Also see Dayton D. McKean, *Pressures on the Legislature of New Jersey*, pp. 38-39. (Columbia Univ. Press, New York, 1938)
53. See the discussion of "Under Representation of Cities" in Austin F. MacDonald, American State Government, pp. 191-3. (Crowell, New York, 1935)
54. *Ibid.* See also the article by Richard L. Neuberger, "Our Rotten Borough Legislatures," 86 *Survey*, February 1950, pp. 53-57.
55. Neuberger, *loc. cit.*
56. The dissenting opinion of Justice Black in *Colegrove v. Green*, 328 *U. S.* 549, 90 *L. Ed.* 1432, is perhaps a forecast of eventual judicial relief. The Justice said that "legislation which must inevitably bring about glaringly unequal representation in the Congress in favor of special classes and groups should be invalidated 'whether accomplished ingeniously or ingenuously.'" He also noted that the provisions of the Constitution on representation were "intended to make illegal a nation-wide 'rotten borough' system as between the states. The policy behind it is broader than that. It prohibits as well 'rotten

boroughs' within the states." In the decision of the Court which declined to grant relief four justices agreed, one with a concurring opinion which upheld the power of the Court to act. Three justices dissented and one took no part in the case. Chief Justice Stone died while the case was before the Court.

57. Neuberger, *loc. cit.*
58. U. S. Senate, Special Committee to Investigate Organized Crime in Interstate Commerce, 82nd Cong., 1st. Sess., Report No. 307. *Third Interim Report*, May 1, 1951, pp. 102-3.
59. James M. Burns, *Congress on Trial*, p. 51. (Harper, New York, 1949) See also the tabulation state by state in *Colegrove v. Green* 328 *U. S.,* 556-559.
60. Elmer C. Griffith, *The Rise and Development of the Gerrymander,* pp. 16-18. (University of Chicago, 1907)
61. Robert C. Carr and others, *American Democracy in Theory and Practice*, p. 225. (Rinehart, New York, 1951)
62. The Apportionment Act of Aug. 8, 1911 (37 *Stat.* 14) required congressional districts to be contiguous and compact. No reapportionment act was enacted after the 1920 census, and in the Act of June 8, 1929 (46 *Stat.* 26) the contiguous-and-compact requirement was deliberately omitted. This law, however, has the valuable feature of providing for automatic reapportionment after each census if Congress fails to take special action.
63. Burns, *op. cit.*, p. 52.
64. These figures are for the 82nd Congress, 2nd Sess. with committees as constituted at the beginning of the session.
65. Representative Madden of Illinois became chairman of the House Committee on Appropriations, being selected over a man senior to him on the committee.
66. Representative Anderson of Minnesota, quoted by Floyd M. Riddick, *The United States Congress: Organization and Procedure*, p. 171. (National Capitol Publishers, Washington, 1949)
67. *Ibid.*, p. 61.
68. Representative Chet Holifield reviewed in detail the arbitrary practices of the Rules Committee in his testimony before the Senate Committee on Expenditures, June 6, 1951. He said, "In practice, the Rules Committee over a period of years developed what I believe to be a pernicious habit of blocking legislation to which a majority of its members objected, instead of facilitating the consideration of legislation in the House. . . .

"I might digress for a moment to say that we have just had an experience of this type on the so-called wheat for India bill. That bill, as it was originally reported by the Foreign Affairs Committee, of which I am also a member, provided that the wheat should be given to the people of India, the starving people of India. When we attempted to get a rule in the House Rules Committee we were obstructed for about four or five months. We were told by a majority of the Rules Committee to go back and rewrite the bill and bring it in with a loan provision in it, rather than a grant provision." *Hearings, Organization and Operation of Congress,* pp. 49 ff.

69. *Ibid.,* p. 51.
70. Cf. George B. Galloway, *Congress at the Crossroads,* p. 112. (Crowell, New York, 1946)

IV. *Morality and the Legislative System: Responsibility and Reason*

1. *Hearings, Organization and Operation of Congress,* p. 51.
2. *Ibid.*
3. Quoted by George B. Galloway, "Proposed Reforms in Congressional Investigations," *University of Chicago Law Review, Spring 1951,* p. 479; reprinted in *Hearings, Organization and Operation of Congress,* p. 643.
4. *Ibid.,* p. 644. Quoted from *Public Opinion,* p. 289. (Macmillan, New York, 1922)
5. Quoted by Galloway, *Hearings, Organization and Operation of Congress,* p. 644. President Coolidge was at that time aggrieved by the aggressiveness of a Senate investigation of the Bureau of Internal Revenue that grew out of a conflict between Senator James Couzens and Secretary of the Treasury Andrew Mellon over the latter's proposed reduction of corporate income taxes. The Senate committee, with Mr. Couzens as the moving spirit, subpoenaed the income-tax records of corporations in which Mr. Mellon was personally interested; and the Bureau of Internal Revenue, with Mr. Mellon as the moving spirit, charged Mr. Couzens with an income-tax delinquency of $10,000,000. (Mr. Couzens proved overpayment and collected $900,000 in refunds.) The complaint of President Coolidge was part of the Couzens-Mellon battle. For a résumé of the episode see Harry Barnard, "Grandaddy of the Tax Scandals," *Nation,* January 19, 1952, pp. 57-8. The President's message appears in full in 65 *Cong. Record,* Pt. 6, pp. 6087-8, April 11, 1924.
6. *Hearings, Ethics in Government,* p. 154.

7. See for example the cross-examination of Robert Heller, a distinguished businessman of active civic interests, and an experienced witness. U. S. House of Representatives, Committee on Armed Services, 81st Congress, 1st Sess., *The National Defense Program—Unification and Strategy, Hearings* . . . October 1949, pp. 588-595. Cross-examinations, of course, have to be experienced to be appreciated.

8. Summarized by Galloway, *Hearings, Organization and Operation of Congress*, p. 644.

9. During 1951, for example, coverage of Russia and Iron Curtain countries, communism, and "loyalty" issues in the *Washington Post* approximated five stories a day and forty-six inches of type. These totals exclude Korean War news and are based on a sample of two days a month, with a week's interval between.

10. A comment of David Lawrence brings out the fact that press and television news channels have a double standard. They print and broadcast statements of Senator McCarthy alleging that persons are communists when made on the floor of the Senate, where, as the law is construed, the news media share in the Senator's immunity. But they have declined to print such allegations when offered to them directly and privately, where the printing and broadcasting of these statements would not be protected by the immunity of the Senate. One might infer that the news media are willing to print and broadcast sensational allegations that are hardly credible, or that they are excessively cautious in disseminating information which the public ought to have. See David Lawrence's report, *Washington Star*, August 9, 1951.

11. *Hearings, Ethics in Government*, p. 274.

12. *Hearings, Organization and Operation of Congress*, p. 598.

13. 96 *Cong. Record*, Pt. 6, p. 795. See the comments also by Senators Smith of New Jersey and Tydings of Maryland.

14. *New York Times*, November 18, 1951.

15. See Senator Taft's summary of the previous action in 95 *Cong. Record*, Pt. 2, 2663-4, March 17, 1949.

16. *Hearings, Organization and Operation of Congress*, p. 269.

17. *New York Times*, July 29, 1951, p. 59.

18. *New York Times*, August 5, 1951, p. 26; August 11, 1951, p. 6.

19. *New York Times*, October 10, 1951, p. 15.

20. Elmer Gertz, "Truman vs. Douglas," *The Nation*, Aug. 4, 1951, p. 87.

21. George B. Galloway, "The Legislative Reorganization Act of 1946," quoted from 45 *American Political Science Review*, 62, (March 1951), in *Hearings, Organization and Operation of Congress*, p. 639.

22. See Representative Clarence Cannon's discouraged comment after the first session of the 82nd Congress, as reported in the *New York Times*, November 11, 1951.

23. These suggested remedies are not original, but have been made in various forms by a number of persons and groups which have studied Congress, among them a distinguished group of political scientists. See the Report of the Committee on Political Parties, of the American Political Science Association, "Toward a More Responsible Two-Party System," 44 *Am. Pol. Sci. Rev.*, September 1950. Supplement.

Simple remedies are sometimes the most difficult to accept. In II Kings, the fifth chapter, it is recorded that when Naaman, "captain of the host of the King of Syria" and a "mighty man of valour," asked of Elisha, the Israelite, what he should do to be relieved of his leprosy, he was told (by messenger) to wash seven times in the River Jordan. "But Naaman was wroth and went away and said . . . Are not Abana and Pharpar, rivers of Damascus, better than all the waters of Israel? May I not wash in them and be clean? So he turned and went away in a rage."

24. See the pamphlet, *Government of the People, By the People, For the People*, U. S. Conference of Mayors, 730 Jackson Place, Washington 6, D. C.

V. *The Executive*

1. Edward S. Corwin, *The Constitution and What It Means Today*, p. 11. (Princeton University Press, 1946)

2. 96 *Congressional Record* 7894-5, June 1, 1950. See Chapter 4, above.

3. *Ethical Standards in Government*, pp. 55-56.

4. Senate Committee on Expenditures in the Executive Departments, Investigations Subcommittee, 81st Cong., 1st Sess. *Hearings* . . . Aug-Sept. 1949. *Influence in Government Procurement*, p. 501.

5. See for example the defense of Donald S. Dawson, as reported in the *New York Times*, February 9, 1951.

6. *Ibid.* Following this attack on the Fulbright Committee Report, Senator Fulbright reported his previous unsuccessful efforts, on behalf of the committee, to convince the President directly that there was something wrong with the RFC, and with the influences brought to bear upon it.

7. Senator Williams reviews parts of the story in his Senate speech of

February 7, 1952, 98 *C. R.* 917-920 (daily edition). The story is also covered in a long interview in the *U. S. News,* December 7, 1951, pp. 24-31.

8. *New York Times,* March 17, 1952.

9. See Senator Williams' speech. 98 *C. R.* 920, February 7, 1952.

10. Mr. Boyle's resignation was announced October 13th. See Democratic National Committee Chairman Frank E. McKinney's denunciation of grafters, in general, not in particular, as reported in the *New York Times,* November 27, 1951.

11. See the press conference defense of Attorney General McGrath and Secretary Snyder as reported in the *New York Times* on December 11, 1951, and February 8, 1952.

12. Plan Nos. 2, 3, 5, 6, and 26 affecting Justice, Interior, Commerce, Labor and Treasury. The President's effort to make the same change in the Department of Agriculture was blocked by Congress.

13. *U. S. News,* Dec. 7, 1951.

14. *Report of the President's Committee on Administrative Management,* p. 29.

15. The Hoover Commission's short report on *General Management of the Executive Branch* deals specifically with this problem.

16. The first effort to make this change in Treasury was first blocked by Congress, but a revised plan was approved. The plan in Agriculture was also blocked by Congress.

17. The phrase is Dean Donald K. David's. See Myles L. Mace, *The Growth and Development of Executives,* p. 190. (Harvard, Graduate School of Business Administration, 1950)

18. In present American usage the under-secretary is a political official. Like the Secretary, his official life span is short.

19. This is the reckoning of the Senate Committee on Expenditures in the Executive Departments. See its report of March 7, 1952. Committee Report No. 12 (Committee Print) 82nd Cong., 1st Sess., *Organization of Federal Executive Departments and Agencies.*

20. *Concluding Report,* pp. 3-4.

VI. *Ethics—Legislative, Judicial, Administrative*

1. Both codes are printed in ʾ62 *Annual Report, American Bar Association,* pp. 1105-1135. Subsequent amendments are on minor points.

2. Deuteronomy 1:16-17.

3. Deuteronomy 16:18-19.

4. A careful study of this episode reveals that "He was rejected not because of his radical writings some twenty-five years earlier, or the charge of Communism, although these caused some newspaper support to be withdrawn and made it easier for his opponents to bring about his defeat. The real issue was federal regulation of the price of natural gas, and his rejection was a victory for the gas and oil interests. Their opposition to Olds was due to the vigorous and effective role which he had played in the development of federal regulation and to his determined opposition to the Moore-Rizley bill, the Kerr bill, and similar ones for which they had pressed in Congress . . ." Senator Aiken declared during the Senate debate, " 'certain public utilities are out to destroy a man for performing his duty. I do not know of anything worse than that. I do not know of anything more detrimental to good government. I do not know of anything to make it more difficult to get men and women to perform the duties of public office.' " Joseph P. Harris, "The Senatorial Rejection of Leland Olds," 45 *Am. Pol. Sci. Rev.*, 691-692, September 1951.

5. *Hearings, Ethics in Government*, p. 213. At the time of President Harrison's election, Mr. Reagan was a member of the Senate (1887-91), but he had previously served in the House 1857-61 and 1875-87. As chairman of the House Committee on Interstate and Foreign Commerce he was the author of the "Reagan Interstate Commerce Bill."

6. A letter from Theodore Roosevelt to Henry Cabot Lodge reprinted by J. M. Mathews and C. A. Berdahl, *Documents and Readings in American Government*, p. 373.

7. *Hearings, Ethics in Government*, p. 344.

8. *Ibid.*, p. 347 ff.

9. *Ethical Standards in Government*, p. 20.

10. U. S. Civilian Production Administration, Bureau of Demobilization, *Dollar-a-Year and Without Compensation Personnel Policies*, Historical Reports on War Administration; War Production Board, Special Study No. 27, p. 41.

11. *Dollar-a-Year and Without Compensation Personnel Policies*, p. 78.

12. *Ibid.*, p. 49.

13. *Public Law 774*, 81st Cong., Sec. 703.

14. *Ibid.*, Sec. 710 (a).

15. *Ibid.*, Sec. 710 (b), (c), (d).

16. Executive Order 10182, November 23, 1950, 15 *Federal Register* p. 8013, and E. O. 10205, 16 *F. R.*, p. 419.

17. *New York Times*, April 15, 1951.
18. House Committee on the Judiciary: Subcommittee on Monopoly Power, 82nd Cong., 1st Sess., Serial No. 1, Pt. 4. *The Mobilization Program*. pp. 995-1023, May-July 1951.
19. There is in addition a much larger number of persons with W.O.C. status who serve occasionally as members of advisory and other committees attached to the field organizations of executive departments, for example, Interior, Agriculture, and Commerce. The number was put above 90,000 in June, 1951. Of the total, 3,866 were attached to the Office of Rent Stabilization. See Paul G. Dembling and Herbert E. Forrest, "Government Service and Private Compensation," 50 *Geo. Washington L. R.* 179, December 1951.
20. E. O. 10182, Sec. 301.
21. *Ethical Standards in Government*, p. 22.
22. The Baruch-Hancock report said, "Speed in shifting . . . productive capacity from war to peace is our most effective attack against the two enemies which threaten in the transition and post-war period— *unemployment and inflation.* . . . We recommend quick, fair and final settlement of terminated war contracts through negotiation by the contractors and the procurement agencies.

    "Any course such as that proposed recently by the Comptroller General would quibble the nation into a panic.

    "The Comptroller's suggestion, as we understand it, was that he review every settlement before payment and that no payment be final until approved by him. . . . If such an audit before payment were decreed, no war contractor would know where he stood, prime contractors would be unable to pay subcontractors, banks would be reluctant to make adequate loans, billions in working capital would be frozen. The delays in settlement could force many concerns into bankruptcy. It would mean unemployment by audit."

    The emphasis of the report was upon speed in contract settlement, clearing government property out of war plants, and disposal of surplus property. See the report submitted to James F. Byrnes, Director of the Office of War Mobilization, by Bernard M. Baruch and John M. Hancock, *War and Postwar Adjustment Policies*, pp. 20-22. (American Council on Public Affairs, Washington, 1944)
23. *Hearings, Ethics in Government*, p. 14.
24. *Ibid.*, pp. 15-16.
25. Senate Committee on Banking and Currency, Subcommittee on Reconstruction Finance Corporation, 82nd Cong., 1st Sess., Senate

Report No. 76, February 5, 1951, *Study of RFC: Favoritism and Influence*, p. 7. This will be cited hereafter as Fulbright Report on *Favoritism and Influence*.

26. *Ibid.*, p. 9.

27. *Ethical Standards in Government*, p. 21.

28. See the comment of the Senate Committee on Expenditures in the Executive Departments, Investigation Subcommittee, 81st Cong., 2d Sess., Senate Report No. 1232, January 18, 1950, *The Five-Percenter Investigation*, p. 14. This document will be cited hereafter as the Hoey Report on *The Five-Percenter Investigation*.

29. For discussion of the Mason frauds see report of the Hoey Subcommittee on *Influence in Government Procurement*, Senate Report No. 611, 82nd Cong., 1st Sess., August 2, 1951.

30. Fulbright Report on *Favoritism and Influence*, pp. 5-6.

31. *Ibid.*, pp. 8-9.

32. See the *Washington Post* report of the Hoey Committee hearings, February 19, 1952.

33. The story has been unfolding for more than a year. Developments were recently summarized, in an effort to clarify the picture, by a Hoey Committee staff member. See the *Washington Post*, e.g., February 20, 1952, and March 14, 1952, from which this material was drawn.

34. See *Favoritism and Influence*, pp. 6-7.

35. It should be noted that strictly speaking the famous fur coat was a matter of comity among two businessmen, Rosenbaum and Young, who presumably were accustomed to do favors for each other. It was not Mr. Young's employment at the time, but his wife's, that brought the government into the picture. See the *New York Times* report on the Fulbright Committee Hearings, February 28, 1951.

36. *Favoritism and Influence*, p. 8.

37. *Ethical Standards in Government*, p. 22.

38. *Ibid.*, pp. 22-23.

39. *The Five-Percenter Investigation*, p. 7.

40. *Ibid.*, p. 9.

41. *Ibid.*, p. 12.

42. *Ethical Standards in Government*, p. 26.

43. *Ibid.*

44. *Ibid.*, p. 23.

45. *The Five-Percenter Investigation*, pp. 21-22.

46. *Ethical Standards in Government*, p. 27.

47. In the Senate debate on the approval of the President's plan reorgan-

izing the Bureau of Internal Revenue (*Congressional Record,* March 13, 1952, pp. 2288-2289) supporters of the plan brought out significant facts:

(1) Moral failures in the Bureau had not touched the seventeen Collectors, of the total of sixty-four, who were career men and had been advanced from the ranks on their merits.

(2) The percentage of failure among the remaining forty-seven political appointees was almost 15 per cent. [It has since increased to 17 per cent.]

(3) The failures among subordinate employees occurred in the districts "where the whole office was a cesspool of politics" because of the faulty leadership, and where many subordinates were hardly *bona-fide* career men.

(4) The rate of failure among the rank and file was less than three-thousandths of one per cent. (If it had equaled that of the politically appointed collectors, the dismissals would have approached 10,000 instead of a figure well under 200.)

48. See *Good Government,* January-February 1952, p. 2.
49. *Ethical Standards in Government,* p. 26.
50. *Ethical Standards in Government,* p. 24.
51. *Ibid.,* pp. 42-45.
52. *Ibid.,* pp. 46-52.
53. *Ibid.,* p. 35.
54. *Hearings, Ethics in Government,* p. 104.
55. *Ethical Standards in Government,* p. 35.
56. *Ibid.*
57. *Ibid.,* pp. 2-3.
58. For the committee's proposals see *The Five-Percenter Investigation,* pp. 22-30.
59. *Ethical Standards in Government,* pp. 37-38.
60. *Ibid.,* p. 38.
61. *Ibid.,* p. 39.
62. Hoover Commission, *General Management in the Executive Branch,* p. 5.
63. See the persuasive comments of Herbert Emmerich, on recent improvements in local and state governments, "A Scandal in Utopia," 12 *Pub. Admin. Review,* pp. 4-5.
64. Report to the Congress on *General Management in the Executive Branch,* pp. 3-5.
65. This summary of reorganization activities in 1949-1952 is taken largely from the report of the Senate Committee on Expenditures

in the Executive Departments, 82nd Cong., 2nd Session, Senate Document No. 91, *Reorganization of the Federal Government*, January 21, 1952. Three additional plans were pending on May 14, 1952.

VII. *Public, Party, and Pressure Politics*

1. William H. Whyte, Jr., "The Wives of Management," *Fortune Magazine*, October, 1951, p. 86 ff, and "The Corporation and the Wife," November, 1951, p. 109 ff.
2. Except in the one-party states of the South, voting in the primary is usually much lighter than in the election which follows. See V. O. Key, *Politics, Parties, and Pressure Groups* (Crowell, New York, 1948), pp. 362, 584-595, for a concise review of "electoral participation."
3. See the discussion of "Money for Lobbying" and "Fund-Raising Techniques" in the General Interim Report of the House Select Committee on Lobbying Activities, 81st Cong., 2nd. Sess., House Report No. 3138, October 20, 1950, pp. 9-23.
4. *Ibid.*, pp. 24-25.
5. *Ibid.*, p. 27.
6. *Ibid.*, p. 38.
7. *Ibid.*, p. 31.
8. *Ibid.*, p. 8.
9. For discussion of "Nominations in the States," see Key, *op. cit.*, pp. 340-372.
10. See the review of nominating procedures in the *New York Times*, February 24, 1952, also Key, *op. cit.*, ch. 13, "National Conventions."
11. See Senator Benton's remarks in the *Hearings, Ethics in Government*, p. 41.
12. See for example Herbert A. Philbrick, *I Led Three Lives*, p. 300. (McGraw-Hill, New York, 1952)
13. *Ethical Standards in Government*, p. 64.
14. *Ibid.*
15. "They Want to Be Good Citizens," *National Municipal Review*, January 1947, p. 29.
16. *Ethical Standards in Government*, p. 62.
17. The adjournment dates since the end of World War II are:
    December 21, 1945
    August 2, 1946
    December 19, 1947

December 31, 1948

October 19, 1949

January 2, 1951 (But there was a long recess, September 23-November 27, 1950.)

October 10, 1951

The last ten sessions of Congress (prior to the second of the 82nd Congress) averaged 335 days in length. If the long recess of 1950 is deducted the average is 328 days. That leaves the member of Congress approximately five weeks a year when Congress is not in session. This time is increased also by short recesses of one or both houses. But they do not alter the fact that being a member of Congress is a full-time job.

18. These figures are taken from the survey reported by Cabell Phillips, *New York Times Magazine*, February 24, 1952.

19. The reputed action of the King Committee chairman in giving a "clean bill of health" to T. Vincent Quinn, district attorney of Queens County and a former member of the House of Representatives, has disturbing overtones. Mr. Quinn's law firm continued to take tax cases and other cases with administrative agencies of the government. Representative Quinn limited his own practice, "with two or three exceptions," to criminal cases, for which the taking of a fee is apparently not prohibited. "In no instance while a member of Congress," he testified, "did he do more than inquire about the status of a case." The disquieting aspect of the Committee's action was the apparent basis for it. According to the *New York Times* reporter, "The inference drawn by many who . . . heard Mr. King's concluding statement was that present members of Congress might become involved if the subcommittee took the position that it was illegal for anybody on the Federal payroll to intervene with Federal agencies in behalf of paying clients." Mr. King was quoted as saying "that 'literally thousands' must have accepted legal fees in 'technical violation'" of the law without any sense of wrongdoing. (John D. Morris, *New York Times*, April 5, 1952.) Apparently no attention was given to the question of propriety. Legality was the criterion applied, and it had to be tempered—but not to the shorn lamb.

20. House Select Committee on Lobbying Activities, 82nd Cong., 1st. Sess., Hearings, Part 5, *Lobbying, Direct and Indirect . . . Committee for Constitution Government*, p. 155 ff.

21. Commission of Inquiry on Public Service Personnel, *Better Government Personnel*, p. 18. (McGraw-Hill, New York, 1935) Quoted from *The Nation's Business*, November, 1928.

22. The statement is attributed to Representative Adolph Sabath by Francis Biddle. See his *The Fear of Freedom* (Doubleday, New York, 1951), for a concise and well-considered review of "The Federal Loyalty Program," pp. 197-245. See also Marie Jahoda and S. W. Cook, "Security Measures and Freedom of Thought," 61 *Yale Law Journal* 295-333, (March, 1952)

23. See Arthur Krock's report of the dismissal of Attorney General Howard McGrath and Newbold Morris, *New York Times*, April 6, 1952. The political opposition in Congress has shown great forbearance in not exploiting this inconsistency of the Administration. The President sent his message to Congress on disclosure legislation on September 27, 1951. (H. Doc. 244, 82nd Cong., 1st Sess., *Cong. Record*, September 27, 1951, p. 12515-516) Mr. Morris was dropped April 3, 1952.

24. See Hugh A. Bone's discussion of "Government Subsidization" in his *American Politics and the Party System* (McGraw-Hill, New York, 1949), pp. 646-648.

25. *Hearings, Ethics in Government*, pp. 466-467.

26. See the optimistic comment on changes in local and state government by Herbert Emmerich, "A Scandal in Utopia," 12 *Public Administration Review*, p. 5 (Winter, 1952).

VIII. *Integrity—Man and the State*

1. *Ethical Standards in Government*, pp. 16-18. This carefully considered recommendation was fully supported by the weight of testimony given to the Committee.

2. E. C. Jenkins, *Philanthropy in America*, p. 173. (Association Press, New York, 1950)

3. *Ibid*. Also see George F. Ketcham, editor, *Yearbook of American Churches*, 1951, p. 251. (National Council of the Churches of Christ, 1951)

4. U. S. Office of Education, *Educational Directory*, 1950-51, Part III, Table 4, p. 12.

5. *Hearings, Ethics in Government*, pp. 72-73.

INDEX

(References to the Notes, pages 311-330, are not included in this Index.)